AF655173

Operation and Management of Multi-Commodity Agro-Processing Centre

CONTENT VIBES
PUBLISHERS • PRINTERS • AGGREGATORS

About the Author

Dr. Arun Kumar is a proficient researcher and author in the field of Agronomy. In his 23 years of academic experience, Dr. Arun Kumar has served in various capacities as Assistant Professor, Junior Agronomist (1998-2005) and Associate Professor (2005 – 2011). Dr. Arun Kumar has also served as the Director Planning at Bihar Agricultural University, Sabour during which he developed the Road Map of the university and headed the PME Cell and Institutional Quality Assurance Cell (IQAC) of the university. He has also served as the Dean (Agriculture), DRI cum Dean (PGS), Comptroller and Director of Research at Bihar Agricultural University, Sabour. During 2021-22, Dr. Arun Kumar has also served as the Vice Chancellor of Bihar Agricultural University. During his tenure as Vice Chancellor, the Bihar Agricultural University and all its constituent colleges were accredited by ICAR and three new colleges were established under the BAU, Sabour. Dr. Kumar has also guided a number of Master's and PhD students and has a number of publications to his credit including 37 Research Papers, 32 Edited/Authored Books, 19 Popular Articles and many more. Dr. Arun Kumar has handled various projects including nine consultancy projects of BAMETI, Patna. He has also chaired/co-chaired technical sessions of various national and international seminars, symposia and conferences. He has also led the state-level committee for the preparation of the agricultural road map of the Bihar State. Considering his outstanding contributions to the field of agriculture, Dr Arun Kumar has been awarded an award for excellent contribution in agriculture sector by his Excellency, the Governor of Bihar. He has done justice to all positions which were previously held by him with such admirable grace and calmness that he is an inspiration to all and Swami Keshwanand Rajasthan Agricultural University, Bikaner is strongly committed to steady development under his able leadership.

Operation and Management of Multi-Commodity Agro-Processing Centre

Arun Kumar
Vice-Chancellor
Swami Keshwanand Rajasthan Agricultural University
Bikaner, Rajasthan, India

CV CONTENT VIBES
PUBLISHERS • PRINTERS • AGGREGATORS

CONTENT VIBES
PUBLISHERS • PRINTERS • AGGREGATORS

1168, Sector 13, Urban Estate
Karnal-132 001, Haryana
Tel: 91-84470 75807, 18440 41168
Email: contentvibesppa@gmail.com
www.contentvibes.in

© 2026, Publisher

Print ISBN: 978-93-67554-67-8

ebooks ISBN: 978-93-67558-23-2

All rights reserved. No part of this publication may be reproduced, stored in a retrieval system or transmitted in any form or by any means, including electronic, mechanical, photocopying recording or otherwise without the prior written permission of the publisher or the copyright holder.

This book contains information obtained from authentic and highly reliable sources. Reasonable efforts have been made to publish reliable data and information, but the author/s, editor/s and publisher cannot assume responsibility for the validity, accuracy or completeness of all materials or information published herein or the consequences of their use.

The work is published with the understanding that the publisher and author/s are not attempting to render any professional services and for the service of the students and professionals in developing countries.

The author/s, editor/s and publisher have attempted to trace and acknowledge the copyright holders of all material reproduced in this publication and apologize to copyright holders if permission and/or acknowledgements to publish in this form have not been taken. If any copyrighted material has not been acknowledged, please write to us and let us know so that we may rectify the error, in subsequent reprints.

Preface

The book "Operation and Management of Multi-commodity Agro-processing Centre" provides a comprehensive guide for managing agro-processing operations effectively. Agro-processing plays a vital role in enhancing the value of agricultural products, improving food security, and creating economic opportunities, especially in rural areas. However, running a multi-commodity agro-processing center requires a multifaceted approach that combines technical expertise, efficient operations, and effective management.

This book discusses the practical aspects of managing such a center, focusing on key areas such as inventory management, raw material sourcing, production processes, quality control, and workforce management. It outlines strategies for handling the complexities that arise from processing various commodities, including perishable goods, and addresses challenges like seasonal demand fluctuations, supply chain management, and maintaining product quality.

The book also emphasizes the importance of adhering to industry standards and regulations, including food safety protocols and environmental considerations. Furthermore, it offers insights into optimizing resource use, reducing waste, and ensuring the financial sustainability of the agro-processing center. Effective leadership and human resource management are also discussed, providing a holistic perspective on how to foster a productive and motivated workforce.

Whether you are a beginner or an experienced professional in the agro-processing industry, this book offers valuable knowledge and practical tips that can be applied to real-world scenarios. With its focus on sustainable practices and continuous improvement, it is an essential resource for anyone involved in the operation and management of multi-commodity agro-processing centers, helping them navigate the complexities of the industry while contributing to the growth of agriculture-based businesses and rural economies.

—Author

Contents

1

Site Selection, Plant Layout and Project Report Preparation

INTRODUCTION

An Agro-Processing Centre (APC) is a facility that processes agricultural products to enhance farmers' income. APCs are capable of both primary and secondary processing, and they also serve as hubs for training, demonstrations, and offering custom services. These centres are designed to help farmers add value to their raw produce, allowing them to establish a stronger presence in the agriculture sector while mitigating the effects of climate change and market fluctuations.The success of any agro-processing venture heavily depends on careful planning and strategic decision-making in its initial stages. One of the most critical factors in ensuring the efficient operation of an agro-processing facility is site selection, which involves evaluating potential locations based on several key parameters such as accessibility, availability of raw materials, labor availability, infrastructure, and proximity to markets. A well-chosen site can significantly reduce transportation costs, ensure a steady supply of inputs, and enhance the overall profitability of the enterprise.

Once the site is selected, the next crucial step is plant layout. A thoughtful and efficient layout maximizes space utilization, streamlines workflows, minimizes waste, and optimizes the use of resources such as water and energy. The layout should facilitate smooth movement of raw materials through various processing stages and ensure the safety of both workers and products. An ideal plant layout not only improves operational efficiency but also adheres to industry standards and regulatory requirements.Additionally, preparing a comprehensive project report is essential for securing financial backing and guiding the implementation of the project. The project report serves as a detailed blueprint, outlining the objectives, scope, financial projections, market analysis, and risk assessments. It provides stakeholders, including investors and lenders, with a clear understanding of the project's viability and potential returns. The process of preparing a project report helps identify challenges, estimate costs, and establish timelines, ensuring that the project progresses in a structured and organized manner.

An APC is equipped with the necessary facilities for processing, storing, and drying various agricultural products such as cereals, pulses, oilseeds, spices, fruits, and vegetables. Processed and packaged food items are produced and marketed under a specific brand name (Kumar and Ilyas, 2003). The ownership and operation of an APC can be managed by an individual, a community, a cooperative, or a voluntary organization. The centre adds value to agricultural products, increasing the marketability of surplus produce from villages or nearby areas, thus enhancing local economic opportunities. In this chapter, we will explore the critical aspects of site selection, plant layout design, and the preparation of a project report, all of which are fundamental to the successful establishment and operation of an agro-processing business.

NEED OF APC

Food grain production in the hills is often insufficient to meet the year-round consumption needs of households, forcing farmers to purchase grains from nearby markets. This issue is primarily due to low productivity, unscientific farming practices, lack of economic incentives, and migration. One significant factor contributing to low productivity is the reliance on rainfed farming, which accounts for approximately 90% of the land area in Uttaranchal (Srinivas and Kumar, 2006). In addition to this, the traditional processing methods lead to significant losses, further compounding the problem. In such circumstances, an Agro-Processing Centre (APC) can play a pivotal role by aiding in processing, value addition, and loss reduction. Moreover, APCs can bridge the gap between producers and consumers by ensuring timely availability of food products at lower costs. The establishment of an APC would create market demand for fresh food grains, encouraging farmers to produce surplus grains, thereby increasing their income and boosting productivity levels. Therefore, beyond reducing losses, the APC would contribute to enhancing the region's overall agricultural productivity.

A MULTI-COMMODITY AGRO-PROCESSING CENTRE (MCAP)

A Multi-Commodity Agro-Processing Centre (MCAP) is a facility or hub that is designed to process a variety of agricultural products (commodities) in one location. These centers are established with the aim of adding value to agricultural produce by processing raw materials into higher-value products. This contributes to both economic growth and food security by enhancing the shelf life, quality, and marketability of agricultural goods.

Key Features of a Multi-Commodity Agro-Processing Centre

- **Diverse Commodity Processing**: The center is equipped to handle and process multiple types of agricultural products, such as fruits, vegetables, grains, pulses, dairy, spices, and more. This flexibility helps farmers by providing a single facility where they can process different kinds of crops.

- **Value Addition**: The primary goal of such centers is to add value to raw agricultural produce. For example, fruits may be processed into juices, jams, or dried products; grains might be turned into flour; dairy products like milk could be converted into butter, cheese, or yogurt.
- **Integrated Facilities**: These centers often include a combination of processing units, packaging, cold storage, and even quality control labs. This integration makes it easier for producers to go from raw harvest to processed goods, improving efficiency and reducing wastage.
- **Market Linkages**: Agro-processing centers also play a crucial role in creating better market linkages for farmers. By processing products, farmers are able to access higher-value markets both locally and internationally. This helps them achieve better income from their produce.
- **Employment and Economic Growth**: These centers typically generate employment opportunities for local communities in processing, packaging, logistics, and marketing. This contributes to the local economy and improves livelihoods.
- **Reduction in Post-Harvest Losses**: Agro-processing centers can reduce post-harvest losses by providing proper storage, packaging, and timely processing of perishable goods. This helps in minimizing wastage of agricultural produce that might otherwise spoil.
- **Technology and Innovation**: These centers often incorporate advanced technologies and best practices in food processing, which helps improve the quality and safety of processed goods. They can also introduce innovation in product development, packaging, and preservation.

Benefits of a Multi-Commodity Agro-Processing Centre

- **Increased Farmer Income**: By adding value to raw agricultural products, farmers can earn better prices for their produce.
- **Reduction in Waste**: Processing agricultural products helps in reducing the volume of waste, especially for perishable items.
- **Economic Growth**: These centers create employment, promote entrepreneurship, and stimulate local economies by encouraging investment in agro-based industries.
- **Sustainable Practices**: Agro-processing can lead to more sustainable agricultural practices by encouraging crop diversification and reducing dependency on raw commodity sales.
- **Export Potential**: Processed agricultural products often have better shelf life and appeal to international markets, opening up opportunities for exports.

Multi-Commodity Agro-Processing Centres are vital for strengthening agricultural value chains, improving the economic standing of farmers, and promoting food security while reducing post-harvest losses and promoting sustainable agriculture.

The concept of an Agro-Processing Centre (APC) revolves around processing grains at the village level to significantly increase farmers' income. These centres are equipped with two or more machines designed for processing agricultural products at the local level, thereby enabling farmers to add value to their produce and improve their economic prospects.

SITE SELECTION

Site Selection for a Multi-Commodity Agro-Processing Centre (MCAP) is a critical process that involves evaluating various factors to ensure the successful establishment and operational efficiency of the center. The goal is to choose a location that optimizes access to raw materials, labor, transportation, infrastructure, and markets, while also minimizing costs and risks.

Key Consideration for Site Selection

1. **Availability of Agricultural Produce**: The site should be located near agricultural regions that produce the commodities to be processed. Proximity to raw material sources helps in reducing transportation costs and ensures the center has a consistent supply of fresh produce.
2. **Diversity of Commodities**: Since the center will process multiple types of agricultural products, the site should be strategically located in an area where a variety of crops and agricultural products are cultivated. This would allow the center to handle different commodities efficiently.
3. **Access to Road, Rail, and Ports**: The site should have good connectivity to major roadways, railway networks, and/or seaports (for export purposes). Efficient transportation is essential for moving raw materials to the center and processed goods to the market.
4. **Proximity to Distribution Networks**: The site should be close to major distribution centers, wholesalers, and retail markets to facilitate easy and timely delivery of processed products.
5. **Availability of Basic Infrastructure**: Access to reliable power, water, and waste disposal systems is essential. Processing agricultural goods often requires significant water and energy input, so ensuring consistent availability is critical for operations.
6. **Cold Storage and Warehousing**: The center should have adequate cold storage and warehousing facilities to handle perishable commodities, especially fruits, vegetables, dairy, and meat products.
7. **Telecommunication Infrastructure**: Efficient communication networks (internet, mobile services) are necessary for operational management, marketing, and distribution coordination.
8. **Skilled and Unskilled Labor**: The site should be in a region where there is access to a sufficient labor force, both skilled and unskilled. Skilled labor is needed for handling complex processing tasks, while unskilled labor will be required for tasks like sorting, packaging, and manual labor.

9. **Labor Costs**: It is essential to consider the local labor costs, as these will impact the overall operational expenses. Choosing a location with affordable labor can significantly reduce operational costs.
10. **Proximity to Consumer Markets**: The center should be near markets that have a demand for processed agro-products, both locally and internationally. Access to urban markets, export hubs, or large retail chains can help maximize sales.
11. **Export Potential**: For agro-processed goods that may be exported, the site should be near ports or have good connectivity to international trade routes.
12. **Adequate Land Area**: The site should have sufficient space for building processing units, storage facilities, and parking. There should also be room for future expansion if the business grows.
13. **Land Ownership and Regulations**: Ensure that the land is available for industrial use and that the legal processes for acquiring land are clear and feasible. Local zoning laws and regulations need to be reviewed for compliance.
14. **Government Policies and Support**: The site should be located in a region where government policies support agro-processing businesses. This may include incentives such as tax benefits, subsidies, or grants for agro-processing industries.
15. **Regulatory Compliance**: Compliance with environmental, health, safety, and food quality standards is necessary. Local and national regulations regarding waste disposal, labor laws, and product certification need to be followed.
16. **Environmental Impact**: It is essential to evaluate the environmental impact of setting up the agro-processing center. Sites should have minimal environmental hazards, and plans should be in place to manage waste, water usage, and emissions. The center should align with sustainable practices to minimize negative impacts on the environment.
17. **Community Impact**: The center should ideally benefit the local community by providing employment and boosting the local economy. It is important to assess local community needs, social dynamics, and potential partnerships with local farmers and businesses.
18. **Proximity to Banks and Financial Institutions**: Financial institutions that offer loans, grants, and financial support for agro-processing industries are important to the success of the center. Having access to these services can make it easier to finance the center's operations.
19. **Incentives and Subsidies**: Local governments or development agencies may provide incentives for agro-processing centers, such as tax breaks, subsidies, or access to grants. Choosing a site in a region with such benefits can help reduce startup costs.
20. **Favorable Climate for Agriculture**: Since the agro-processing center will rely on agricultural raw materials, it is important to consider the local climate conditions. A favorable climate can ensure consistent production of agricultural commodities throughout the year.

21. **Climate Resilience**: Assess whether the location is prone to natural disasters like floods, droughts, or cyclones, which could disrupt agricultural production and supply chains.

Selecting a site for a Multi-Commodity Agro-Processing Centre is a complex decision that requires a thorough understanding of the region's agricultural potential, infrastructure, labor availability, market access, and government policies. A well-chosen site can significantly enhance the efficiency, sustainability, and profitability of the center, while a poor choice can lead to higher costs, logistical challenges, and business failure. By carefully evaluating these factors, the agro-processing center can be positioned to successfully meet both local and global demand for processed agricultural products.

PRINCIPLE OF AGRO-PROCESSING CENTRE ESTABLISHMENT

The fundamental principle behind establishing an Agro-Processing Centre (APC) is the availability of surplus produce, which can be estimated using the following equation:

$$S = Pt - (Un + L)$$

Where,S=Surplus Produce

P_t = Total Production

U_n= Total utilization of produce by the population to meet their various need

L = Total losses during various operations.

The type and capacity of the processing centre, as well as the machinery and labor requirements, are determined based on the availability of surplus produce. The activities carried out at the Agro-Processing Centre (APC) are primarily influenced by the raw materials available, the processed products that can be produced, and the market potential. These factors also serve as the foundation for estimating the capital investment required, along with the necessary land and building space.

Steps for Setting up an Agro-Processing Centre

Prioritization of Commodities

Commodities were prioritized based on the per centage of area cultivated with each crop. After assessing the prioritization, a detailed discussion was conducted with local communities, potential farmers, opinion leaders, and market stakeholders. Ultimately, crops like wheat, rice, finger millet, barnyard millet, lentil, soybean, bhatt, pigeon pea, linseed, mustard, turmeric, coriander, and chilies were chosen for processing, packaging, and marketing under the brand name "HIMRAJ."

Selection of Equipment

The equipment selection was based on the prioritized food and other commodities for the centre. Factors such as weight, power source, operational ease, safety, and ease of maintenance were also considered while selecting the equipment for the Agro-Processing Centre (APC).

Characteristics Considered in Selecting the Entrepreneur for the APC

Entrepreneurship refers to the ability to organize and manage factors of production—land, labor, and capital—to create new goods and services (Stoner et al., 1995). Entrepreneurs recognize opportunities others might overlook and view change as a natural and positive force for growth.

Establishment of the APC

Suitable locations and potential entrepreneurs were systematically identified in and around the Almora centre. A committee was formed to select the entrepreneur and location. After meeting several entrepreneur groups and conducting surveys, an NGO in Takula village was chosen as the key entrepreneur due to several advantages, including its location, infrastructure, and willingness to start the APC. The village is situated on the Bareilly-Bageshwer national highway, centrally located and surrounded by a cluster of villages. The site is equipped with infrastructure like a 3-phase power supply, water, road access, and a vibrant rural market.

Equipment Installed at APC, Takula

Seven post-harvest machines were selected and installed based on their feasibility and sources, as outlined by Kacharu et al. (1987). The equipment was chosen considering the region's food grain surplus and its availability. After extensive consultations with entrepreneurs, state officials, and scientists, the appropriate machines were selected and installed to meet the specific requirements of the area.

Table 1.1: Equipment installed at APC, Takula

SNo	Agro-processing Equipment and Facilities	Approx. Cost (₹ 000 INR.)	Technical Specifications
1	Mini Rice Mill unit (with cleaner, sheller, and polisher) with 10 hp electric motor	75	Milling capacity: 2.0 q/hr, Power source: 5 hp, 3-phase electric motor
2	Grain cleaner/Grader	10	Cleaning and grading capacity: 1.0 q/hr, Power source: one man or 0.5 hp single-phase electric motor
3	Mini Dal Mill (Pulse milling plant)	16	Milling capacity: 90.0 Kg/hr, Power source: 1.0 hp single-phase electric motor
4	Grain mill (Plate type attachakki of 300-350 mm diameter)	15	Grinding capacity: 100.0 kg/hr, Power source: 5 hp, 3-phase electric motor
5	Mechanical oil expeller (6 volt)	65	Expelling capacity: 40.0 kg/hr

SNo	Agro-processing Equipment and Facilities	Approx. Cost (₹ 000 INR.)	Technical Specifications
6	Millet thresher cum pearler	8	Threshing capacity: 35-40 kg/hr, Pearling capacity: 70.0 kg/hr
7	Masala Chakki (Spices grinder)	5	Grinding capacity: 5.0 kg/hr, 8-10 hp electric motor, 3-phase electric motor
	Total	219	

PLANT LAYOUT

The plant layout design plays a crucial role in ensuring the smooth flow of materials, efficient utillization of space and safety. The placement of equipment was arranged according to the available space. To ensure the efficient operation of all the machines, it was essential to run them simultaneously using a single power source. As a result, the shaft length was slightly extended beyond the recommended size to accommodate this requirement.

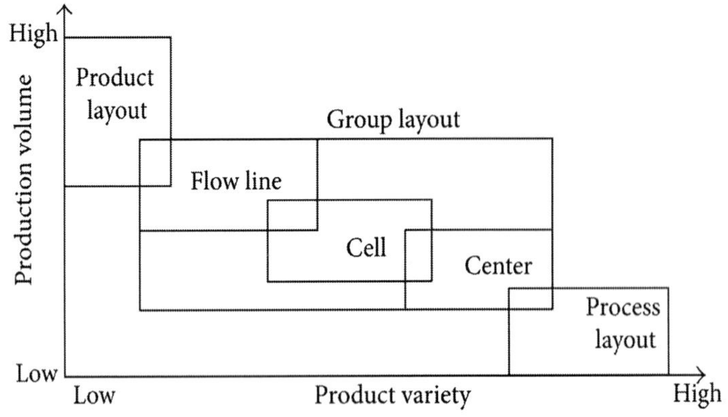

Figure 1.1: Layout Types

A plant layout is designed to optimize the physical arrangement of various components within a facility to efficiently achieve the desired output, both in terms of quantity and quality. An ideal plant layout allocates space and organizes equipment in a way that minimizes overall operating costs. There are three primary types of layouts—product layout, process layout, and group layout—commonly used in manufacturing systems. Group layouts can be further divided into flow line, cell, and center layouts.

Layout Efficiency

A govel layout improves productivity and minimizes waste. To evaluate the effectiveness of a layout, key performance indicators (KPIs) are employed. Common KPIs include travel distance (m), distance traveled multiplied by weight (mkg), goods movement, personnel movement, overall equipment efficiency (OEE), energy efficiency, and waste generation. However, it is essential to identify and integrate KPIs that are specifically relevant to food manufacturing when assessing layout efficiency. This ensures that food safety concerns are adequately addressed. Incorporating these KPIs allows for a more accurate evaluation of improvements in the efficiency of food manufacturing processes when layout adjustments are made.

Food Processing Technology

The primary objective for food manufacturers is to produce products that are not only safe but also wholesome, free from harmful microorganisms, chemicals, and foreign contaminants. Given that food is perishable and degrades over time, food processing aims to slow down this natural deterioration by choosing suitable processing techniques, formulations, packaging, and storage conditions. To ensure food safety, processing plants take specific measures to eliminate microbial, chemical, and physical contamination risks. Consequently, food safety becomes a critical concern, and the layout design of these facilities must focus on preventing both direct and cross-contamination of the products being produced. Unlike other manufacturing plants, food processing plant layouts must prioritize food safety alongside production efficiency. This distinction underscores that food processing facilities require a unique approach to layout design, integrating specific safety considerations with operational efficiency. Thus, food processing plants introduce a new layer of complexity to the typical layout design process.

Quality Standards Applicable for the Food Processing Industry

Numerous guidelines are available to regulate food manufacturing processes. In the food processing sector, Quality Assurance (QA) systems are employed to enhance product quality and reduce costs, while Hazard Analysis and Critical Control Points (HACCP) programs are specifically focused on ensuring food safety. Both HACCP and Good Manufacturing Practices (GMP) are management-based approaches that help maintain high hygiene standards within plants. HACCP systems implement process control by identifying critical points in production where contamination risks need to be monitored and managed. This system is widely recognized in the food industry as an effective means of establishing sound production, sanitation, and manufacturing practices that ensure food safety. Consequently, it can be concluded that the integration of QA and HACCP systems together promotes improvements in both production efficiency and product safety.

A key aspect that warrants attention in the food processing industry is the relationship between hygiene practices and the layout of processing plants. While food hygiene has been studied across various disciplines, a considerable body of knowledge exists, but it has not been systematically linked to the evaluation and design of food processing plant layouts. Existing literature on layout planning has insufficiently addressed the influence of hygiene factors, particularly in the context of food processing companies, highlighting a gap in how layout designs impact sanitation and food safety practices.

Development of Framework

A systematic approach is essential in layout design to ensure it aligns with production requirements. To initiate this process, gathering sufficient information is critical. The complexity of layout design increases when practical constraints are present, such as the need to demolish existing structures, expand current facilities, or manage the intricacies of a manufacturing process while maintaining the plant's capacity and flexibility. Additionally, the cost and time limitations for implementing a new layout are often overlooked in existing literature, but these factors are crucial considerations. Therefore, understanding these constraints is vital when designing a layout.

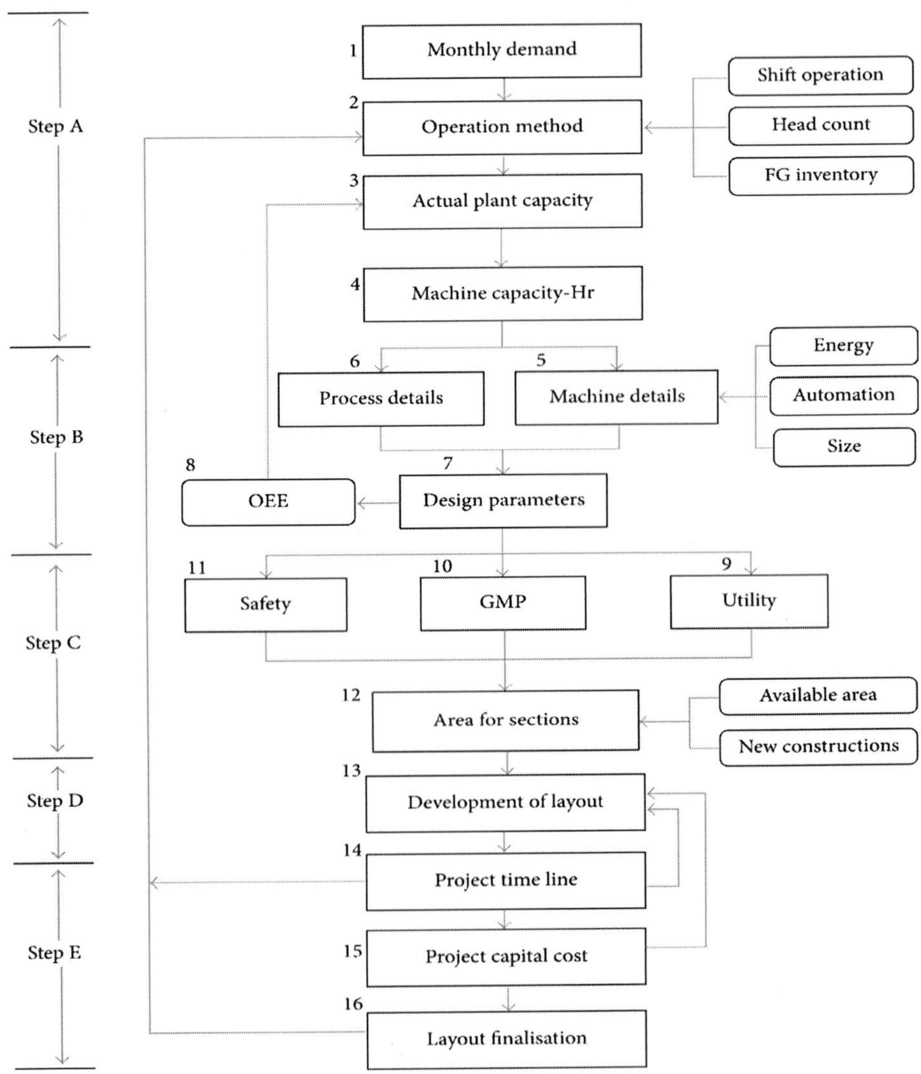

Figure 1.2: Proposed Framework

The framework proposed in given Figure was developed to assist industrial designers in gathering necessary information in a structured way. This framework consists of five main steps: Step A focuses on determining the required machinery capacity, Step B addresses the design parameters of the manufacturing process, Step C generates space requirements for various sections of the layout, Step D evaluates layout alternatives, and Step E involves selecting the most feasible layout from the available options.

Step A. Details of six items are to be known to derive the machinery capacity: monthly demand, shift operation information, headcount of personnel, finished goods inventory, actual plant capacity, and machine capacity. Here, shift operation, head count, and the finished goods inventory constitute the operation method.

Step B. This is to consolidate the process details and machine details for the layout design. Energy requirement, level of automation, and the size of machines are the determining factors of machine details. Process and machine details decide the design parameters for the layout design. When the OEE is known, this information can be used to feed information to obtain the actual plant capacity.

Step C. This helps to identify the required floor area for each section in the layout. In order to decide this, safety, GMP, and utility areas need to be assessed. The available area and possible new construction for additional area are then searched and finally the optimum mix of areas for the different sections is determined.

Step D. Layout development is carried out at this stage. A suitable layout design tool has to be used to develop an optimum solution to the facility layout problem. Relationship diagrams, from-to matrix, and other layout development methods can be used to develop the layout. This is where a model for layout planning can have a positive impact.

Step E. The final step takes care of the practical aspects that affect the layout. The financial feasibility and feasibility as a project to implement the selected layout are emphasised in this step.

Development of the Model

A model can be created to assist Step D in the framework for the food industry. The process of layout generation and evaluation is often challenging and time-consuming due to the complex and multi-objective nature of the task, as well as the difficulties in data collection, as noted by L. C. Lin and G. P. Sharp in their work, "Application of the integrated framework for the plant layout evaluation problem." Research, both past and emerging, is focused on developing methodologies to address these challenges. For instance, C. S. Tak and L. Yadav propose an algorithmic approach to layout design. However, algorithmic approaches tend to focus mainly on minimizing flow distance to reduce material handling costs, while procedural methods heavily rely on the experience of experts. Consequently, neither an algorithmic nor a procedural approach alone is always effective in solving practical design challenges.

Food processing factories must adhere to guidelines established by regulatory authorities. These guidelines outline the minimum industry requirements, and Good Manufacturing Practices (GMP) are developed based on these guidelines and the latest industry advancements. Food manufacturing factories must comply with these mandatory GMP to ensure product safety and hygiene standards. As a result, these factories share many similarities, which can be leveraged to develop a standardized model layout applicable to food processing plants.

As previously mentioned, the food industry's regulations must be incorporated into the design of factory layouts, and the segregation of work areas is critical in food processing. This is because the industry is characterized by a constant fluctuation in product volume, type, and mix, driven by changing market demands. Additionally, many critical control points in the food industry have been identified as potential hazards during the manufacturing process. Proper controls must be in place to mitigate contamination risks, and the layout of the site plays a key role in this risk mitigation.

The basic sections of food processing facilities include primary manufacturing, secondary packing, warehouses, utility areas, and administrative spaces. The hazards identified in Hazard Analysis and Critical Control Points (HACCP) include biological hazards (e.g., bacteria, yeasts, moulds), chemical hazards (e.g., cleaning chemicals, lubricants), and physical hazards (e.g., glass, insects, pests, metal, and dust). Layouts for food processing plants should be designed to minimize risks related to these hazards.

Section	Colour	Code R, G, B
Primary		255, 255, 0
Secondary		0, 255, 0
Administration		0, 255, 255
Utility		255, 0, 255
Stores		255, 191, 127

Figure 1.3: Colour Scheme to Identify the Five Basic Sections of a Layout

The primary manufacturing area, where the product is exposed to the environment, poses the greatest hygiene risk during the manufacturing process. Therefore, risk mitigation measures are critical to prevent contamination. Environmental factors such as humidity, temperature, particulate levels, and barometric pressure must be monitored and controlled in this section. The primary manufacturing area should also be fully separated from other sections to minimize contamination risk. Employees entering this area must adhere to GMP requirements, including uniform changes, and suitable facilities for this process should be provided. Moreover, separate pathways for personnel and materials entering the factory should be maintained, as this is a GMP and safety standard requirement.

The remaining four sections should be strategically placed to support primary manufacturing while maintaining food safety standards. It is essential to clearly define these five sections in the layout design, with a color scheme to easily identify each section. The food processing industry involves many simultaneous activities and often requires complex layouts, which can take various forms. The proposed color scheme will help simplify the design process by providing a visual representation that aids in the understanding of the layout.

Layout Model

The "diamond model" layout for food manufacturing was created by strategically arranging the five key sections mentioned earlier. Unlike traditional layout methods, which primarily focus on optimizing adjacency or minimizing travel distances between departments, this model places greater emphasis on food safety (or GMP) as the primary criterion for department placement. While traditional optimization factors are still considered, they are secondary to ensuring that the layout adheres to stringent food safety standards.

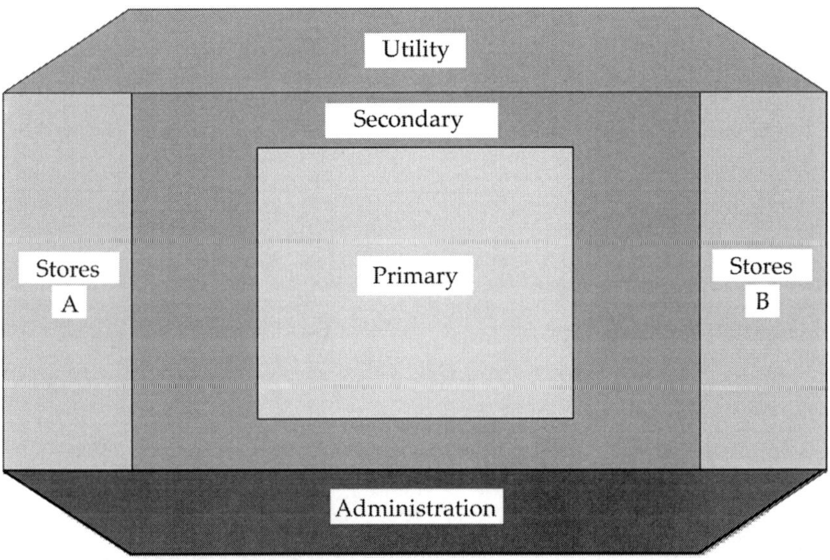

Figure 1.4: Diamond Model

Existing layouts present in the food industry were observed (n=4) and evaluated in designing the model layout. Many layouts indicate that the high risk and low risk areas are protected from the external environment by only a solid wall. This can lead to pest ingression, cross contamination, and direct contamination. Typically, utility systems are positioned away from high-risk areas, meaning HVAC ducts, steam lines, and compressed air lines must pass through wall openings to reach these zones. This creates a potential risk for the food processing plant. However, this risk can be effectively mitigated by placing the secondary manufacturing area around the primary manufacturing zone. The secondary manufacturing area should then be enclosed by other sections of the facility to act as a barrier, preventing external contaminants from reaching the primary and secondary manufacturing areas. This layout reduces the chances of contamination—whether biological, chemical, or physical. Finally, utility, administration, and warehouse areas should be connected to the secondary manufacturing area to further streamline the flow of operations and enhance safety.

The diamond model layout, Ensures proper material and personnel movement within the facility. The material flow progresses from left to right. Raw materials and packing materials are received on the left side of the layout, processed into finished goods, and then moved to the storage area on the right. Personnel enter the facility through the administration area, located at the bottom. This layout effectively minimizes the risk of cross-contamination and optimizes the movement of both personnel and goods throughout the factory floor.

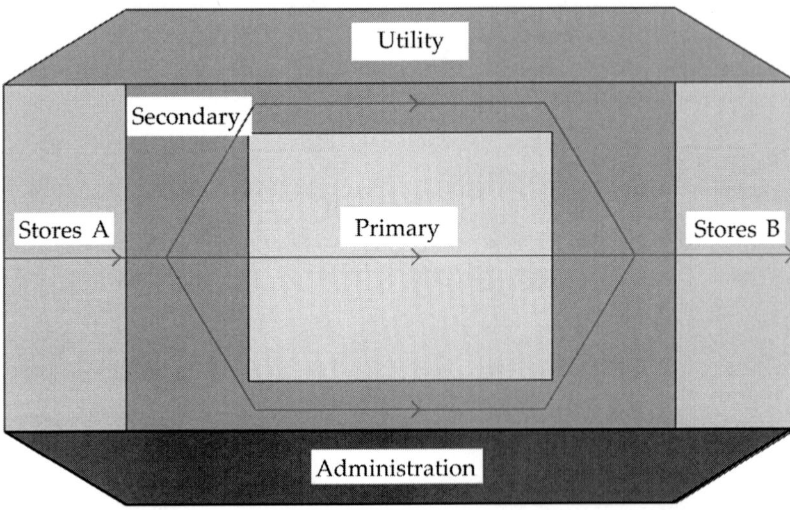

Figure 1.5: Material Movement in Diamond Model

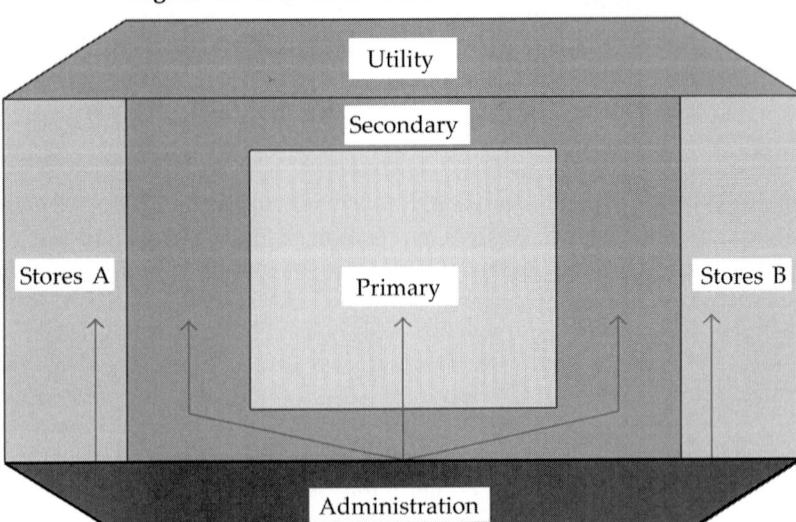

Figure 1.6: Personnel Movement in Diamond Model

Figure illustrates the five key areas of a food processing factory, which encompass all essential functions of typical food processing operations. The space allocation for each of these areas is determined based on the specific space requirements dictated by the manufacturing process. These requirements are identified through the application of the framework, which helps in determining the appropriate space distribution in the layout.

Primary Manufacturing Area

The product that moves from the secondary manufacturing area is exposed to the facility environment in the primary manufacturing area, significantly raising the contamination risk. Therefore, it must be the most safeguarded area of the manufacturing process. To address this, the model places the primary manufacturing area at the center of the layout, isolating it from the external environment as much as possible.

Typically, the product enters the primary area via pressurized air locks. Personnel must also enter through air locks and undergo gowning changes. They are required to wear head covers, shoe covers, masks, and gloves as appropriate to the manufacturing process before accessing the primary manufacturing area. In addition, hand-wash stations should be set up at the entry point to this area. To further minimize contamination, air curtains should be installed at the entrances to prevent outside air from entering the high-risk zone.

As noted, the primary manufacturing area is where the product is most exposed to contamination risks. Therefore, the air within this section must be conditioned according to specific standards. The particle count in the air is controlled using high-efficiency particulate air (HEPA) filters, and the relative humidity is regulated based on process requirements. The air pressure is maintained at a slightly higher level than that in the secondary manufacturing area to prevent particulates from entering the primary manufacturing space. The pressure differential between the low-risk and high-risk areas is kept between 5 and 15 Pa, ensuring that air flows from the high-risk area to the low-risk area at a speed of 1.5 m/sec or higher through openings.

Secondary Manufacturing Area

The product is initially exposed to the facility environment in the secondary manufacturing area. Raw materials enter this area from the stores. The product, which is typically in its primary packaging when it reaches the secondary manufacturing area, undergoes final packaging there. Once completed, the product in its final packaging is sent to the finished goods warehouse. To prevent contamination through air leakage, air locks must be placed between the stores and the secondary manufacturing area. These air locks also serve to keep pests from entering the secondary manufacturing space.

Personnel access to the secondary manufacturing area is from the administration area, and entry is also through air locks. A gowning procedure is usually required to change into designated clothing before entering the secondary manufacturing area. Therefore, the gowning area should be strategically located within the administration section of the layout.

The air quality within the secondary manufacturing area is controlled to meet the specific requirements of the manufacturing process. The same pressure differential is maintained between the primary and secondary manufacturing areas to ensure air flows from the high-risk to the low-risk area. Additionally, it is advisable to maintain positive pressure (e.g., 0.02 mm H_2O) relative to the utility, stores, and office areas. This positive pressure prevents outside air from entering the secondary manufacturing area, thus safeguarding the product from contamination.

Warehouse

The warehouse is responsible for holding both raw materials and packing materials for the manufacturing process, as well as finished goods. It is divided into two sections: Store A and Store B. Store A is designated for raw materials and packing materials, which remain in a quarantine area until they pass quality checks. Once cleared, they are released for use in manufacturing. Store B holds finished goods, which are only released after they pass quality checks.

The environmental conditions in the store areas are tailored to suit the specific needs of the materials and products. For instance, the stores can include cold rooms, chilled rooms, or air-conditioned spaces, depending on the requirements of the raw materials and finished goods.

Goods movement within the warehouse follows a one-way direction. There is no backtracking or criss-crossing of material flow, ensuring a streamlined process. As depicted in Figure 5, raw and packing materials enter Store A and progress through the manufacturing process before reaching Store B as finished goods. To prevent cross-contamination, personnel movement should be restricted or carefully controlled. Appropriate changing room facilities must be strategically located to maintain hygiene standards.

Utility Area

This area accommodates all utilities and the engineering department of the organization. The utility equipment includes components like air handlers for the heating, ventilating, and air conditioning (HVAC) system, boilers, air compressors, chillers, and water purification plants, all of which support the manufacturing process. Observations indicate that frequent direct access to the secondary packing area from the utility area is not necessary. As such, sealed emergency exit doors can be installed, if required, to maintain the separation and prevent unnecessary access.

Administration Area

This area houses facilities such as the main administration office, employee changing rooms, canteens, washrooms, toilets, and first aid rooms. Employees use the changing rooms in the administration area to change into their factory uniforms and sanitize their hands before entering the secondary manufacturing area. After changing, employees access the stores through a separate entrance. This area is not designated as a production space. Offices are also located here, and the layout can be designed so that these offices have a direct view of the manufacturing area through glass panels. This arrangement provides good visibility of the production process while preventing cross-contamination. A designated visitors' viewing area of the production process can also be located in this section.

Personnel and Goods Movement

Employee movement within the facility in the diamond model is illustrated by arrows in Figure 1.6. Employees working in different sections can access these areas through the administration area. Those assigned to the primary and secondary manufacturing areas enter via air locks. Access to the primary manufacturing area is exclusively through the secondary manufacturing area.

Raw and packing materials first arrive at the warehouse and are stored in Store A. These materials are then moved to the secondary manufacturing area, where tasks such as removal of packaging, weighing, and batch preparation occur.

Next, the raw materials, now ready for processing, are transferred to the primary manufacturing area. Once the manufacturing process is complete and primary packing is finished, the product moves to the secondary packing area. Secondary packing operations, such as pasting labels, printing information, packing into shippers, shrink wrapping, and palletizing, are carried out here. Finally, the finished product is transferred to Store B, ready for dispatch.

PROJECT REPORT PREPARATION

A project report serves as a comprehensive document out lining the details of the business and the implementation plan. Agricultural services are essential for supporting farmers and agribusinesses while promoting sustainable agriculture. By offering access to information, technology, and equipment, agro-services help farmers enhance their productivity, reduce costs, and contribute to global food security.

An agricultural service center project report is an important document that provides the necessary guidelines for obtaining licenses, setting up the business, and securing financial support from banks. It serves as a comprehensive guide, addressing all queries and providing quick solutions to potential challenges.

Agricultural Services Centers (ASCs) are dedicated facilities that offer a wide array of services to farmers, agribusinesses, and rural communities. Typically established by government bodies or non-governmental organizations, ASCs play a crucial role in promoting sustainable agricultural practices and improving the economic well-being of rural populations.

Types of Services

Types of Services Offered by Agricultural Service Centers:

- **Soil Testing**: Analysis of soil composition and fertility to determine the appropriate fertilizers and ideal crop rotation plans. This helps optimize soil health and crop production.

- **Crop Management**: Implementation of best practices for planting, growing, and harvesting crops to maximize yield and quality. Techniques like precision planting and nutrient management may be used to enhance efficiency.
- **Financial Planning**: Creation of financial plans and budgets tailored to agricultural businesses. This includes managing risks and exploring opportunities to ensure the financial health and growth of the farm.
- **Market Analysis**: Assessment of market trends and demand for agricultural products. This enables farmers to make informed decisions regarding crop selection and the timing of sales for maximum profitability.
- **Technology and Equipment**: Provision of access to advanced technology and equipment, such as tractors, seed drills, and irrigation systems. This equipment is essential for improving productivity, efficiency, and sustainability in farming.
- **Environmental Sustainability**: Promotion of farming practices that minimize environmental impact. This includes reducing pesticide use, enhancing soil conservation, and supporting other sustainable agricultural practices that protect natural resources.

How to Download Agro Service Centre Project Report

Gone are the days of waiting for expert consultations. Now, you can easily access your agro service centerstartup sample report by downloading it instantly in PDF format.

First Step

- Click "Add to Basket"
- Proceed to Checkout
- Complete the Payment

Second Step

- Once your payment is successful, you will receive a link to download the report.
- You can download the report immediately using this link.

Benefits of Agricultural Services Centers (ASCs)

- **Improved Agricultural Productivity**: ASCs equip farmers with valuable information, technology, and expertise, helping to boost agricultural productivity and ensure greater food security.
- **Increased Income**: By enhancing yields, lowering costs, and connecting farmers to new markets, ASCs contribute to higher income levels and better livelihoods for farmers.
- **Empowered Rural Communities**: ASCs empower rural communities, especially women and youth, by offering educational resources, training, and promoting gender-sensitive approaches to farming.

- **Enhanced Environmental Sustainability**: ASCs support sustainable agricultural practices by advising farmers on soil and water conservation, pest control, and the adoption of environmentally friendly technologies.

Current and Future Projection of Agricultural Services Centers in India

Agricultural Services Centers (ASCs) are crucial in helping farmers and agribusinesses in India thrive. These centers offer a variety of services like expert guidance, market insights, financial aid, training, and access to essential equipment and technology. In recent years, the Indian government has significantly invested in establishing and upgrading ASCs to foster sustainable agriculture and enhance the well-being of rural communities. This approach helps improve agricultural practices, boosts rural economies, and ensures food security for the growing population.

Current Status

Currently, there are over 10,000 Agricultural Services Centers (ASCs) across India, catering to a vast number of farmers and agribusinesses. These centers offer valuable services, including expert advice on soil and water management, crop selection and rotation, pest and disease control, and the adoption of modern technologies. In addition to technical support, ASCs also provide market information and essential financial services such as credit and insurance, enabling farmers to manage their finances effectively and grow their businesses. These centers play a vital role in improving agricultural productivity and enhancing the livelihoods of rural communities.

Future Projections

Despite the challenges, the future of Agricultural Services Centers (ASCs) in India looks highly promising. The Indian government has made significant commitments to invest in the growth and expansion of these centers, with a target of establishing 100,000 ASCs by 2025. Furthermore, the growing adoption of precision agriculture and other advanced technologies is expected to boost the demand for ASC services, as farmers increasingly seek ways to enhance their productivity and operational efficiency. This progress will likely contribute to the overall development of the agricultural sector and support sustainable farming practices across the country.

Role of Technology in Agro Service Business

Technology plays a crucial role in transforming the agro service business by providing farmers with access to real-time data and resources that enhance their productivity. Mobile applications and digital platforms allow farmers to easily access weather forecasts, market prices, pest and disease alerts, and farming best practices. This timely information helps farmers make informed decisions on crop management, leading to better yields and reduced losses. Additionally, the integration of precision agriculture technologies like drones, sensors, and GPS mapping helps farmers optimize resource use, monitor soil health, and manage irrigation more efficiently.

In the agro service sector, technology also enables better connectivity between farmers and service providers. Through online platforms, farmers can directly connect with agricultural experts, suppliers of seeds, fertilizers, and equipment, and even financial institutions offering loans and insurance. This streamlines the supply chain, reduces the time spent searching for resources, and makes it easier for farmers to access products and services that were once out of reach, especially in rural areas. Moreover, the use of blockchain technology is gaining traction to ensure transparency and traceability in agricultural supply chains, ensuring that consumers and businesses can trust the origin and quality of the products.

Furthermore, technology plays a pivotal role in enhancing the sustainability of agriculture. By using data analytics and AI-based solutions, agro service businesses can offer tailored recommendations to farmers on crop rotation, soil fertility, and sustainable practices. These technologies can help mitigate the environmental impact of farming, reduce pesticide usage, and improve water conservation. Through continuous innovation, technology is helping to reshape the agro service business into a more efficient, sustainable, and accessible model that ultimately benefits both farmers and the broader agricultural ecosystem.

The future of Agricultural Services Centers (ASCs) in India looks bright, as they are poised to play a pivotal role in shaping the country's agricultural landscape. With government investment and the growing reliance on technology, ASCs will increasingly help farmers access critical resources and information, boosting productivity and efficiency. The incorporation of digital platforms and mobile apps is expected to bridge gaps in rural areas, making ASC services more accessible and comprehensive, while enhancing market connectivity and financial inclusion for farmers. This evolving model promises to drive sustainable agricultural practices and improve rural livelihoods across India.

HOW MUCH DO I NEED TO INVEST FOR STARTING AGRO SERVICE CENTRE IN INDIA

The expenses associated with establishing an Agro Service Centre (ASC) in India can vary based on several factors such as location, the scale of the operation, the services provided, the necessary equipment, and the budget for marketing and advertising. Understanding these costs is crucial for determining the financial feasibility of your business. This article offers a detailed breakdown of the various costs involved in starting an ASC in India.

- **Rent for Office or Facility Space**: Rental costs for office or facility space can differ greatly depending on the area and the size of the facility. For instance, setting up an ASC in a metropolitan area will typically incur higher rent compared to rural regions. On average, the monthly rent for such spaces in India can range between 50,000 and 500,000 Rupees.
- **Equipment and Supplies**: The type of equipment and supplies needed for an ASC depends on the services offered. For instance, if services such as soil testing and seed procurement are provided, you'll need to invest in machinery like tractors, plows, seed drills, and irrigation systems. Additionally, supplies

such as seeds, fertilizers, and pesticides will be necessary. The cost of these items can range from 500,000 to 5,000,000 Rupees.

- **Marketing and Advertising**: To ensure that potential customers are aware of your services and to reach your target audience, you'll need to allocate a budget for marketing and advertising. These costs can vary significantly based on the strategies you implement. The marketing and advertising expenses typically range between 50,000 and 500,000 Rupees.
- **Licenses and Permits**: To legally operate an ASC, you will need to secure the required licenses and permits. This includes business registration, a trade license, and an agricultural service center license. The fees for obtaining these licenses can vary from 10,000 to 100,000 Rupees.
- **Staffing Costs**: Depending on the scale of your ASC, you'll need to hire staff such as technicians, agricultural advisors, and administrative employees. Salaries and benefits can differ based on the qualifications and experience of the staff. On average, staffing expenses can range from 50,000 to 500,000 Rupees per month.
- **Other Costs**: There are several additional costs to consider, such as utilities, insurance, and office supplies. These costs typically range between 10,000 and 50,000 Rupees per month.

Additionally, seeking financial support through investors, grants, or loans can help ease the financial burden of starting an ASC.

In conclusion, the initial investment required to start an Agro Service Centre in India can range from a few million Rupees to several million Rupees, depending on the scale, services, equipment, and marketing efforts. Having a clear understanding of the costs and formulating a detailed financial plan will be key to ensuring the success and long-term sustainability of your ASC.

How Much Space is Needed to Start an Agro Service Centre?

The space required to establish an Agro Service Centre (ASC) depends on multiple factors, including the range of services provided, the number of customers served, and the size of the inventory. A general estimate of the area needed for an ASC can be determined based on the following key aspects:

- **Sales Area:** This section is designated for displaying agricultural inputs like seeds, fertilizers, pesticides, and other related products. The size of this area depends on the variety and quantity of products you intend to sell and the space required for their proper arrangement.
- **Storage Area:** This space is essential for keeping agricultural inputs such as fertilizers, seeds, pesticides, and other supplies. The storage area size depends on the quantity of inventory you plan to maintain for smooth operations.
- **Office Area:** This section serves as the administrative hub for handling record-keeping, accounting, and customer support functions. The office space requirement will be influenced by the number of employees and the tasks they are expected to perform.

- **Training and Demonstration Area:** This part of the facility is dedicated to educating farmers and rural communities on the use of agricultural inputs and demonstrating best farming techniques. The space required for training and demonstrations will vary based on the activities planned and the number of participants expected.

In summary, the space requirement for an ASC depends on factors such as the services offered, customer volume, and inventory size. A typical ASC requires an estimated 1,000 to 1,500 square feet; however, the actual area may differ based on individual business needs.

How to Select the Right Location for an Agro Service Centre?

Choosing the right location for an Agro Service Centre (ASC) is a crucial decision that can impact the business's success. A well-chosen location can help attract customers, lower operational costs, and ensure long-term sustainability. Below are key factors to consider when selecting a location for your ASC:

- **Accessibility:** The ASC should be easily accessible to farmers and rural communities, preferably located near major roads, highways, or public transportation hubs to facilitate smooth customer visits.
- **Proximity to Agricultural Land:** Establishing an ASC close to farming areas makes it more convenient to offer services to farmers and reduces travel time and costs for soil testing, seed procurement, and other agricultural support services.
- **Market Potential:** Evaluating the market potential of a location is essential. This includes analyzing the number of farmers in the area, the demand for agricultural services, and the overall customer base to ensure sufficient business opportunities.
- **Competition Analysis:** It is important to assess the level of competition in the area. If there are existing ASCs nearby, evaluating their performance can help determine whether you should establish your business there or explore a different location or service differentiation strategies.
- **Operating Costs and Cost of Living:** The cost of running a business varies by location. Urban areas generally have higher rental, labor, and operational costs compared to rural regions. Factoring in these expenses is crucial for financial sustainability.
- **Availability of Skilled Labor:** Hiring qualified agricultural technicians, advisors, and administrative staff is vital for running an ASC efficiently. Choosing a location where skilled labor is available can help ensure smooth operations.

Selecting the right location for an Agro Service Centre requires careful evaluation of accessibility, proximity to agricultural zones, market potential, competition, cost-effectiveness, and labor availability. A well-researched decision will contribute significantly to the business's success.

How to Effectively Promote an Agro Service Centre?

Marketing and advertising play a vital role in the success of an Agro Service Centre (ASC). Implementing effective promotional strategies can enhance visibility, attract more customers, and ensure business growth. Here are some key approaches to marketing an ASC:

- **Develop a Strong Brand Identity**: Creating a unique brand image that differentiates your ASC from competitors is essential. Your brand should reflect the core values and services offered while maintaining consistency across all marketing materials.
- **Target the Right Market:** Identifying your target audience, primarily farmers and rural communities, allows you to develop tailored marketing strategies. This may include advertisements in local newspapers, agricultural journals, radio stations, and distributing educational materials that highlight the benefits of your services.
- **Engage with Local Communities:** Building relationships with local farmers and communities can boost business credibility. Participating in local events, supporting community initiatives, and collaborating with agricultural organizations can enhance your reputation and trust among potential customers.
- **Utilize Social Media Platforms:** Platforms such as Facebook, Instagram, and Twitter are powerful tools for engaging with customers. Posting updates, sharing customer testimonials, and offering exclusive deals can increase visibility and attract new clients.
- **Network with Agricultural Organizations:** Establishing connections with agricultural cooperatives, farmer associations, and local agribusiness groups can expand your reach and enhance service awareness. Participating in industry events and agricultural fairs can also generate business opportunities.
- **Offer Promotional Discounts and Deals:** Attracting new customers through promotional offers and discounts can encourage them to try your services. Rewarding loyal customers with special deals can also help build long-term relationships and repeat business.
- **Create Informative Educational Materials:** Producing brochures, pamphlets, and videos explaining ASC services and their benefits can be an effective marketing tool. These materials can be distributed in person or shared via email and social media.

In conclusion, a well-planned marketing strategy is crucial for the success of an Agro Service Centre. By establishing a strong brand identity, targeting the right audience, engaging with local communities, leveraging social media, networking with industry groups, offering promotions, and providing educational resources, an ASC can effectively increase its customer base and drive business growth.

Essential Machinery and Equipment for an Agro Service Centre

Agro Service Centres (ASCs) require a diverse range of machinery and equipment to effectively support farmers and rural communities. The specific equipment needed depends on the services provided, but certain essential tools and machines are crucial for efficient agricultural operations. Below are some of the key pieces of equipment commonly used in an ASC:

- **Tractors:** These are fundamental for various farming activities such as plowing, planting, and harvesting. The size and type of tractor required will depend on the ASC's service offerings and the scale of farming operations it supports.
- **Irrigation Equipment:** Devices like sprinklers and drip irrigation systems are vital for efficient water management. They help in conserving water, enhancing crop yields, and improving overall farm productivity.
- **Power Tillers:** These lightweight tillers are essential for soil preparation, weeding, and other farming tasks. They are particularly useful for small-scale farmers and areas with space constraints.
- **Seed Drill Machines:** These machines facilitate precise seed placement, reducing manual labor and increasing the efficiency of sowing operations.
- **Harvesters:** Designed for crop harvesting, harvesters significantly enhance the efficiency of harvesting processes while reducing labor costs, making them indispensable for ASCs serving large-scale farms.
- **Sprayers:** Used for applying pesticides, herbicides, and fertilizers, sprayers play a crucial role in maintaining crop health and ensuring high yields.
- **Fertilizer Spreaders:** These machines distribute fertilizers uniformly across fields, reducing manual labor and enhancing the effectiveness of fertilization.
- **Power Generators:** In areas with unreliable electricity supply, power generators provide a consistent energy source for operating equipment and ensuring uninterrupted ASC services.
- **Tools and Specialized Equipment:** Basic hand tools like spades, hoes, and pruning shears are essential for routine agricultural tasks. Additionally, specialized instruments such as soil testers and moisture meters are critical for providing valuable insights into soil conditions and farm management.

The specific machinery and equipment required for an Agro Service Centre depend on the range of services it offers. However, investing in essential tools like tractors, irrigation systems, tillers, seed drills, harvesters, and power generators enables ASCs to provide high-quality services, improve agricultural efficiency, and contribute to the success of farmers and rural communities.

Government Guidelines and Licensing Requirements for Starting an Agro Service Centre in India

Starting an Agro Service Centre (ASC) in India involves complying with various government regulations and obtaining necessary licenses to ensure legal and sustainable operations. Below are the key government guidelines and licensing requirements for ASCs:

Government Guidelines for ASCs

- **Business Registration**: All ASCs must be registered with relevant government authorities, such as the Registrar of Companies or the Department of Agriculture.
- **Licensing Requirements**: Certain services, such as seed distribution or pesticide usage, require specific licenses.

- **Environmental Compliance**: ASCs must adhere to environmental regulations by ensuring the use of eco-friendly fertilizers and chemicals.
- **Labor Laws Compliance**: ASCs must follow labor laws, including minimum wage requirements and employee working conditions.
- **Tax Regulations**: ASCs must comply with tax laws, such as corporate and income tax payments, and GST registration.
- **Insurance Coverage**: ASCs must obtain insurance policies to safeguard against financial risks and liabilities.
- **Food Safety Regulations**: If an ASC deals with food production and distribution, it must meet food safety and hygiene standards.
- **Import/Export Regulations**: ASCs involved in international trade must comply with relevant import/export regulations.
- **Agricultural Support Policies**: ASCs can benefit from government subsidies, tax incentives, and other agricultural promotion schemes.

By adhering to these guidelines, ASCs can operate legally, offer high-quality services to farmers, and contribute to the agricultural sector's growth.

Licenses and Permits Required for ASCs

- **Business Registration**: An ASC must register as a sole proprietorship, partnership, or private limited company.
- **Trade License**: A trade license from the local municipal corporation is mandatory.
- **Environmental Clearance**: ASCs engaging in activities that impact the environment require clearance from regulatory authorities.
- **Pesticide License**: ASCs dealing with pesticides must secure a pesticide license from the Central Insecticides Board and Registration Committee.
- **Seed License**: If an ASC is involved in seed production and distribution, a seed license from the Department of Agriculture is required.
- **Fertilizer License**: ASCs handling fertilizers must obtain a fertilizer license from the Department of Agriculture.
- **Labor License**: ASCs employing workers must acquire a labor license from the Department of Labor.
- **Tax Registration**: An ASC must obtain a Taxation Identification Number (TIN) and register under the Goods and Services Tax (GST) framework.
- **Insurance**: Obtaining comprehensive insurance coverage is necessary to protect the ASC from unforeseen risks.

Complying with these licensing requirements ensures that ASCs operate legally, maintain high service standards, and contribute effectively to rural agricultural development.

Major Challenges faced by agro service centers

Despite these initiatives, several challenges persist in fully harnessing the potential of ASCs in India. A significant hurdle is the limited accessibility of these centers in many rural areas, especially in remote and hard-to-reach locations. Furthermore, a considerable number of farmers lack the essential knowledge and technical expertise required to effectively utilize the services provided by ASCs, which can hinder their overall impact and effectiveness.

MODEL PROJECT REPORT FOR AGRO-PROCESSING CENTRE

Executive Summary

The Agro-Processing Centre (APC) aims to facilitate the processing of agricultural products to enhance their value and increase the income of local farmers. This center will focus on adding value to farm produce such as fruits, vegetables, grains, and other locally grown crops by processing them into marketable products like juices, jams, flour, and packaged food. The facility will serve as a crucial support structure for the rural agricultural economy and help in reducing post-harvest losses.

Key Objectives

- To provide a sustainable market for local agricultural products.
- To reduce post-harvest losses by processing farm produce.
- To generate employment opportunities for the local community.
- To contribute to food security by offering nutritious, value-added products.

Introduction

Background

Agriculture is the backbone of the economy, especially in rural areas. However, post-harvest losses, limited access to processing technologies, and lack of proper infrastructure often result in the wastage of agricultural produce. The Agro-Processing Centre is envisioned to bridge this gap by offering advanced processing technologies and providing farmers with better value for their produce.

Need for the Project

- **Post-Harvest Losses**: A significant portion of agricultural produce is wasted due to lack of storage and processing facilities.
- **Income Generation**: Farmers often sell their produce at low prices during harvest seasons. Processing can increase the shelf life and value of their products.
- **Market Access**: By processing agricultural products, the centre will open up access to national and international markets.

Market Analysis

Target Market

The key market for processed products includes:

- **Domestic consumers**: People seeking value-added, nutritious, and locally produced food products.

- **Retailers**: Supermarkets, local grocery stores, and online marketplaces.
- **Export markets**: Potential export of processed products to international markets where demand for quality, organic, and processed food is rising.

Market Demand

There is an increasing demand for processed food products due to changing lifestyles, increased awareness of food quality, and the growing interest in healthy, sustainable, and locally sourced products. Additionally, the government is encouraging agro-processing to reduce reliance on imported food products.

Product Line

The Agro-Processing Centre will produce a variety of products, such as:

- **Fruit Juices and Concentrates**: Made from locally sourced fruits like mango, orange, and guava.
- **Pickles and Jams**: Processed from vegetables and fruits.
- **Flour**: Milling of grains such as wheat, maize, and rice.
- **Ready-to-Eat Snacks**: Packaged food items, such as chips, granola, and packaged fruits.
- **Dried Vegetables & Fruits**: For longer shelf life and wider distribution.

Infrastructure and Location

Location

The centre will be located in close proximity to farming communities, ensuring easy access to raw materials. Ideally, it should be situated near transport hubs to facilitate distribution.

Facility Design

The centre will be equipped with modern processing machinery, storage facilities, and packaging units. The facility will be divided into different sections:

- **Processing Area**: For washing, cutting, and packaging the produce.
- **Storage Area**: For raw materials and finished products.
- **Quality Control Lab**: To ensure that all products meet food safety standards.
- **Administrative Offices**: For management, marketing, and other operations.

Technology and Equipment

The centre will use advanced equipment for food processing, including:

- Juicers, Extractors, and Pasteurizers for juice processing.
- Dehydrators for drying fruits and vegetables.
- Milling machines for grinding grains into flour.
- Packaging machines for sealing products.

Production Process

Fruit and Vegetable Processing

- **Raw Material Procurement**: Locally sourced fresh fruits and vegetables.
- **Cleaning and Sorting**: Washing and sorting produce based on quality.
- **Processing**: Techniques like juicing, canning, and drying, depending on the product.
- **Packaging**: Products will be packaged according to industry standards to ensure hygiene and shelf life.
- **Distribution**: Finished products will be distributed to various retail outlets.

Flour and Grains Processing

- **Grain Procurement**: Sourcing wheat, maize, and rice from local farmers.
- **Milling**: Grinding grains into flour and other derivatives.
- **Quality Control**: Testing flour for standardization.
- **Packaging**: Ensuring the packaging is both eco-friendly and durable.

Financial Plan

Capital Investment

Initial capital investment will cover the purchase of land, construction of the facility, procurement of machinery, and initial working capital. The total estimated cost is:

Table 1.2: Initial Capital Investment.

Item	Cost (INR)
Land & Building Construction	30,00,000
Equipment and Machinery	50,00,000
Working Capital	20,00,000
Other Infrastructure Costs	10,00,000
Total	1,10,00,000

Revenue Model

The primary sources of revenue will be from the sale of processed products. The following assumptions have been made for the financial projections:

- Average production capacity: 500 tons of processed product per month.
- Expected price per unit: INR 50 per kg.
- Expected revenue per month: INR 25,00,000.

Operational Expenses

Key operational expenses will include:

- **Raw Material Costs**: Purchase of agricultural produce.

- **Labor Costs**: Wages for employees at various stages of production.
- **Utilities and Maintenance**: Electricity, water, and other infrastructure maintenance costs.

Profitability Projections

The Agro-Processing Centre expects to achieve break-even within 2-3 years, with steady growth in profit margins as production capacity expands and economies of scale kick in.

Sustainability and Environmental Impact

Waste Management

The centre will implement a waste management system to recycle waste and reduce environmental impact. This includes:

- **Organic Waste**: Used for composting or converted into animal feed.
- **Packaging Waste**: Recycled or disposed of in an eco-friendly manner.

Energy Efficiency

The facility will use energy-efficient equipment and explore renewable energy sources like solar power to minimize energy consumption and carbon footprint.

Conclusion and Recommendations

The Agro-Processing Centre project offers a valuable opportunity to enhance the economic well-being of local farmers, minimize post-harvest losses, and generate stable employment. By processing raw agricultural produce into value-added products, the center can contribute to a more sustainable and profitable agro-processing ecosystem, benefiting both farmers and the broader agricultural industry.

Recommendations

- Collaborate with local farmers for a steady supply of raw materials.
- Focus on product innovation to cater to diverse consumer preferences.
- Explore government schemes and funding opportunities for agro-processing.
- Invest in research and development to improve processing techniques and product shelf life.

Annexures

- **Annexure 1**: Detailed Financial Projections (5 years)
- **Annexure 2**: Marketing Plan
- **Annexure 3**: List of Required Equipment and Suppliers
- **Annexure 4**: Employee Hiring Plan and Job Descriptions

2

Manufacturing and Management of Primary Processing Centre

INTRODUCTION

A Primary Processing Centre (PPC) is a facility that offers essential infrastructure for the initial processing of agricultural produce, including grading, sorting, packaging, and storage. These centers are strategically located near production zones within raw material catchment areas and are supported by Collection Centers (CCs) in nearby villages.

The establishment and efficient management of a Primary Processing Centre (PPC) play a crucial role in enhancing the value of raw agricultural products, improving their marketability, and minimizing post-harvest losses. A well-operated PPC integrates modern processing technologies, optimized resource utilization, and streamlined logistics to ensure high-quality output and long-term sustainability. Advanced processing methods such as drying, milling, juicing, and canning help maintain product quality and nutritional integrity while reducing waste. Additionally, a robust management framework is essential for supervising operations, implementing quality control measures, and maintaining an efficient supply chain that connects local farmers to the processing facility. The effectiveness of a PPC extends beyond technical efficiency, as it also fosters community empowerment through job creation, skill enhancement, and active participation, thereby contributing to both economic development and sustainable agricultural practices. By harmonizing these elements, a PPC serves as a critical hub for agricultural progress, granting farmers improved market access, decreasing reliance on unprocessed exports, and generating value-added products that align with consumer demand.

The manufacturing and management of a Primary Processing Centre (PPC) play a crucial role in transforming raw agricultural produce into value-added products that enhance marketability, reduce post-harvest losses, and improve farmers' income. A well-established PPC serves as a key link between agricultural production and end consumers by providing essential processing facilities such as cleaning, sorting, grading, milling, drying, juicing, and packaging. These processes not only increase the shelf life of agricultural products but also ensure that they meet quality and safety standards required for both domestic and international markets.

The manufacturing aspect of a PPC involves the selection and implementation of modern agro-processing technologies that optimize efficiency while maintaining product integrity. Advanced machinery and equipment, such as seed cleaners, dehuskers, pulverizers, and cold storage units, enable large-scale processing with minimal wastage. The use of sustainable practices, including energy-efficient systems and waste management solutions, further enhances the operational viability of PPCs.

On the other hand, the management of a PPC involves overseeing the entire supply chain, from sourcing raw materials directly from farmers to ensuring the timely distribution of processed products. Effective management requires strategic planning, workforce training, quality control measures, and adherence to regulatory standards. Additionally, logistics, inventory management, and financial planning are key components that contribute to the success of a PPC.By integrating efficient manufacturing and management strategies, PPCs can significantly contribute to the agro-processing industry, promote rural employment, and support sustainable agricultural practices. A well-managed PPC not only improves market access for farmers but also strengthens the overall food supply chain, ensuring that agricultural produce is utilized optimally. This chapter explores the various facets of manufacturing and managing a PPC, highlighting best practices, technological advancements, and management strategies essential for its success.

The development and management of a Primary Processing Centre (PPC) within the agro-processing sector involve converting raw agricultural materials into refined, market-ready goods. This transformation is vital for adding value to agricultural produce, prolonging its shelf life, and ensuring it meets consumer and retailer quality standards. A well-functioning PPC integrates cutting-edge processing technology with strategic management to facilitate seamless operations, optimize resource allocation, and uphold sustainability. Core processes in a PPC typically include cleaning, sorting, milling, juicing, drying, and packaging, depending on the specific agricultural products being processed. Managing a PPC entails overseeing the entire supply chain, from sourcing raw materials directly from farmers to distributing the final processed goods. Effective management practices involve coordinating production schedules, maintaining processing equipment, ensuring compliance with food safety regulations, and organizing logistics to guarantee timely market distribution. Quality assurance is a key priority, with stringent controls enforced at every stage of processing to ensure products are safe, nutritious, and consistent in quality. Additionally, resource management plays a significant role, focusing on waste reduction, energy conservation, and the adoption of eco-friendly practices, such as water efficiency and recycling initiatives.

A thriving agro-processing PPC relies on skilled labor and active community involvement. By providing employment opportunities and specialized training, these centers ensure operational efficiency while contributing to local economic development. Establishing a well-connected ecosystem that bridges technological advancements with local agricultural practices enables PPCs to enhance farmers' incomes, support food security initiatives, and drive sustainable economic growth in the agro-processing industry.

PRIMARY PROCESSING CENTRE (PPC)

A Primary Processing Centre (PPC) in agro-processing is a specialized facility designed for the initial transformation of raw agricultural produce into more refined and usable forms. These centers primarily focus on enhancing the quality, longevity, and market appeal of agricultural commodities through fundamental processing techniques. By adding value through minimal but essential processing, PPCs play a crucial role in reducing post-harvest losses and improving economic returns for farmers. The primary processing operations carried out in these facilities typically include cleaning, sorting, grading, drying, milling, crushing, and packaging, among others, depending on the nature of the raw materials being processed. Through these activities, PPCs ensure that agricultural products meet industry standards, are easier to store and transport, and become more suitable for further processing or direct consumption.

Essential Functions of a Primary Processing Centre

- **Cleaning and Sorting:** Raw agricultural products, such as fruits, vegetables, grains, or pulses, are cleaned to remove dirt, pesticides, or other contaminants. Sorting ensures that only high-quality produce proceeds to further stages of processing.
- **Grading:** Products are graded based on size, quality, and ripeness to meet market specifications.
- **Milling and Grinding:** Grains like wheat, maize, and rice are milled into flour or other products such as cornmeal. This helps create products that have a longer shelf life and are easier to transport.
- **Drying:** Perishable products like fruits, vegetables, or herbs may be dried to prevent spoilage, enhance their shelf life, and reduce transportation costs.
- **Juicing or Crushing:** Fruits and vegetables may be processed into juices, purees, or concentrates, which are used in the production of beverages or processed food products.
- **Packaging:** The processed products are packaged in various forms (e.g., bulk, retail) to ensure hygiene, preservation, and easy distribution.

Goals of a Primary Processing Centre

- **Value Addition:** Enhancing the economic value of raw agricultural products by processing them into higher-value products.

- **Reduction of Post-Harvest Losses:** Minimizing spoilage and wastage that occur from improper storage or handling by providing timely processing.
- **Improved Market Access:** Providing farmers with an organized platform to sell their produce at better prices through value-added products.
- **Job Creation:** Generating employment opportunities for the local workforce, especially in rural areas, through processing activities.

Categories of Products Processed at a Primary Processing Centre

- **Grains and cereals:** Milling of wheat, rice, maize into flour or meal.
- **Fruits and vegetables:** Canning, drying, juicing, or packaging for the retail market.
- **Spices and herbs:** Grinding and packaging for use in food processing or retail.
- **Oilseeds:** Crushing and extraction of oil.

SIGNIFICANCE OF A PRIMARY PROCESSING CENTRE IN AGRO-PROCESSING

A Primary Processing Centre (PPC) acts as the initial stage in converting raw agricultural produce into market-ready commodities, serving as a critical link between farm production and the end market. These centres significantly enhance the efficiency of the agricultural value chain, promote food security, and contribute to rural economic development by connecting farmers with larger and more diverse markets.

Equipped with modern technology and advanced processing machinery, PPCs help minimize post-harvest losses, enhance the market potential of agricultural products, and enable farmers to secure better prices for their produce. By improving product quality and reducing wastage, these facilities directly contribute to strengthening the economic stability of farming communities, thereby enhancing their overall livelihoods.

Upon arrival at the PPC, agricultural produce requires a well-equipped unloading facility to ensure seamless handling. This infrastructure is crucial in directing fresh produce toward manual sorting and grading sections in the shortest time possible while minimizing losses. Once graded, sorted, cleaned, and packed, the processed produce is stored in a warehouse until it is ready for dispatch. Efficient logistics management ensures that the products are loaded onto transport vehicles at the right time, facilitating smooth transfer to Central Processing Centres (CPCs). It is imperative to keep losses at the loading stage to an absolute minimum to maintain product quality and maximize economic benefits.

Containers

To ensure the safe transportation of perishable goods, it is proposed to use collapsible plastic crates for the transfer of products between the Primary Processing Centers (PPCs), Central Processing Centre (CPC), and Collection Centers (CCs). The crates will rotate continuously between these centers, optimizing the movement of goods. To meet an annual procurement target of 20,000 MT per year, the average daily procurement will be around 68 MT. However, procurement is expected to fluctuate, with peak seasons possibly reaching up to 100 MT per day. During these peak periods, the demand for crates will rise, requiring approximately 7,000 crates to handle a single day's procurement. Therefore, a total of 7,000 crates is planned for the Sikaria Mega Food Park (P) Ltd., with a budget allocation of Rs 25 lakhs for the entire park.

Measurement of Raw Material

Each Primary Processing Centre (PPC) will be equipped with weighing scales within the sorting and grading area. These scales will help quantify the amounts received, the amounts rejected, and the final quantities of products that are sorted and graded for packaging.

Sorting

The primary objective of sorting is to ensure that the agricultural produce meets the quality criteria. After the unloading and weighing process, the produce will be directed to the sorting area where it will be segregated to ensure that only the produce of the required quality is sent to the Central Processing Centre (CPC). Produce that does not meet the quality standards of the respective units will be set aside for alternate handling.

Grading

Grading is essential for categorizing produce based on differentiating parameters such as size. Even when the produce meets similar quality standards, it may be required by different units based on size specifications. This activity will ensure the segregation of processable inputs, with table-grade produce being set aside for retail sale or as directed. The grading process will be done manually using tables at each Processing Centre (PPC), with a total of 10 tables planned for the facility.

Clearing

Washing ensures that raw materials are clean, which helps extend their shelf life by preventing decay due to dirt or other contaminants. It also reduces the need for intensive washing at the Central Processing Centre (CPC). Washing is product-specific and will be applied selectively to those items that require it. After washing, the produce will proceed to the packing phase.

Packing

The cleaned raw materials will be properly packed to ensure their preservation for either cold storage or temporary warehouse storage before being sent to the Central Processing Centre (CPC). The packing procedure will vary depending on the type of product and will be designed to account for transportation time and potential road hazards to minimize wastage during transit.

Storage Facilities

Once packed, the materials will be stored in a warehouse for temporary storage until they reach the required quantity for shipment. The goods will then be transported to the Central Processing Centre (CPC) near Agartala when sufficient volume is ready for loading onto trucks.

Ripening Chambers

Ripening chambers will be developed at the Central Processing Centre (CPC) and Primary Processing Centre (PPC) locations, depending on the availability of raw materials such as mangoes, bananas, and papayas in the surrounding areas. These chambers will ensure proper ripening and quality control of the produce before further processing.

PRODUCTION OF PRIMARY PROCESSING CENTRE

The manufacturing of a Primary Processing Centre (PPC) involves the establishment of facilities where raw materials (often agricultural or natural resources) undergo initial processing before they are further refined or used in various industries. The main purpose of a Primary Processing Centre is to add value to raw materials, turning them into products that can be used for secondary or tertiary processing or directly in consumer markets. Here's an overview of how the manufacturing process for a PPC might be structured:

Strategy and Design

- **Site Selection**: Identify a location close to the source of raw materials to minimize transportation costs.
- **Facility Layout**: Design the layout of the processing facility to optimize workflows, ensure safety, and adhere to regulatory standards.
- **Capacity Planning**: Determine the processing capacity required based on expected volumes and future growth.
- **Environmental Impact**: Assess and plan for waste management, water usage, energy consumption, and pollution control.

Infrastructure Advancement

- **Construction**: Build the physical infrastructure, including processing units, storage areas, warehouses, and offices.
- **Utilities Setup**: Ensure reliable access to power, water, and waste management systems. This may involve setting up electricity generation, water treatment plants, and waste disposal systems.
- **Transportation**: Construct or establish transportation systems (rail, road, or sea) for incoming raw materials and outgoing products.

Installation of Equipment and Machinery

- **Processing Machines**: Install machinery for primary processing operations, such as grinders, mills, crushers, sorters, and separators. The specific equipment will depend on the type of raw materials (e.g., agricultural crops, minerals, or timber).

- **Automation Systems**: Implement automated controls for improving efficiency, minimizing human error, and ensuring the safety of operations.
- **Maintenance Systems**: Set up maintenance schedules and facilities to keep equipment in good working condition.

Personnel Management

- **Hiring**: Recruit skilled workers, operators, technicians, and managers who can handle the day-to-day operations of the PPC.
- **Training**: Provide specialized training on machinery, safety protocols, environmental compliance, and best practices to improve productivity and reduce accidents.

Procurement Material

- **Supply Chain Management**: Establish relationships with suppliers of raw materials (e.g., farmers, mining companies, or logging operations) to ensure a steady and reliable supply of inputs.
- **Quality Control**: Implement quality control measures at the raw material reception stage to ensure that only suitable materials enter the processing system.

Operational Processing

- **Initial Processing**: Depending on the industry, this may include cleaning, sorting, grading, cutting, milling, or extracting valuable substances from the raw materials.
- **Value Addition**: Some primary processing steps may include creating semi-processed goods that are suitable for further processing (e.g., turning wheat into flour or cotton into yarn).
- **Packaging**: If the primary product is ready for market or further processing, packaging systems are implemented to prepare it for transport.

Quality Control and Assurance

- **Testing**: Ensure that the processed material meets specific standards in terms of quality, safety, and compliance with local and international regulations.
- **Documentation**: Maintain records for tracking production processes, raw material sources, and finished products to facilitate quality assurance and traceability.

Logistics and Distribution

- **Storage**: Finished goods or partially processed materials are stored in appropriate conditions (e.g., temperature control, humidity control) to maintain product integrity.

- **Transportation**: Organize the logistics for distributing processed goods to secondary processors, wholesalers, or directly to consumers.

Sustainability and Environmental Issues

- **Energy Efficiency**: Implement energy-efficient systems (e.g., renewable energy sources, waste heat recovery).
- **Waste Management**: Manage by-products and waste materials through recycling, composting, or disposal according to local regulations.
- **Sustainable Practices**: Adopt sustainable practices, such as reducing water usage, minimizing emissions, and ensuring compliance with environmental standards.

Continuous Enhancement

- **Monitoring**: Continuously monitor the operations for efficiency, quality, and compliance.
- **Upgrades**: Regularly update the facility and equipment to stay competitive, improve productivity, and meet emerging standards.
- **Feedback Loops**: Incorporate feedback from customers, employees, and regulatory bodies to refine processes and products.

The overall goal of a Primary Processing Centre is to add enough value to raw materials to make them suitable for use in more advanced manufacturing or for direct consumption.

MANAGEMENT OF PRIMARY PROCESSING CENTRE

Managing a Primary Processing Centre (PPC) involves overseeing its day-to-day operations, ensuring efficiency, quality control, and profitability, while also adhering to environmental and safety regulations. The management structure typically involves multiple levels of responsibility, from senior executives to on-the-ground operators. Here's a detailed overview of how to effectively manage a Primary Processing Centre:

Leadership and Organizational Framework

- **Management Team**: A PPC typically has a management team comprising senior leaders who are responsible for high-level strategic planning and decision-making, such as the CEO, Plant Manager, and Operations Manager.
- **Departments**: The center may be divided into key functional areas, such as:
- **Operations**: Responsible for the daily running of the facility.
- **Production**: Oversees the processing of raw materials.
- **Quality Control**: Ensures the processed goods meet safety and quality standards.
- **Logistics**: Manages transportation and storage of raw materials and finished products.
- **Human Resources**: Manages staffing, training, and employee welfare.
- **Finance and Accounting**: Tracks costs, revenues, budgets, and financial performance.

- **Maintenance**: Ensures machinery and equipment are functioning optimally.
- **Safety and Compliance**: Ensures adherence to health, safety, and environmental regulations.

Strategic Planning and Objective Formulation

- **Defining Objectives**: Establish short-term and long-term operational goals. These could be related to production efficiency, quality standards, sustainability, or market expansion.
- **KPI (Key Performance Indicators)**: Set measurable targets for various aspects of performance, such as processing capacity, waste reduction, uptime, and labor efficiency.
- **Budgeting**: Develop and manage the budget for both capital and operational expenses. This includes setting aside funds for equipment upgrades, facility maintenance, and any emergency funds for operational disruptions.

Management of Production and Operations

- **Production Scheduling**: Develop a production schedule based on raw material availability, customer demand, and equipment capacity. This ensures the PPC operates efficiently without downtime.
- **Raw Material Management**: Ensure that raw materials are delivered on time and are of the required quality. This involves working closely with suppliers and managing inventory.
- **Process Optimization**: Constantly monitor and refine processing workflows to maximize output while minimizing waste, downtime, and energy consumption.
- **Capacity Management**: Manage the balance between production capacity and demand, ensuring that the facility can handle fluctuations in order volume without overburdening resources.

Quality Control and Assurance

- **Quality Standards**: Set specific quality control measures to ensure products meet both customer and regulatory standards. This includes regular testing, inspections, and process evaluations.
- **Feedback Loops**: Implement a feedback system where any defects or issues in the products are reported back to the production line for immediate resolution.
- **Training**: Provide ongoing quality control training to staff at all levels, ensuring that quality assurance protocols are followed consistently.

Management of Maintenance and Equipment

- **Preventative Maintenance**: Establish and enforce a regular maintenance schedule for machinery and equipment to reduce the likelihood of downtime due to mechanical failures.

- **Repairs and Replacements**: Create a system for managing repairs and ensuring spare parts are available when needed.
- **Lifecycle Management**: Plan for the replacement or upgrading of older equipment to improve efficiency, reduce costs, and stay competitive.

Human Resources Management

- **Staffing**: Hire skilled workers for various roles within the PPC, including machine operators, technicians, managers, and administrative staff.
- **Training and Development**: Offer ongoing training programs to improve skills, enhance safety knowledge, and keep up with technological advancements in processing methods.
- **Employee Engagement**: Foster a positive work environment through clear communication, recognition programs, and addressing employee concerns.
- **Health and Safety**: Ensure that all staff are trained on safety protocols and that a safe working environment is maintained. Regularly conduct safety audits and implement improvements.

Management of Inventory and Supply Chain

- **Raw Materials Procurement**: Develop long-term relationships with suppliers to ensure a stable supply of quality raw materials at the best prices.
- **Inventory Control**: Implement systems for tracking raw materials, in-process items, and finished products to reduce waste and ensure efficient use of resources.
- **Logistics Coordination**: Manage transportation for incoming raw materials and outgoing finished products. This includes dealing with logistics providers and optimizing transportation routes to reduce costs.

Sustainability and Environmental Compliance

- **Waste Management**: Ensure that waste products (e.g., by-products, packaging, or scraps) are managed according to environmental regulations. This could involve recycling or finding uses for waste materials.
- **Energy Efficiency**: Implement energy-saving measures, such as energy-efficient equipment, renewable energy sources, and optimizing energy consumption.
- **Regulatory Compliance**: Stay updated with environmental laws and regulations that apply to primary processing industries. Ensure that all operations are in full compliance to avoid fines or shutdowns.

Financial Management

- **Cost Control**: Track operational costs closely and find areas to improve efficiency and reduce expenses. This includes energy costs, raw material costs, labor costs, and maintenance expenses.

- **Revenue Generation**: Monitor the pricing strategy for finished products and services, considering market trends, competitors, and cost structures.
- **Financial Reporting**: Regularly generate financial reports to assess the profitability of the PPC, review budgets, and identify opportunities for growth or cost reduction.

Risk Management and Contingency Planning

- **Identifying Risks**: Assess risks that could disrupt operations, such as raw material shortages, machinery breakdowns, or supply chain disruptions.
- **Contingency Plans**: Develop contingency plans for handling emergencies, such as accidents, natural disasters, or equipment failures. This includes having backup suppliers and systems in place.
- **Insurance**: Ensure that the PPC is adequately insured against operational disruptions, accidents, property damage, and liabilities.

Orgoing Enhancement and Innovation

- **Process Improvement**: Encourage a culture of continuous improvement using methods like Lean Manufacturing or Six Sigma to reduce waste, improve quality, and streamline processes.
- **Innovation**: Stay ahead of market trends by researching and adopting new technologies or processing methods that can improve efficiency or product quality.
- **Feedback Systems**: Regularly solicit feedback from employees, customers, and suppliers to improve operations and product offerings.

Customer Relationship Management

- **Customer Satisfaction**: Maintain high levels of customer satisfaction by ensuring timely delivery of quality products.
- **Market Research**: Understand customer needs and market trends, adapting operations to meet changing demands.
- **Communication**: Ensure clear and transparent communication with customers, addressing concerns promptly and fostering long-term relationships.

Effective management of a Primary Processing Centre requires a balance of operational efficiency, quality control, cost management, and regulatory compliance. Strong leadership, clear communication, and a dedication to orgoing enhancement are Essential to the success and sustainability of the center

3

Preparation of Grain Pulse and Oilseed- Based Products

INTRODUCTION

The production of products from grains, pulses, and oilseeds entails a series of processes aimed at converting raw agricultural materials into products that are ready for use or consumption. These processes typically take place in dedicated facilities like grain mills, pulse processing units, and oilseed crushing plants, where various types of equipment are employed at different stages of production. Below is an introduction to the main processes and an overview of the equipment commonly used for these operations.

The preparation of grain, pulse, and oilseed-based products plays a vital role in transforming raw agricultural produce into consumable goods, contributing significantly to food security and nutrition. These products are integral to the daily diets of people around the world, and the processes involved in their production are designed to enhance quality, shelf life, and marketability. The procedures that go into preparing these products vary depending on the type of raw material, but all involve a series of specialized steps that are typically carried out in dedicated processing facilities.Grain mills, pulse processing units, and oilseed crushing plants are the primary settings where these transformations take place. Each of these facilities is equipped with specific machinery to perform tasks such as cleaning, milling, sorting, and packaging, with the aim of creating high-quality end products that are ready for distribution. The operation of these different pieces of equipment is crucial for ensuring consistency in quality, efficiency in production, and minimal wastage.

The processing of grains, pulses, and oilseeds involves several stages, such as cleaning to remove impurities, grinding or crushing to break down the raw materials, and packaging for storage or shipment. Each stage requires different equipment, such as mills for grains, crushers for oilseeds, and sorting machines for pulses. Understanding the operation of these machines is essential for anyone involved in the agro-processing industry, as it allows for better management of production, cost control, and maintenance. By familiarizing oneself with the equipment used in these processes, one can ensure that the products meet industry standards and fulfill consumer needs while optimizing resource use and reducing waste.

PREPARATION OF GRAIN-BASED PRODUCTS

Grains like wheat, rice, maize, barley, and oats are staple foods and raw materials for various processed products. The preparation of grain-based products can range from simple cleaning and milling to more complex processing operations like baking, brewing, and making cereal products.

Essential Procedures

- **Cleaning**: Grains are cleaned to remove impurities, stones, dust, and other foreign materials. This step is crucial to ensure the quality of the final product.
- **Milling**: Grains are ground into flour, semolina, or other products, depending on their intended use (e.g., flour for baking, rice for consumption, or cornmeal for various foods).
- **Flaking or Rolling**: Grains like oats may be flaked or rolled into thinner sheets for use in breakfast cereals or snacks.
- **Packaging**: After processing, grains or flour are packaged for distribution and sale.

Apparatus Vtilized

- **Grain Cleaners**: Machines like vibratory sieves, air blowers, and rotary cleaners are used to clean grains.
- **Roller Mills**: Used for grinding and milling grains into flour or meal.
- **Hammer Mills**: A type of grinding equipment often used for smaller grains or in coarse milling operations.
- **Flakers/Rollers**: Used to flatten and roll grains into flakes (commonly used for oats or barley).
- **Packaging Machines**: These machines are used to package the final products in bags, boxes, or other containers.

GRAIN PROCESSING

Wheat milling is a detailed and intricate process designed to transform wheat grains into wheat flour that can meet various needs while separating the by-products. The milling process generally consists of several essential stages and principles:

- **Crushing and Grinding**: Initially, wheat grains are crushed and ground progressively, stripping the endosperm from the bran flakes. The endosperm is then ground into flour with a specific degree of fineness. This step primarily focuses on separating the endosperm from the wheat bran and germ, which is crucial to ensure that the flour quality meets required standards.

- **Separation Principle**: The core principle in the milling process is achieving maximum separation of the endosperm from the bran and wheat germ. The quality of the flour, especially the ash content, is a critical parameter for evaluating the milling process. To produce high-quality flour, particularly with low ash content, more grinding passes are required with less force, which helps increase the particle size difference between the endosperm and the bran after grinding.
- **Peel Grinding System**: This system is responsible for removing the outer layers of the wheat grains and sorting them into wheat residue, oatmeal, wheat heart, and coarse flour. Further milling is done to remove the wheat residue, wheat heart, and meal from the bran flakes, ensuring that the bran remains as intact as possible to maximize separation of the endosperm and bran.
- **Heart Grinding System**: After the wheat husks are separated, the grains are processed to extract the wheat heart and coarse powder. The wheat heart is sent to the heart grinding system for further milling into fine flour, while the rest of the grains are handled by the relevant systems for better product yield.
- **Slag Grinding System**: This system processes the flour grains mixed with wheat hulls, separating the wheat hulls from the endosperm. It helps extract the wheat heart and coarse flour of superior quality, which are then sent for further refinement.
- **Powder Cleaning System**: By utilizing a combination of air sieves, the powder cleaning system sorts pure powder grains, bran powder grains, and bran chips. These are sent to the appropriate grinding systems for further processing to ensure the purity of the final product.
- **By-products**: Wheat germ, an important by-product of the milling process, holds high nutritional value. It can be developed and used as a valuable food resource due to its health benefits.

The overall wheat milling process transforms raw wheat into fine flour suitable for a wide range of applications while separating valuable by-products like wheat germ. The entire milling process is purely physical, involving a multi-step cycle to maintain the purity and high quality of the flour.

Similarly, corn flour milling involves processing corn to extract starch or produce corn flour, incorporating steps such as grinding, sieving, flour cleaning, and more. The key stages of corn milling include:

- **Material Selection and Cleaning**: The corn is first thoroughly washed to remove dust, impurities, and any unwanted parts such as husks. The cleaned corn kernels are then soaked to soften them, with substances like sodium sulfite often added during the soaking to aid the process.
- **Grinding and Separation**: Specialized equipment such as vertical grinders and flow plate sedimentation methods are used to grind the corn into a slurry, from which the germ and endosperm are separated.
- **Starch Extraction and Post-processing**: After extracting wet corn starch through precipitation and drying, it can be further processed into a variety of products, including items like corn vermicelli.

Throughout this process, a range of equipment and techniques ensures the corn is processed efficiently into high-quality starch or flour, which can then be used in various food applications.

MECHANICAL APPARATUS FREQUANTLY UTILIZED IN GRAIN PROCESSING

Grain Cleaning and Screening Equipment

Cleaning and screening are the first steps in the grain processing workflow, designed to eliminate impurities, dust, and unwanted particles from the grains. Our company manufactures cleaning equipment such as cyclone dust collectors, magnetic separators, and vibrating screens. These devices effectively remove contaminants and dust, enhancing the quality and nutritional value of the grains. They also minimize waste and loss during further processing stages and significantly improve production efficiency.

Grinding Equipment

Grinding is a crucial stage in grain processing, converting grains into powder for subsequent use. Our company offers grinding machinery, including horizontal stone mills, vertical stone mills, and rolling mills. These machines are crafted from premium quality stone and alloy steel, ensuring fine grinding capabilities, high output, and low energy consumption. Our grinding equipment finds applications in various industries such as food production, pharmaceuticals, cosmetics, and animal feed.

Crushing Equipment

Crushing equipment plays a pivotal role in grain processing, as it is used to reduce grains into powdered form. Our range of crushing machines includes hammer crushers, gear crushers, and ball mills. These devices are known for their high crushing efficiency, simple operation, and ease of maintenance. They are widely used in sectors like food production, pharmaceuticals, chemicals, and agriculture.

Drying Equipment

Drying is an essential part of grain processing, helping to preserve the quality and extend the shelf life of grains by lowering their moisture content. Our drying equipment lineup includes air dryers, conventional dryers, and vacuum dryers. These machines provide uniform drying results, consume less energy, and are simple to operate, ensuring optimal moisture levels for grain preservation.

Packaging Equipment

Packaging is the final step in the grain processing process. Packaging equipment is used to package food, beverages, animal feed, and other products into their final forms, preserving product quality and ensuring long-term storage. Our company manufactures packaging machines such as weighing packaging machines, sealing machines, and vacuum packaging machines. These devices are known for their efficient packaging, speed, and ease of use, making them ideal for large-scale production environments.

CEREALS PROCESSING

Wheat Processing

Wheat, often regarded as the fundamental "bread grain" of European civilization, has been a staple source of human food for over 6,000 years. In India, wheat ranks as the second most important food grain after rice. However, it is estimated that approximately 10 per cent of the wheat crop is lost during various stages, including harvesting, threshing, transportation, or storage. As production continues to rise, these losses become increasingly significant. The losses during storage are both quantitative and qualitative, making it essential to reduce such wastage, especially in storage systems. Promoting the motto "grain saved is a grain produced" among farmers and traders is vital to minimizing these losses.

Following rice, wheat is the second-most important food crop in India. With a decrease in acreage devoted to coarse cereals such as sorghum, minor millets, pearl millet, finger millet, and barley, the dietary preferences of people are shifting towards rice and wheat. Wheat's significance in modern society is growing due to its versatility in producing ready-to-eat or easy-to-prepare foods. Even in traditionally rice-eating regions, wheat has gained popularity. The rising number of milling, baking, and confectionery units across the country further highlights wheat's expanding role. As various types of foods demand specific wheat qualities, wheat consumption will continue to increase, thereby boosting the demand for diverse varieties of wheat.Traditionally, when harvesting wheat, the crop is cut and tied into sheaves, which are then stacked in the field. Exposure to wind and sunlight helps reduce the moisture content from around 16 per cent within a few days. Once the moisture level is sufficiently low, the sheaves are collected, stacked, and threshed. The resulting grain, with a moisture content of 14 per cent or less, can be safely stored.

The most crucial step in wheat processing is milling. Milling refers to the process of grinding grains into flour, meal, or any other consumable form suitable for human or animal consumption. In India, a significant portion of wheat is used to make atta and maida. The scope of milling encompasses a wide array of processes, depending on the type of grain and the end product being produced.

Wheat Grain Structure

The wheat grain is composed of several distinct parts. The outer layers, known as the pericarp and testa, are hard and indigestible. Beneath these layers lies the aleurone layer, which contains a higher proportion of protein than the flour itself. At the lower end of the grain is the embryo, attached to a small structure called the scutellum. The majority of the grain, approximately 85 per cent, is made up of the endosperm, from which flour is derived.

It is essential to note that the milling of wheat is a physical process. The composition of the wheat kernel, which includes bran, germ, and endosperm, is as follows:

- Bran: 12%
- Germ: 3%
- Endosperm: 85%

Objective of Flour Milling

The goal of flour milling is to initially separate the endosperm from the bran and germ in the largest chunks possible, and then reduce these endosperm chunks into flour-sized particles through a series of milling processes. The germ is relatively easy to remove because it contains oil, making it putty-like and prone to flattening under the force of the rolls. In contrast, bran is much more challenging to separate. Like endosperm, bran is easily ground into a fine powder, making it difficult to separate it from the powdery endosperm. Flour that is contaminated with wheat bran tends to be brownish, rather than white, and is not suitable for food purposes.

The successful separation of bran from endosperm relies on the following principles:

- When wheat is soaked in water, the bran becomes tough and rubbery, while the interior endosperm softens and becomes friable.
- When the wheat berry is sheared by the corrugations of the first roll or break, it splits open, releasing some endosperm and flour, thus progressively removing the remaining endosperm from the bran in successive break rolls.

Most wheat mills achieve about 70% flour yield from a theoretical yield of around 85% total endosperm. The by-products of milling, including grain shorts and bran, make up roughly 30% of the mill stream.

Process of Wheat Milling

The wheat milling process is divided into five primary stages, which are as follows:

- Wheat Reception and Storage
- Wheat Cleaning
- Tempering or conditioning
- Milling of wheat into flour and its by-products
- Storage of the finished products

Wheat Reception and Storage

The Selection of wheat plays a essential role for the flour miller. Without sound wheat that is unspoiled and free from insect contamination, the miller is unable to produce an adequate product. The type of wheat chosen depends on its intended use, whether for bread, cakes, cookies, pastries, or biscuits, with the primary factor being the protein content. The flour typically contains a lower per centage of protein than the wheat from which it is milled, as the wheat is brought in with approximately one per cent higher protein content than desired in the finished flour.

It is also important to note that, like other cereal grains, wheat is subject to government inspection and grading. This grading system is valuable to the milling process, as it not only evaluates the soundness of wheat for milling purposes but also limits contamination by other cereal seeds, weed seeds, and foreign matter.

Wheat is stored in large, concrete-lined silos at the mill. Prior to storage, the wheat undergoes initial cleaning and drying to remove impurities and foreign material. If necessary, moisture is reduced to prevent heating during storage. Excess moisture can lead to heat production from microbial growth, caused by their respiration processes. Thus, wheat must be stored dry, typically with no more than 14.5 per cent moisture content.

The drying process occurs in three stages:

- The wheat is preheated to the desired temperature, with the grain temperature not exceeding 48°C when the moisture content is at 17 per cent, and 39°C when moisture is under 17 per cent.
- Water is removed through heat vaporization.
- Finally, the grain is cooled through water evaporation.

Wheat Cleaning

Since the grain impurities have already been removed during storage, the techniques used in the cleaning house are more refined. Wheat is cleaned by eliminating loose foreign materials and dirt that are attached to the surface of the grain.

Upon entering the cleaning house, the wheat is weighed and then passed through a separator set to remove fine impurities and dust. Small items such as sticks, stones, sand, and dust are filtered out, and lighter impurities like wheat chaff are removed using an air current. After this, the wheat passes over magnetic separators to remove any metal particles that may have found their way into the wheat mix. Another cleaning machine used to remove other cereal grains and weed seeds is the disc separator. This separator features different types of plates that can discharge wheat at various points along the route.

The next step in the cleaning process involves removing dirt from the surface of the wheat through scouring. Scourers come in various designs, but typically the wheat is treated by paddles against an emery-coated surface. The intensity of the treatment is controlled by adjusting the clearance between the paddles and the stationary emery surface. Dirt and the outer coating of wheat bran are then removed by air aspiration.

The final cleaning step is water treatment. Water is used to dissolve dirt and allows stones and pieces of metal to sink. In some cases, this step also helps reduce microbiological contamination of the wheat. Additionally, this process generally increases the wheat's moisture content by approximately one per cent.

Tempering or Conditioning

Tempering involves adding water to both the bran and the endosperm, resulting in the bran becoming tougher and more rubbery, while the endosperm becomes less vitreous. This process enhances milling efficiency. During tempering, water is added to raise the moisture content of the wheat to 15-19% for hard wheat and 14.5-17% for softer varieties. Over time, the water diffuses into the bran, causing it to lose its friable characteristics and take on a leathery texture.

Conditioning, in contrast to tempering, always involves the use of heat. The goal is to quickly diffuse water into both the bran and endosperm. Wheat conditioning typically involves four sections. The first section heats the wheat to the proper temperature, which is critical since excessive heat can affect gluten quality. A temperature of 45°C is typically the maximum allowed. In the second section, moisture is added, and the wheat is held at the appropriate temperature. The third section cools the wheat to room temperature, while the final section provides a holding bin where the moisture in the wheat can equilibrate before milling.

In some conditioning methods, all of the water can be added at once. The wheat passes through the preheating and cooling sections in 1.5 hours or less. However, the wheat is held in the final holding bins for 8 to 18 hours, with longer times used for harder wheat varieties.

One particular conditioning method rapidly heats the wheat by injecting steam and holding it at a temperature of 49°C for about one minute. Following this, the wheat is quickly cooled by plunging it into cold water and then sent through a centrifugal machine to remove the surface water. This method is very fast and has the advantage of preventing the bran coat from drying out, as it is not cooled with air or evaporation.

Wheat Grinding

Wheat grinding is carried out between pairs of rolls that move in opposite directions at different speeds, with a notable gap between them. Unlike crushing, the primary method of reducing the size of the wheat is shearing. The faster roll runs at speeds of 250 to 450 rpm, roughly 25 times faster than the slower roll, contributing to the shearing process.

The roller milling area is divided into two main sections: the break section and the reduction section. In the break section, the bran is broken open, and the endosperm is milled away. This process often involves multiple steps. After each break, the mixture of free bran, free endosperm, free germ, and bran with attached endosperm is separated. The bran still attached to endosperm is sent to the next break roll, and the process is repeated until as much endosperm as possible is separated from the bran. The separated endosperm is then directed to the reduction rolls, where it is further reduced to the proper particle size for flour production.

The rolls in the reduction section are similar to the break rolls but have smooth surfaces rather than corrugated ones. After each reduction of endosperm, the resulting material is returned to the second roll for further processing, and this step is repeated until the desired particle size is achieved.

Element of Wheat Mill

Break Rolls

The surface of the break rolls is always fluted to achieve the necessary grinding effect. The sawtooth flutes spiral around the roll, with the number of flutes per unit length increasing from the first to the fourth break. The first break typically has 4-5 flutes per cm, while the fourth break has approximately 12 flutes per cm.

Break Sifting System

After each set of break rolls, there is a sifting system known as scalping. This system can be divided into two parts:

- **Plansifier**: This consists of flat sieves stacked in layers, with the sifter rotating in a plane parallel to the floor. As the sifter moves in a circle about 9 cm in diameter, the smaller particles pass through the sieve below, while the larger particles move across the sieve to a collecting trough for removal. Plansifiers can have up to 12 sieves stacked on top of each other, and each sieve has four separate compartments. In Plansifiers, larger pieces of bran with adhering endosperm are first removed at the top and sent to the next break roll. Subsequent sieves become finer, removing bran and germ, while finer layers eliminate endosperm middling and the bottom collects flour. Coarse separations use wire mesh screens, while finer separations use cloth. The finest sieves can reach up to 196 mesh per inch, with openings as small as 0.060 mm.
- **Purifier**: The middlings still contain tiny bran particles, which are removed by passing the product through a purifier. The purifier uses air currents to carry the bran away. Essentially a long oscillating sieve inclined downward, it becomes coarser from head to tail. Air is blown through the sieve from the bottom, causing the flour to stratify into endosperm chunks of various sizes. At the bottom are the smallest pure middlings, followed by larger middlings, then endosperm and bran particles. The larger pieces of endosperm still adhering to bran, along with endosperm chunks, move to the top, and light bran particles settle at the very top.

The sieves are designed so that only endosperm particles pass through to the reduction rolls, while composite particles of bran and endosperm, as well as pure bran, are sent back to the break rolls or mill feed. Typically, purifiers are used for four break rolls in the scalping system. For example, fine middlings from the first, second, third, and fourth breaks usually undergo a double purification process, while coarse middlings require only one purification treatment.

Reduction Rolls

The reduction system consists of two key components: roll mills and sifting machines. The primary function of the reduction rolls is to reduce endosperm middlings into flour-sized particles and to assist in removing the remaining bran and germ particles. The roll stands in the reduction system are divided into coarse rolls and fine rolls, based on the gap between the rollers. Coarse rolls are specifically used to produce uniform-sized middlings for further reduction into flour. These rolls are often referred to as sizing rolls, and the middlings sent to them are called chunks. Once the middlings are sized by the sizing rolls, they are directed to the fine rolls for grinding into flour.

Following each reduction process, the resulting product is passed through sifters, where finished flour is separated, and the oversized material is sent back to the reduction rolls for additional processing.

Reduction Sifting System

Plansifiers are positioned after the reduction rolls and serve the purpose of separating the stock into coarse rolls, with the fine middlings being sent back to the fine rolls, while the flour is extracted from the middling system. Purifiers are commonly placed behind the coarse reduction rolls, where their primary function is size grading, as opposed to purification.

It is essential to avoid over-grinding the flour in the reduction system, as excessive grinding can damage starch granules, rendering the flour unsuitable for baking. Over-grinding can be identified by a high maltose value.

Scratch System

In this setup, if the mill is functioning correctly, the scratch system can be bypassed. However, if the mill is not performing optimally, the scratch system is employed to ensure the proper separation of the endosperm from the bran. The scratch system serves as an extension of the break system and is used primarily as a backup system.

CORN PROCESSING

Corn (Zea mays) is a versatile crop used for both human and animal consumption, as well as for industrial applications. It is processed into various food and feed ingredients, beverages, and industrial products. Typically harvested when its moisture content ranges between 18% and 24%, corn kernels must be dried to safe moisture levels of about 12% to prevent losses.

Mechanical harvesting and shelling can sometimes cause external damage, such as the breaking of the pericarp and the germ, which makes the kernels susceptible to biotic factors like insects, mites, pathogens, fungi, and microorganisms during storage before processing. To minimize deterioration and microbial growth, maintaining low moisture content and proper storage temperatures is crucial. Maize is consumed in various forms, including maize grits, polenta, corn bread, popcorn, and maize flakes, and is also widely used in beverage production. A corn kernel is made up of the endosperm, germ, pericarp, and tip cap.

Milling of Corn

Dry milling and wet milling are the two primary methods used for processing corn. In the dry milling process, various end products are produced, such as germ for oil extraction, husk and de-oiled germ for cattle feed, and grits for breakfast foods. On the other hand, the wet milling process produces products like starch, germ, and feed.

Dry Milling Method of Corn

The dry milling process is divided into two methods: the non-de-germing method (traditional) and the de-germing method (modern). In the traditional method, the entire kernel is ground into meal using a stone grinder without removing the germ, resulting in a product that is high in fiber and protein. After grinding, the hull and germ are separated from the meal by sifting.

In the de-germing method, the kernels are moistened with a small amount of water and then tempered to reach equilibrium. After the kernels are dried, the hull, germ, and tip cap are removed to obtain corn grits. The germ is used for oil extraction, while the de-oiled germ and hull are repurposed as cattle feed, known as hominy feed. The yield from endosperm products and hominy feed is approximately 70% and 30%, respectively.

Tempering – De-germing (TD) Method of Dry Milling

The main objectives of this method are:

- To eliminate nearly all the germ and hull, ensuring the endosperm contains as little fiber as possible,
- To recover the maximum amount of the endosperm as large, clean grits without any dark specks, and
- To recover the maximum amount of germ as large, pure particles.

The key unit operations involved in the tempering and de-germing process are outlined below:

Cleaning

Cleaning is the initial and most crucial operation required for the success of subsequent milling processes. Dry cleaners, which include aspirators and sieves, and wet cleaners, which comprise a washing and destining unit along with a mechanical dewatering unit known as a whizzer, are used for cleaning corn. Iron particles are removed through the use of a magnetic separator.

Hydrothermal/Conditioning Treatment

Cold or hot water, or steam in a predetermined quantity, is added to the corn kernels either in one, two, or three stages, with appropriate time intervals after each stage. The tempering period varies depending on the hydration methods used. Similarly, tempering temperatures range from room temperature to approximately 50°C, depending on the method. Both cold and hot water are utilized to add moisture, and occasional heat in the form of open steam is applied as needed. The ideal moisture content for de-germing in the de-germer is between 21-25%.

De-Germing

De-germing is a crucial process aimed at removing the germ, hull, and tip cap from the kernel to obtain grits. After de-germing, the resulting products consist of a mixture of kernel components, separated to varying degrees, with endosperm particles ranging from grits to flour. The Beall de-germer features a rotating cast iron conical roller mounted on a horizontal shaft within a conical cage.

Drying and Cooling of Degermer Stock

The de-germed products must be dried to a moisture content of 15 to 18 per cent for optimal grinding and sifting. Typically, rotary steam tube dryers are used for this drying process, although rotary louver-type dryers can also be employed.

The stock is heated to approximately 50°C. For cooling the dried products, counter-flow or cross-flow rotary dryers, vertical gravity coolers, or fluidized bed coolers may be used.

Rolling and Grading

The next step is the recovery of various primary products. Further separation of the germ and husk from the endosperm takes place during the gradual size reduction in roller mills.

The germ, husk, and endosperm fragments are then separated using sifters, aspirators, specific gravity table separators, or purifiers. Sifting is a crucial operation and is sometimes referred to as scalping, grading, classifying, or bolting, depending on the method and purpose. Sifting is essentially a size separation process using sieves. Scalping refers to the coarse separation of the product after it leaves the roller mill or de-germinator. Grading or classifying involves separating a single batch of stock (typically endosperm particles) into two or more groups based on particle size. Bolting is the process of removing hull fragments from cornmeal or flour.

Wet Milling Method of Corn

For wet milling, the raw corn should have a moisture content of 15-16 per cent and be physically intact. Corn that is cracked, heat-damaged, or infested with insects and pests (especially those treated at temperatures around 75°C during drying) is unsuitable for the wet milling process. Heat-damaged corn, in particular, negatively impacts the quality of the oil extracted from the germ. During the steeping process in wet milling, sufficient moisture is added to the corn to prepare it for the subsequent degerming, grinding, and separation operations.

The wet milling process involves several key steps:

- Cleaning,
- Soaking,
- Germ separation and recovery,
- Grinding and hull recovery, and
- Separation of starch and gluten.

Cleaning

Corn is screened and aspirated to remove impurities like dust, chaff, cobs, stones, insect-infested grain, broken, and other foreign materials. The storage bins receive the cleaned grains.

Steeping

The main goals of steeping are to remove solubles, mostly from the germ, to make it easier to separate the gluten and germ from the starch granules, and to soften the kernel for grinding. When used for stepping, water impregnated with SO_2 (also known as acidulated water with H_2SO_3) aids in stopping some fermentation, which induces a protracted sleeping process. For a duration of 28 to 48 hours, depending on the plant, the steeping is done at roughly 50° C. The moisture content of the steeped corn reaches approximately 45%.

Germ Recovery

The de-germing unit receives the softened and wet kernels, which contain roughly 45% moisture. This machine tears the soft kernels apart and releases the germs without grinding them by using a rotating plate with projected teeth and a stationary metallic plate. The pulpy mixture comprising germ, husk, starch, and gluten is separated using the old-fashioned floatation method. The newer method involves passing the mixture through hydroclones, where centrifugal force separates the germ because it is lighter.

Milling and Fibre Recovery

Starch, gluten, and hulls are present in the mixture following the separation of the germ and the screening of the coarse particles. The remaining starch is then released by grinding the horny endosperm and hulls. Particle size is significantly reduced as the material to be ground enters the machine through a rotating rotor and is flung out with tremendous force against the impactors at the rotor's periphery as well as against a stationary impactor.

Here, the starch is easily released with very little hull size reduction. The coarser hulls and fibers are eliminated from the milled slurry by passing it through a sequence of hexagonal reels that contain ground starch, gluten, and hulls.

Starch-Gluten Separation

After the starch and gluten slurry is concentrated, the gluten particles—which are lighter than the starch particles—are separated using a high-speed centrifugal separator. This process is divided into two phases, with various hydroclone types of equipment performing the second stage of centrifugation. After filtering, the resulting starch is dried to create dry starch.

Processing of Rice

Paddy (*Oryza sativa L.*) is one of the most significant food grains globally, with nearly 2/3 of the world's population partially or entirely relying on rice as their primary food source. India stands as the second-largest rice producer in the world. A paddy grain consists of several layers, with the main components being the husk, bran layers, starchy endosperm, and the embryo or germ. The rice husk, also known as hull, acts as a protective coating for the seed and is indigestible for humans. The bran, which is the hard outer layer of the grain, is made up of the aleurone, nucellus, seed coat, and pericarp. Along with the germ, it forms a vital part of the whole grain and is frequently produced as a by-product during milling. The embryo or germ is rich in protein and is commonly removed along with the bran during the milling and polishing process. The starchy endosperm is what is typically referred to as white rice. A paddy grain consists of approximately 20% husk, 5-7% bran layers, and around 3% embryo by weight.

Rice milling involves transforming the rough rice grain into a form suitable for human consumption, and this process requires great care to avoid kernel breakage and maximize recovery. When only the husk is removed from the paddy, the result is brown rice. Brown rice can be further milled to eliminate the bran layers, producing the more visually appealing white rice.

Method of Rice Milling

Historically, the hand pounding method was commonly used for milling paddy. In this traditional approach, paddy was pounded in a stone or wooden pestle and mortar. After pounding, the grains were winnowed to separate the de-husked kernels from the un-husked ones. The un-husked grains would then undergo another round of pounding in the pestle and mortar. These methods, however, were labor-intensive, time-consuming, and required significant manual effort. The hand pounding process removed the husk and a small portion of the bran, resulting in brown rice that retained its nutritional benefits due to the presence of the bran layers.

However, hand pounding gradually became obsolete with the introduction of hullers for milling paddy. One of the most widely used hullers is the Engleberg huller, in which paddy is passed through two or three cycles to produce milled rice. The Engleberg huller works by mechanically cutting the husk and often the bran layers using a rotating knife and a stationary blade. While this method is faster than hand pounding and reduces manual labor, it is considered crude because it causes a high amount of rice breakage, resulting in a lower yield of whole grains (head rice). Additionally, the by-product bran is removed along with the husk. Rice is separated from the husk and bran through sieving and bowling, but the milling process tends to generate a greater quantity of broken rice compared to hand pounding, thus reducing the overall milling outturn.

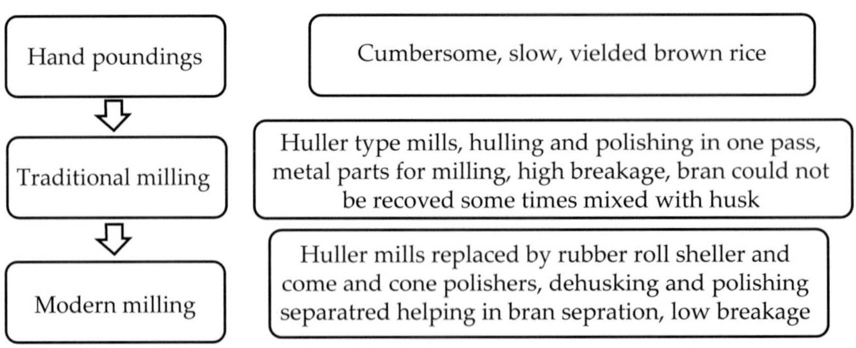

Figure 3.1: Overall Milling Outturn.

Bran, a by-product, is rich in dietary fiber, essential fatty acids, starch, protein, vitamins, and minerals, as well as antioxidants beneficial for human health. Pure rice bran contains 18-21% oil. Recognizing the value of this by-product for oil extraction and other food and industrial purposes, the government emphasized the recovery of rice bran, which led to the modernization of rice milling. The aim was to improve rice yields and produce higher-quality by-products like bran and husk. A key objective of modern rice milling is to maximize whole grain rice production, as the market value of whole kernels is higher. To achieve this, it is crucial to minimize breakage during processing.

Modern rice mills have replaced the Engleberg huller with rubber roll shellers. In a rubber roll sheller, two counter-rotating rolls remove the husk through frictional rubbing, effectively separating the husk from the brown rice. Furthermore, most modern mills polish the brown rice to remove the bran layers. Polishing typically involves two to four stages, with cone polishers used to remove the bran.

In both traditional and modern rice milling methods, rice is processed in either its raw or parboiled form. Parboiling refers to the partial boiling of rice, where the rice undergoes soaking and steaming. This process causes the starch in the rice to gelatinize, and water-soluble vitamins and minerals become an integral part of the rice starch. As a result, the rice becomes tougher, reducing the likelihood of breakage during milling. Although parboiling offers several benefits, it is primarily done based on consumer preferences. When a milling plant produces parboiled rice, it must include a dedicated section for the parboiling and drying processes in addition to the regular milling operations.

Modern Rice Milling Processes

The key steps involved in the modern rice milling process, along with the definitions of each process, are outlined below:

Table 3.1: The Modern Rice Milling Process

Pre cleaning	Sieve separator, magnetic separator and winnowers	Clearing the paddy of all contaminants and unfilled grains. This also entails taking the paddy's metal components out.
De-stoning	Vibratory separator	Separating from paddy
Parboiling	Paddy is partially boiled by soaking, steaming, and then drying. enhances the nutritional value by causing the starch inside the rice grain to gelatinize. It enhances the recovery from milling.	
Dehusking	Rubber roll sheller	Removing husk from paddy with minimum damage to the rice grain
Husk aspiration	Aspirator	Separating the husk from brown rice/unhusked paddy
Paddy separation	Specific gravity separator	Separating the unhusked paddy from brown rice
Whitening	Cone polisher	Removing all or parts of the bran layer and germ from brown rice using cone polishers

<table>
<tr><td>Polishing</td><td colspan="2">Enhancing the appearance of milled rice is achieved by eliminating any remaining bran particles and polishing the outer surface of the milled kernels using cone polishers.</td></tr>
<tr><td>Grading</td><td>Vibratory sieve grader</td><td>Separating small – large brokens from head rice</td></tr>
<tr><td>Color sorting</td><td>Colour sorter</td><td>Removing the discolored rice from the white rice</td></tr>
<tr><td>Bagging</td><td colspan="2">Getting the milled rice ready for delivery to the client</td></tr>
</table>

Cleaning and Grading

The paddy needs to be cleaned of chaff, lighter impurities, foreign grains of varying sizes, sand, stones, debris, and any metal pieces that may be present. The various cleaning processes and the machinery used for these operations are outlined in Table below.

Table 3.2 Machinery used in Cleaning Paddy

Machinery	Operation
Vibratory sieve	For removing foreign of different sizes
De-stoner	For removing stones
Magnetic separator	For removing the metal parts in the paddy bulk
Winnower	For removing lighter impurities

Cleaning paddy is essential to deliver high-quality rice that meets consumer expectations in the market. Removing metal parts and stones is crucial as they can damage the milling machines. Many of these cleaning operations can be carried out with one or two machines.

Parboiling

Parboiling is an optional pre-milling process applied to paddy. It is a hydrothermal treatment in which paddy is soaked in water and then subjected to gelatinization by steaming. This process includes soaking, steaming, and drying. There are several methods of parboiling, such as the household method, single steam method, double steam method, hot water soaking method, and pressure parboiling method, among others. Commercial-scale operations generally adopt the single steaming, double steaming, and hot soaking methods. Below are some popular parboiling methods:

- **Single Steaming Method**: In the single steaming method, paddy is soaked in water at room temperature for 1-3 days in cement cisterns. Once soaking is complete, the water is drained, and the paddy is steamed in batches.

- **Double Steaming Method**: The double steaming method begins with steaming the raw paddy. After this, the paddy is added in batches to water for soaking at room temperature in a cement tank. The steaming of the paddy raises the temperature of the soaking water to above 50–60°C, and the paddy is gradually cooled to room temperature over a day. After 24 hours, the water is drained, and the paddy is steamed for the second time.
- **Hot Soaking Method**: In this method, raw paddy is immersed in hot water at 90-95°C. The water is circulated to maintain the temperature between 65-70°C for 5 to 6 hours. After soaking, the water is drained, and the paddy is steamed in the same vessel.

Steaming and Drying

In modern rice milling, steaming is carried out separately using a dedicated steaming unit. The steam is typically generated from a boiler unit under pressure. After steaming, the soaked paddy is dried. Modern rice mills typically use LSU (Low-Speed Under-Air) dryers with hot air generated from steam-heated exchangers for the drying process.

The purpose of this process is to bring about physical, chemical, and organoleptic modifications in the rice, resulting in economic, nutritional, and practical advantages.

Advantages of Parboiling

Advantages of Parboiling are as follows:

- The milling yield increases, and the quality improves, as there are fewer broken grains.
- The grain structure becomes more compact and vitreous, even when some kernels are fully or partially chalky.
- The milled rice appears translucent and shiny.
- Parboiled paddy and milled parboiled rice have a longer shelf life compared to raw rice, as germination is no longer possible, and the kernel becomes harder, making it resistant to insect infestation and moisture absorption from its surroundings.
- The grains remain firmer when cooked and are less prone to becoming sticky.
- The rice absorbs more water during cooking, leading to greater swelling.
- After cooking, the rice absorbs less fat from added ingredients.
- When cooked, the rice remains fresh for a longer period and does not spoil as easily.
- Parboiled rice retains more proteins, vitamins, and minerals, which are distributed throughout the endosperm during the parboiling process.
- Parboiled rice becomes easier to digest after cooking.
- Less solids remain in the cooking water after cooking.

- Shelling parboiled paddy is easier compared to raw paddy.
- Rice bran obtained from parboiled rice contains a higher per centage of oil.

Disadvantages of Parboiling

Below are the disadvantages of Parboiling:

- The heat treatment during parboiling reduces some natural antioxidants, which leads to a higher rate of rancidity in parboiled rice during storage compared to raw rice.
- Parboiled rice takes longer to cook than raw rice and may have a characteristic off-flavor that may not be preferred by those accustomed to eating raw rice.
- The parboiling process requires additional capital investment.
- Despite the extra costs associated with parboiling, the higher yield of head rice from the process results in additional profit for the miller and ensures a lower price for consumers. Additionally, the higher nutritional value of parboiled rice justifies the large-scale adoption of the parboiling process. Generally, fine scented varieties of paddy that have good milling quality are not subjected to parboiling.

Traditional Method of Parboiling

The traditional parboiling process involves soaking paddy in water at room temperature for 24-28 hours or more, followed by steaming in kettles under atmospheric pressure and drying in the sun. In the boiling method, paddy is soaked in regular water for 24-72 hours before being steamed. In the double boiling method, steam is first injected into raw paddy in the steaming kettle before soaking. The hot paddy raises the temperature of the soaking water to 45-50°C, which reduces the soaking time to 24 hours. Afterward, the soaked paddy is steamed. Sometimes, the soaking water itself is heated to about 50°C before adding the raw paddy, eliminating the need for initial steaming. However, the traditional method of parboiling has several disadvantages:

- Prolonged soaking leads to fermentation, resulting in an undesirable smell.
- It facilitates the growth of mycotoxins, which are harmful.
- Sun drying is unreliable and inconsistent.
- There are significant losses due to consumption by birds, rodents, and insects during drying.
- The drying process is unhygienic.
- It requires large drying yards.
- The labor requirements are high.

Modern methods used in various countries have been effective in overcoming these limitations.

Modern Method of Parboiling (CFTRI)

Parboiling tanks are filled with clean water, which is then heated to approximately 85°C by passing steam through coils inside the tank. In some cases, hot water is prepared separately in a different tank and pumped into the parboiling tank.

Paddy is quickly added to the hot water, causing the temperature of the paddy-water mixture in the tank to remain around 70°C. The soaking water can be recirculated back into the hot water tank to maintain a steady temperature of 70°C. After soaking for about 3 to 3.5 hours, the soaking water is drained out, and the water discharge valve is kept open to remove any condensation that forms during steaming. The soaked paddy is then exposed to steam at a pressure of approximately 4 kg/cm^2 via an open steam coil. Soaking and steaming occur in the same tank. The process is considered complete when the husk splits, indicating successful parboiling. The parboiled paddy is then removed by opening the bottom door and can be dried either under the sun or using a mechanical dryer.

PULSE-BASED PRODUCTS PREPARATION

Particularly in vegetarian diets, pulses like lentils, chickpeas, peas, and beans are a significant source of protein. In order to create a variety of goods for industrial or culinary applications, processing pulses usually entails cleaning, dehulling, splitting, and occasionally roasting or frying.

Processes

- **Cleaning**: To get rid of any potential dirt, stones, or other contaminants, pulses are carefully cleaned.
- **Dehulling**: To improve texture and facilitate digestion, the pulses' outer skin, or hull, is removed.
- **Splitting**: To make dishes like split peas or lentil dals, some pulses, like lentils, are split.
- **Roasting or Frying**: To create snacks or improve their flavor profile, some pulses are roasted or fried.
- **Milling**: Pulses are ground into meal or flour, which is then used to make a variety of food items.

Equipment Used

- **Pulse Cleaners**: These devices clean pulses using gravity separators, air classifiers, and sieves.
- **Dehullers**: specialized devices, such as impact or abrasive dehullers, that remove the hulls from pulses.
- **Splitters**: Devices that divide pulses into smaller pieces or in half. In order to prepare pulses for snacks or other foods, industrial ovens or fryers are utilized.
- **Pulse Mills**: Pulses are frequently ground into flour or meal using hammer or pin mills.

PROCESSING METHODS FOR DRY PEAS, LENTILS & CHICKPEAS

Legumes undergo multiple stages before becoming ready for use either as a plated dish or as an ingredient in food preparation. These stages can include cleaning, drying, sorting, splitting, milling, and fractionating. Depending on the type of pulse and its intended application, additional processes like de-hulling (decorticating), puffing, roasting, and grinding might also be incorporated.

Once the field-dried pulse product reaches the processing facility, it is visually inspected for its color and overall quality. Following inspection, it is transferred to storage bins. Proper storage of the freshly received product is crucial for maintaining quality and ensuring the crop's optimum preservation. Each type of crop may have specific storage needs, so humidity and temperature levels are carefully regulated to create the best preservation environment while preventing pest or fungal infestations.

Upon being released from the receiving bins for the initial air cleaning stage, magnets are employed to remove metal debris and stones from the product. Additionally, many processors perform a second and final screening using rare earth magnets to ensure the removal of any remaining metal before the product is bagged.

After processing is completed, the product is bagged and shipped to customers. The quality control procedures may vary across processors, including inspection and packaging methods before dispatch.

Pulses may be shipped either after cleaning or undergo further processing. One common procedure is de-hulling and splitting, which removes the seed coat, making the pulses more digestible and enhancing other qualities.

Typically, pulses are soaked overnight in cold water for 4 to 12 hours to improve de-hulling and splitting. The soaking process can be accelerated by using warm or hot water, which also helps reduce seed hardness. However, heating incurs additional costs for processors and needs to be carefully controlled to maximize yield and avoid microbial problems. Pulses with thick, tough seed coats are often mechanically abraded or cracked before soaking to aid moisture absorption, resulting in faster cooking and more digestible cotyledons.

In some Asian regions, food legumes are stored at ambient temperatures for several days after soaking. This allows them to germinate, activating enzymes that partially *hydrolyze* the proteins, starch, and oligosaccharides. It also inactivates tannins, releases minerals, and produces vitamins. The sprouted grains are then consumed directly or processed further by dehulling, roasting, and grinding for use in various food products.

Pulses can be consumed either whole or as ingredients, such as in the form of flour. For flour production, whole legumes or hulled splits are either ground dry into flour or ground wet into a batter, which can be combined with cereals or millet for use in other food products. The properties of the resulting product, including mouthfeel, texture, and more, are influenced by factors like the pulse composition, grinding fineness, particle size grading, and cooking conditions.

Cleaning

Following this, most pulse processors employ a de-stoner to remove heavier contaminants such as stones, metal pieces, and glass. In a de-stoner, the pulses are spread across a perforated deck, and air is passed through the perforated surface to create an air cushion. This cushion allows the pulses to float gently toward the outlet of the machine due to gravity. Heavier particles, like stones, will sink to the bottom of the stream, where they are pushed upward by the vibratory motion of the deck. The stones are then expelled from the machine's upper side. Some de-stoners are also equipped with a stratification step before the main deck to further separate the impurities.

Figure 3.2: Legume Processing is Cleaning

The initial stage in legume processing is cleaning. This process typically begins with the use of a screen cleaner and aspirator to remove both coarse and fine impurities, as well as dust. Screen cleaners come in various types and sizes but generally feature flat sieves with either slotted or round holes, designed to separate impurities based on their size.

These tables function by floating the pulses over an air cushion and classifying them based on differences in density. The gravity tables effectively filter out these impurities, ensuring that only the desired pulses remain.

For split peas, the process begins with cleaning and de-stoning after the dried product is received, followed by steaming and tempering. These steps ensure the peas are prepared for a uniform split in the pea splitter, reducing shattering and other product losses. In some cases, steaming and tempering are done right before the splitting process.

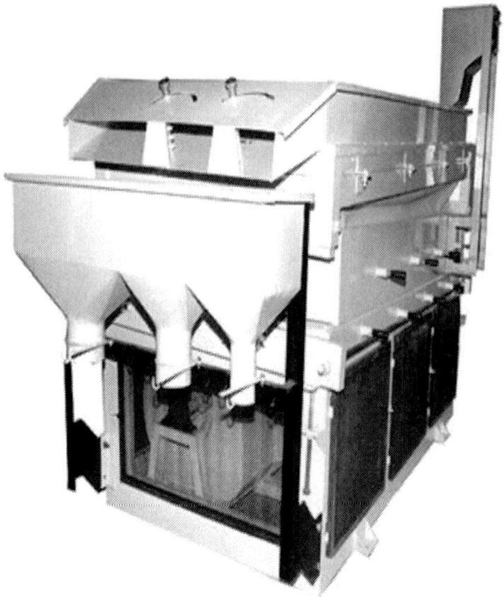

Figure 3.3: Processors Use Gravity Tables to Separate Light-Density Foreign Materials, such as Pebbles, Dirt, and any Undeveloped, Broken, or Damaged Pieces.

To further enhance quality, most processors use optical sorters at the end of the cleaning line to remove difficult defects and discolored pulses before packaging.

Sorting

Optical sorters play a crucial role in ensuring uniform color and enhancing the cleaning process by removing foreign materials and preventing cross-contamination.

Figure 3.4: Sorting.

Pulses are sorted based on various criteria such as size, density, and color. Size sorting is typically performed on separators, where chickpeas, for instance, are processed through five sieves ranging from 6 millimeters to 10 millimeters.

Gravity tables are used to grade pulses according to their density, specifically removing immature seeds. After this, the product usually undergoes a metal detection system followed by a final air-blast cleaning and bagging process. Additionally, passing the products through magnets that act as pre-screeners helps processors maintain food safety standards before the final packaging.

Dehulling

Dehulling legumes typically involves two key steps: (1) loosening the hull, either by the dry or wet method, and (2) removing the hull and cleaning the seeds. The hull can be loosened through various techniques, including:

- Prolonged sun drying to loosen the hull.
- Applying small amounts of edible oil, followed by sun drying and tempering.
- Soaking the legumes in water for several hours, followed by coating them with red-earth slurry and sun drying.
- Soaking in water for several hours to loosen the hull before processing into food products.
- A combination of the above methods.

Figure 3.5: Dehulling.

There are several methods for decorticating food legumes. The oldest and most widely used technique involves spreading the seeds out to dry in the sun or mixing them with a small amount of water before pounding them in a mortar using a pestle.

Dehulling (also known as decortication) produces refined cotyledons with improved appearance, texture, and cooking qualities, making the legumes easier to digest and more efficiently utilized by the body. However, the process can be time-consuming, depending on how tightly the hull adheres to the *endosperm*, due to the thin layer of gums and *mucilages* (gelatinous substances in plants).

The success of dehulling is influenced by the variety, harvest season, and location where the legumes are cultivated. Larger, bold-grain varieties are easier to dehull and yield a higher product, making them more favored by millers. In contrast, smaller varieties require repeated pre-dehulling treatments and more complex processes. Legumes such as dry peas, lentils, and chickpeas, which have easier-to-remove hulls, typically need less drying and fewer oil or water treatments.

Freshly harvested legumes, with their higher moisture content, are more challenging to process. These are either stored for a period to reduce moisture or treated with lime water or a solution of sodium carbonate to loosen the hull.

The hull is then winnowed away, leaving the clean cotyledons. Commercial mills use similar methods but on a much larger scale, designed for higher yield and greater operational efficiency.

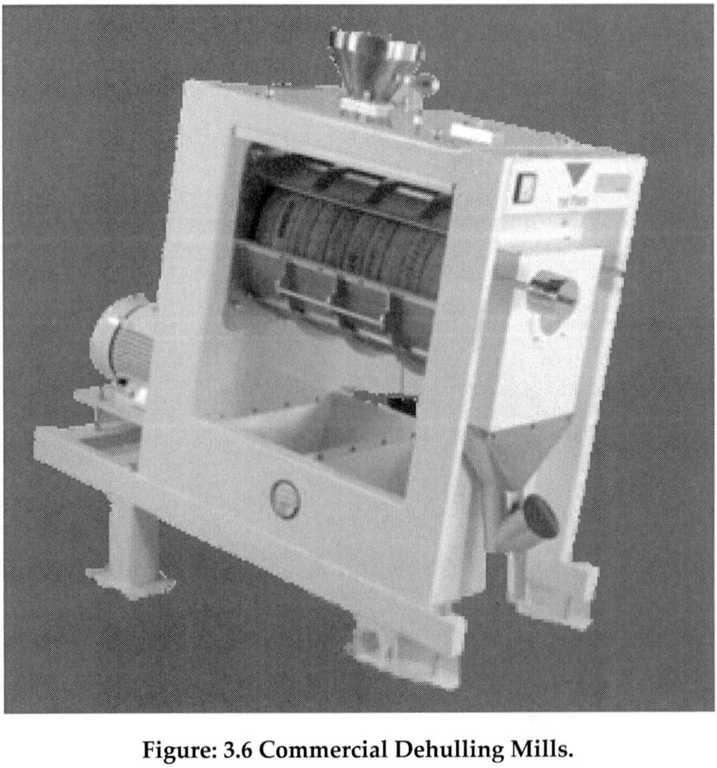

Figure: 3.6 Commercial Dehulling Mills.

Smaller processors typically achieve around 50 per cent removal of the hull in the first attempt using traditional dehulling methods.

This process is repeated several times until most of the grain is converted into dehulled, split cotyledons. However, achieving complete hull removal can be challenging with this method, and breakage is a common issue.

An alternative dehulling method involves adjusting the moisture content of the grain to help loosen the hull. The grain is first exposed to heated air in a tempering bin for a specified period, depending on the variety. Gradual aeration raises the moisture content to a critical level. After this, an abrasion-type hulling machine is used to remove the hull, while minimizing damage to the endosperm. If the grain is to be split, the dehulled grain is then moved on to a splitting machine.

Splitting

A lot of the processes are automated, especially the decorticating and splitting processes. Although splitting and dehulling are more successful when done separately, they are frequently done in tandem. Before dehulling, adding water promotes splitting. However, this procedure frequently leaves hull fragments on the split cotyledons (dhal), which must subsequently be removed using polishing equipment. The germ, which forms between 2 and 5 per cent of the seed, is usually lost during splitting.

Figure 3.7: Splitting

Acquaintance with Operation of Different Equipment

Each piece of equipment plays an essential role in the processing of grain, pulse, and oilseed products. Understanding the operation of these machines is crucial for ensuring the efficient functioning of a processing facility:

- **Automation and Control**: Many modern processing plants incorporate automated systems to manage machinery and track performance. These systems can monitor input quality, optimize output, and help reduce labor costs.
- **Safety Protocols**: Operating heavy machinery and handling raw materials necessitate strict adherence to safety protocols. Employees should be well-trained in machine operation and safety measures to prevent accidents such as malfunctions, fires, or injuries from moving parts.
- **Maintenance**: Consistent maintenance is vital to maximize the lifespan and efficiency of machinery. A preventive maintenance schedule should be established, covering tasks like cleaning, lubrication, and part replacement.
- **Efficiency and Quality Control**: Operators should be trained to oversee production efficiency and product quality, making adjustments to machinery settings as needed to ensure consistent and high-quality output.

A variety of procedures and specialized tools are needed to prepare products based on grains, pulses, and oilseeds. In order to guarantee product quality, maximize efficiency, and uphold safety, management and operators play a crucial role in supervising the operations of this machinery. The efficient operation of any processing facility depends on an understanding of the various machines used in these processes.

PREPARATION OF OILSEED-BASED PRODUCTS

Oil is extracted from oilseeds, such as sunflower, soybean, canola, cottonseed, and mustard, and used in industrial applications, cooking oils, and food products. Meal extraction, refinement, and occasionally the creation of oilcakes for animal feed are additional steps in the preparation of oilseed products.

Processes of Oilseed-based Products

- **Cleaning and Conditioning**: To make oil extraction easier, seeds are cleaned to get rid of dirt and foreign objects and then conditioned by heating or moistening.
- **Crushing or Expelling**: To extract the oil, oilseeds are mechanically pressed or crushed. Usually, solvent extraction techniques or a mechanical expeller are used for this.
- **Refinement**: To make the extracted oil fit for human consumption, it is refined to get rid of contaminants, color, and odor.
- **Press Cake/Meal Production**: Following the extraction of oil, the solid residue (press cake or meal) may be further refined or turned into animal feed.
- **Packaging**: For distribution, the refined oil is packaged.

Equipment Used

- **Seed Cleaners**: Equipment such as air cleaners, sieves, and destoners that are used to clean oilseeds.
- **Oil Expellers/Presses**: High-pressure mechanical devices that extract oil from seeds. Equipment for solvent extraction, which involves dissolving the oil from seeds using a solvent (typically hexane).

- **Refining Equipment**: By eliminating contaminants like colorants, gums, and free fatty acids, these devices purify crude oil. They consist of units for deodorizing, bleaching, neutralizing, and degumming.
- **Oil Mills**: These are employed in the refining and mechanical pressing of oil.
- **Packaging Machines:** Oilseeds and oils are packaged for retail or commercial use, just like grain-based products.

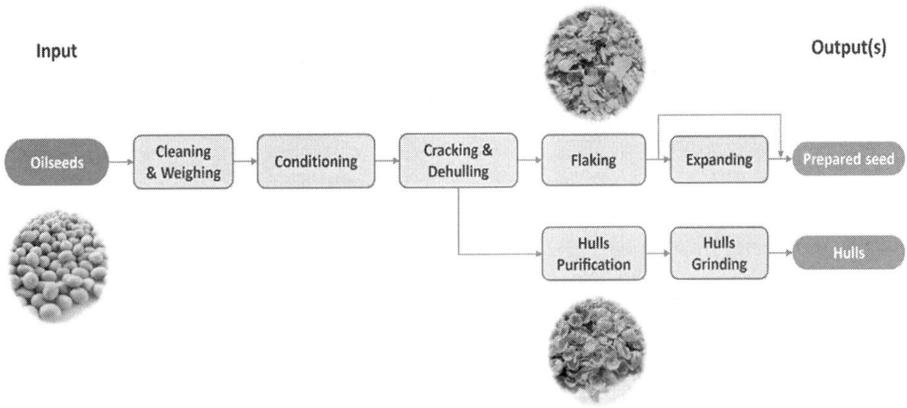

Figure 3.8: Preparation of Oilseed-Based Products.

Oil Extraction Techniques

Oilseed processing and extraction methods are designed to maximize oil quality while minimizing undesirable components, ensuring high extraction efficiency, and producing valuable meal byproducts. Several techniques exist for extracting oil from oilseeds, with two of the most common being solvent extraction and mechanical extraction using a screw press.

In the United States, mechanical oil expression is not widely used due to its lower oil recovery rates. However, screw presses remain a preferred choice for small-scale processors due to their lower initial investment costs. In contrast, solvent extraction using hexane has become the standard method in modern large-scale oilseed processing facilities. These solvent-extraction plants have capacities ranging from 100 to 9,000 metric tons per day.

Emerging extraction techniques, such as supercritical fluid extraction, water-based extraction, and enzyme-assisted water extraction, are gaining interest, particularly for the production of specialty and gourmet oils. These alternative methods offer potential advantages in terms of sustainability and oil purity.

Solvent Extraction

Solvent extraction involves the selective dissolution of oil by exposing oilseeds to a liquid solvent, making it the most efficient method for oil recovery. The effectiveness of the process depends on factors such as the preparation of oilseeds before extraction, operating temperature, process mode (batch vs. continuous, co-current vs. counter-current), and the design of the equipment. In commercial solvent extraction, the residual oil content in the meal is typically reduced to less than 1%.

The selection of a solvent is based on its oil solubility, cost, and safety considerations. Common solvents used for oil extraction include light paraffinic petroleum fractions, pentane (boiling at 88-97°F), hexane (146-156°F), heptane (194-210°F), and octane (215-264°C). Among these, hexane is the most widely used solvent in large-scale vegetable oil extraction. However, one significant drawback of these solvents is their high flammability, necessitating strict fire safety measures to minimize explosion risks in extraction facilities.

Additionally, the 1990 Clean Air Act classified hexane as a hazardous air pollutant, prompting the oilseed processing industry to explore alternative solvents such as alcohol and water. However, alcohols and water have limitations, including lower oil solubility, higher energy requirements for solvent recovery and meal drying, and a negative impact on soybean protein functionality.

The solubility of oil in a solvent increases with temperature, which also improves viscosity and diffusivity. As temperature rises, viscosity decreases while diffusivity increases, leading to shorter extraction times and lower energy consumption for solvent recovery. However, excessive heat may degrade or denature certain oil and meal components. Therefore, the choice of operating temperature is determined by the type of oil being processed and the desired specifications of the final product.

Traditional solvent extraction consists of three primary stages: oil extraction, desolventizing of meal and oil, and meal toasting. These steps ensure efficient oil recovery while maintaining the quality and usability of the extracted oil and byproducts.

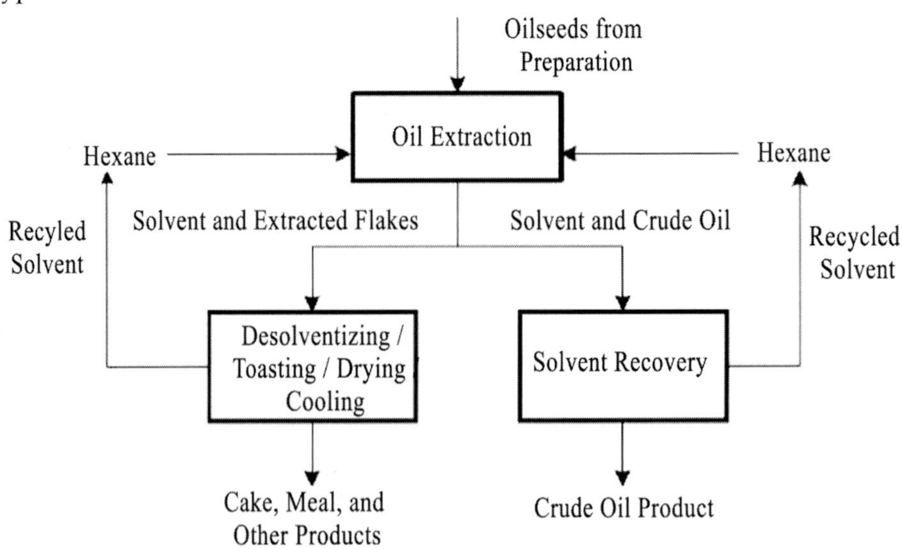

Figure 3.9: Simplified Flow Diagram of a Hexane-Based Oil Extraction Process.

During the 1800s, small-scale batch oil extraction systems were widely used in Europe, where a single vessel served both for extraction and meal desolventizing. Even today, batch extractors are employed for recovering specialty and high-value oils, as well as for extracting oil from spent bleaching clay. Two common batch extractor designs include a rotating drum and a vertical cylindrical kettle with a vapor-tight cover and a low-speed agitator.

The introduction of large-scale continuous processes began in the early 1920s. Modern commercial solvent extraction of oilseeds now primarily relies on two types of continuous extractors: immersion and percolation.

In immersion-type extractors, flaked oilseeds are fully submerged in solvent, ensuring thorough oil extraction. To maximize efficiency, the particle size should be as small as possible to increase seed-solvent contact. However, this design poses challenges in effectively separating solids from miscella (the oil-solvent mixture), making it more suitable for small-scale operations.

Percolation-type extractors, on the other hand, involve the formation of a fixed bed of flaked seeds over which the solvent is sprayed. The solvent percolates through the seed bed, washing out the oil. Here, the seed particles must be large enough to allow proper solvent drainage and prevent blockage, which can otherwise reduce extraction efficiency.

Early percolation designs featured basket-type extractors, where flaked seeds were placed in perforated-bottom baskets supported by an endless chain inside a sealed housing. These baskets moved in a slow, continuous cycle (approximately one revolution per hour). As each basket was filled at the top, solvent was sprayed over the seeds while the basket descended. Upon reaching the top on the opposite side, the baskets were inverted to discharge spent flakes into a hopper, which transferred them to a meal desolventizer via a conveyor belt.

While basket-type extractors proved functional, they were bulky and required extensive maintenance. Consequently, modern extraction systems have shifted towards horizontal and rotary-type designs. Horizontal extractors operate on the same principle as basket-type extractors but use a rotating horizontal plane instead of a vertical movement, making them more efficient and easier to maintain.

Meal and Oil Desolventizing

Following oil extraction, the removal of residual solvent from the meal (spent seeds) is performed in a desolventizer-toaster (DT), which is typically divided into three sections: pre-desolventizing, desolventizing, and toasting. The meal is heated to a temperature sufficient to evaporate the solvent while ensuring that its nutritional value remains intact. The DT consists of multiple trays stacked vertically, with sweep arms attached to a rotating shaft that moves the meal around for uniform processing.

Even after passing through the DT, the meal may still retain some moisture, which necessitates further drying. In some cases, desolventizing and drying occur in a single piece of equipment known as a desolventizer-toaster-dryer-cooler (DTDC), which integrates multiple steps into a streamlined process.

Simultaneously, solvent recovery from the miscella (oil + solvent mixture) takes place in distillation columns. The process includes an additional stripping column, indirectly heated with steam, which eliminates any remaining solvent and moisture from the oil. The solvent vapors generated during distillation and stripping are condensed and recycled back to the extractor, optimizing efficiency and reducing solvent loss.

Once the stripping phase is completed, the extracted oil undergoes a refining process to eliminate undesirable components, ensuring the final product meets quality and safety standards for consumption or industrial applications.

Mechanical Oil Extraction

The first mechanical oil expression devices used in oilseed processing were lever and wedge presses. A hydraulic press was used in the first cottonseed oil mill built in the United States in the 1920s. Between the press's head block and ram, seeds in filter bags were manually placed into horizontal, perforated boxes. Hydraulic pressure was applied to the ram to press the boxes together. Via the filter bag, oil was forced out. After that, the spent cake filter bag was manually taken out of the hydraulic press. Filter bags were replaced by cages in later iterations of the hydraulic presses. Up until the 1950s, hydraulic presses were in use. Continuous solvent extraction plants and continuous screw presses, which require less work, have taken their place. Hydraulic presses are still used in the olive oil industry today.

The mechanical screw press consists of a vertical feeder and a horizontal screw, the diameter of the body of which increases to exert pressure on the oils as they advance through the length of the press. The cylinder surrounding the screw has slots along its length, which allow the internal pressure to increase to first expel the air and then drain the oil through the cylinder. The oil collects in a trough under the screw and the oil-soaked cake is discharged to the bottom of the screw. The main advantage of screw pressing is that it allows large quantities of oilseeds to be processed with a minimum of labor and allows continuous oil extraction. Maintenance of screw presses is difficult. The moving parts and the high pressure and temperature created in the press increase consumption. The major improvement in the mechanical design of screw presses has been the development of construction materials that extend the life of the most worn parts. Equipment parts that once lasted three months before needing to be replaced can now last up to two years. Today, much larger screw presses have been built. Previous capacities of 5 tons per day are now over 100 tons per day for full press and over 800 tons per day for pre-press applications.

An increasing number of small-scale crushing mills utilizing extruding-expelling (E-E) technology have been established as farmer-owned cooperatives or on-farm operations to process locally grown soybeans and other oilseeds. The E-E method employs a dry extruder that generates heat through friction before the screw pressing stage, eliminating the need for costly steam-heated dryers, cookers, and steam-generating equipment. The resulting partially defatted meal, which typically retains 6-7 per cent residual oil content, is commonly incorporated into livestock feed rations.

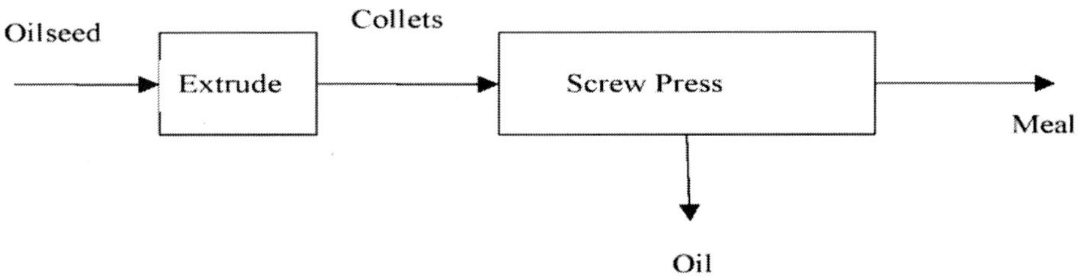

Figure 3.10: Process Flow Diagram of an Extruding-Expelling (E-E) System

Expanders are utilized to transform oilseeds into porous pellets known as collets, enhancing the efficiency of solvent extraction. Collets are larger, denser, and stronger than flakes, allowing better solvent penetration and improved micella (oil + solvent) drainage in the extraction process. The increased bulk density of collets also optimizes space usage within the extractor, enabling higher processing capacity in oilseed plants.

For seeds with high oil content, such as sunflower, safflower, peanut, canola, and rapeseed, pre-pressing is necessary to reduce meal oil content to approximately 16-18% before solvent extraction, as these seeds contain excessive oil to form suitable flakes or collets. In contrast, soybeans, with their lower oil content of 18-20%, do not require pre-pressing.

A new screw press system, Hivex, integrates pre-pressing and collet formation into a single unit, eliminating the need for separate extruders and pre-press machines. This innovative design incorporates a drainage cage and a pressing screw within the expander barrel, streamlining the oilseed processing workflow.

Aqueous Extraction

Aqueous extraction (AE) is a traditional oil extraction method widely practiced in developing countries. A technique known as water-flotation has historically been employed to extract coconut and palm oil. The process involves heating the oil-bearing material, grinding it with or without water, and then boiling it to release the oil. The extracted oil, which rises to the surface, is collected and heated further to eliminate any remaining moisture. This method is generally considered satisfactory for traditional, non-commercial applications, yielding approximately 50% oil extraction efficiency.

In addition to oil extraction, AE can also be used to recover high-quality proteins. To enhance oil and protein extraction yields while operating under milder processing conditions, enzymes or surfactants are sometimes added to the extraction medium. However, this approach comes with certain limitations. Finely ground seeds can generate dust, which poses an explosion risk if the processing area lacks adequate ventilation.

Additionally, AE has lower extraction efficiency compared to other methods, and the process requires breaking emulsions that may form to effectively separate oil and water phases. The costs associated with enzymes and surfactants, as well as the challenge of treating aqueous effluents, further limit the widespread adoption of this method in large-scale commercial operations.

Supercritical Fluid Technology

Public concern and government attention to the environmental and human health risks of organic solvents and residues in oil and oil products have catalyzed the search for alternative solvents for the treatment of cooking oil. Ethanol, isopropyl alcohol, acetone, isohexane, and supercritical fluids (SCF) have been investigated as alternative solvents. SCF technology has been investigated as an alternative technique to oil and oilseed processing methods for more than two decades. The supercritical carbon dioxide (SC-CO_2) technique, which uses carbon dioxide above its critical pressure (7.3 MPa) and critical temperature (31 °C) as a solvent, has been the solvent of choice for most food applications. The unique advantage of SC-CO_2 is the ease of removing the solvent from the extract. When the pressure is released from the system, the carbon dioxide returns to the gas phase and the oil precipitates from the CO_2-oil mixture. The carbon dioxide is recycled; therefore, the CO_2 released from the system does not pose an environmental problem.

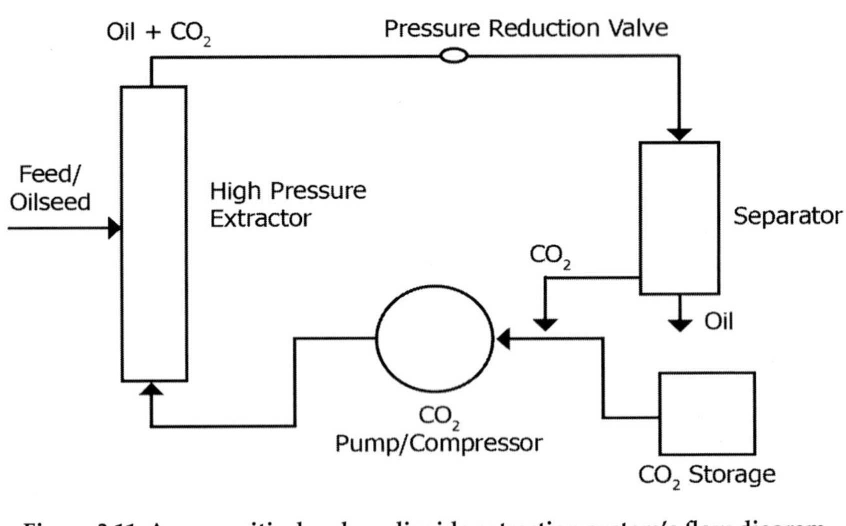

Figure 3.11: A supercritical carbon dioxide extraction system's flow diagram.

Although, the industrial applications of SC-CO_2 technology are constantly growing, most of the applications currently concern high value-added products. The economic feasibility of SC-CO_2-based processes is still hampered by the investment cost of high-pressure vessels. However, savings can be made through simplified separations and reduced solvent costs for supercritical fluids. The non-toxicity of SC-CO_2 and the significant reduction in process waste streams make this technology unique in terms of compliance with increasingly stringent health and environmental regulations.

4

Preparation of Products Using Flour Mill

INTRODUCTION

In order to turn grains into flour and create a variety of food products, including bread, cakes, pasta, and other baked goods, a flour mill is used to prepare goods. Depending on the type of grain (wheat, corn, *etc.*) and the intended end product, the process also entails cleaning, milling, and occasionally additional flour refinement.

GRAIN SELECTION AND CLEANING

To get rid of dust, stones, husks, and other foreign objects, the grains must be cleaned before milling:

- **Cleaning**: To guarantee that only premium grains are fed into the milling process, grains (usually wheat, corn, or other cereals) are cleaned using devices like air separators, sieves, or rotary cleaners.
- **Pre-conditioning**: In certain situations, moisture is added to the grains to condition them, softening them and increasing milling efficiency.

Wheat Flour Production Process A Step by Step Approach

Grading

Using cutting-edge equipment, the skilled millers evaluate and analyze the wheat when it gets to the flour mill. Wheat samples are prepared for chemical and physical examination. When grading wheat, many factors are taken into account, but the most crucial one is the protein content. Following this procedure, millers keep the same-grade wheat in silos until they need it for milling.

Purifying

To get rid of impurities, such as sticks, stones, and other fine materials, the wheat is meticulously cleaned. The purified wheat is now prepared for conditioning.

Conditioning

At this stage, the pure wheat is soaked in water after removing the bran. Conditioning is done before milling the wheat, as it is important to maintain uniformity of moisture content throughout the grain. The wheat is left in the conditioning bins for 24 hours. The conditioning step is important because it promotes the release of the inner endosperm during the milling process.

Gristing

In this step, the conditioned wheat and cleaned wheat are combined. In essence, various batches of wheat are combined to produce the precise type and quality of flour needed.

Separating

- The resulting grain then passes through a series of grinding rollers, which rotate continuously at different speeds. Don't worry, the rollers don't actually crush the grain, but rather split the seeds in two, separating the interior from the outer husk.
- Then the pieces of wheat kernel are separated by a complex set of sieves. The white particles of the endosperm, i.e. the semolina, are passed through a series of smooth reducing rollers, to grind the white flour forever.

Milling

The grain is ground using a machine that crushes it into small pieces. The grain is then passed through sieves and after repeated grinding and sieving, it becomes fine flour, wheat germ, and wheat bran. These three elements can be sold separately, to produce different types of flour, or they can be used together to produce whole wheat flour.

Flour Processing

To obtain enriched flour, vitamins and minerals are also added. To obtain self-raising flour, salt and hardening agents must be added. In a month or two, the flour is fully mature. All that remains is to pack the flour in paper bags, in the quantity you want to distribute later. This is the journey of the grain that turns into the familiar and widely used flour in the home.

MILLING PROCESS

After the beans are cleaned and packaged, the next step is the actual milling process, in which the beans are ground into flour. There are different types of milling methods, each suited to different products.

Roller Milling for Wheat

- **Crushing**: The grain is passed through a series of rollers to break it into smaller pieces. This process gradually removes the outer layers of the grain (the bran) and separates the endosperm (the part used to make flour) from the germ.

- **Reduction**: After crushing, the remaining material is further ground with finer rollers to produce the desired flour texture. This may involve multiple passes through the rollers.
- **Sieves and screens**: After milling, the flour is passed through a flour mill to separate the flour into different grades (e.g. fine, semolina or coarse). The kernels and germ are often removed at this stage to produce refined flour.

Stone Milling Traditional Method

- **Grinding**: Grain is ground between two large stone wheels in a stone mill, which crushes the grain evenly and slowly while retaining more bran and germ.
- **Whole Grain Flour**: Since the endosperm and a large portion of the outer bran and germ are still present, the resulting flour is usually whole grain. Stone milling frequently results in flour that has a more nutty flavor and a coarser texture.

Impact Milling for Corn or Other Grains

- **Grinding**: Using high-speed hammers or blades to strike the grain, impact mills reduce the grain to fine particles. This process yields a coarser flour and is frequently applied to corn.

FLOUR REFINING (OPTIONAL)

To produce a finer, more consistent product, some types of flour undergo additional refinement to get rid of extra bran, germ, and other contaminants:

- **Bleaching and Enrichment**: To enhance their appearance and nutritional value, some flours are bleached or enhanced with extra nutrients like vitamins and minerals.
- **Fortification**: To avoid nutrient deficiencies in the populace, flour in certain nations is fortified with vital nutrients (such as iron and folic acid).

PRODUCT PREPARATION FROM FLOUR

Following production, the flour can be used to make a wide range of goods, particularly in the food and bakery industries. The kind of flour used, its characteristics, and any additional ingredients or additives that may be added determine the kind of product that is produced.

Bread and Bakery Products

- **Mixing**: Flour is mixed with water, yeast, salt, and other essential ingredients to form a dough. For whole wheat or specialty bread, additional components such as honey, seeds, or oils may be incorporated to enhance flavor and texture.
- **Kneading**: The dough undergoes a kneading process to develop gluten, which contributes to its elasticity and structure. This step is crucial for ensuring proper rising and achieving the soft, airy texture characteristic of bread.

- **Fermentation:** The dough is left to rise for several hours, allowing yeast to ferment the natural sugars present in the flour. This fermentation process produces carbon dioxide, which causes the dough to expand, creating a light and fluffy consistency.
- **Baking:** The risen dough is placed in an oven and baked at a controlled temperature. The heat solidifies the structure, forming the final texture and crust of the bread.

Pastries, Cakes and Cookies

- **Mixing:** For cakes, cookies and pastries, flour is combined with sugar, eggs, butter and other ingredients as specified in the recipe. These products typically have a higher fat content compared to bread, contributing to their rich and tender texture.
- **Baking:** Like bread, the dough or batter is baked at suitable temperatures. However, cakes and cookies generally require shorter baking times at lower temperatures than bread, allowing them to achieve a soft, moist texture and a golden-brown finish.

Pasta Products (Using Semolina Flour)

- **Dough Preparation:** Semolina, a coarser type of flour, is commonly used in pasta making. It is combined with water and, in some cases, eggs to create a dough.
- **Shaping:** The dough is then rolled into sheets and molded into various pasta shapes, such as spaghetti, penne, or ravioli, depending on the desired form.
- **Drying:** Pasta is dried to lower its moisture content, which helps to preserve it for extended storage before it is packaged for sale.

Other Flour Products

- **Cereal Products:** Flour is used to produce various breakfast cereals, including puffed cereals, flakes, and other processed cereal-based products.
- **Flatbreads:** For making flatbreads like tortillas or naan, flour is combined with water, salt, and occasionally oil, then rolled out into thin sheets and cooked on a hot surface.

PACKAGING

Once the flour or the final product is prepared, the last step involves packaging for distribution, which includes:

- **Flour Packaging:** Flour is packaged in bags of varying sizes, typically using materials such as paper, plastic, or cloth sacks for retail sale.
- **Finished Products:** Baked goods, pasta, and other flour-based products are packaged in suitable containers, such as plastic wrap, boxes, or bags, for retail or wholesale distribution.

TYPES OF FLOUR AND THEIR USES

Different types of flour are prepared for different culinary uses and can be classified according to their protein content, milling process, and intended use:

- **All-purpose flour**: Used for most baking applications, such as cakes, cookies, and breads.
- **Bread flour**: Highest protein content, ideal for leavened products like bread.
- **Pastry flour**: Lowest protein content, perfect for delicate baked goods like pastries and cakes.
- **Whole wheat flour**: Contains the whole grain, which provides more fiber and a nutty flavor.
- **Oat flour**: A coarse flour made from durum wheat, commonly used in pasta and some types of bread.

EQUIPMENT IN FLOUR MILLS

- **Cleaning equipment**: Vibrating separators, air classifiers, destoners, and magnetic separators are used to clean grain.
- **Milling equipment**: Roller mills, stone crushers, hammer mills, or impact crushers are used to grind and process grain into flour.
- **Screeners and sifters**: They are used to separate different grades of flour and remove impurities.
- **Mixers and kneaders**: They are used to mix flour with other ingredients in the preparation of dough.
- **Cooking Ovens**: Convection or bridge ovens used to bake finished products.
- **Packaging Machinery**: Automated systems for filling and sealing flour or finished products into bags or other containers.

The preparation of products using a flour mill involves a systematic process that begins with the cleaning of grains and ends with the packaging of finished products. The milling process itself can vary depending on the type of grain being processed, and the final product can range from bread flour to pasta, breakfast cereals, and other processed foods. The efficiency of the flour mill and the proper operation of various equipments are essential for producing high-quality flour and products.

THE MANUFACTURING PROCESS

The grain is brought to the mill and inspected. Grain samples are taken for physical and chemical analysis. The grain is graded based on several factors, the most important being protein content. The grain is stored in silos with grain of the same quality until it is needed for milling.

Purifying the Wheat

In this work, basic theories were transformed into a series of mechanical devices that formed a flour mill. At the end of the book, a drawing depicted how these devices created a continuous production line that eliminated the need for human labor throughout the entire process. Evans, who was the son of a miller, operated a mill with his brothers and developed the systems and perfected the operations that eventually led to the creation of an automated grain mill.

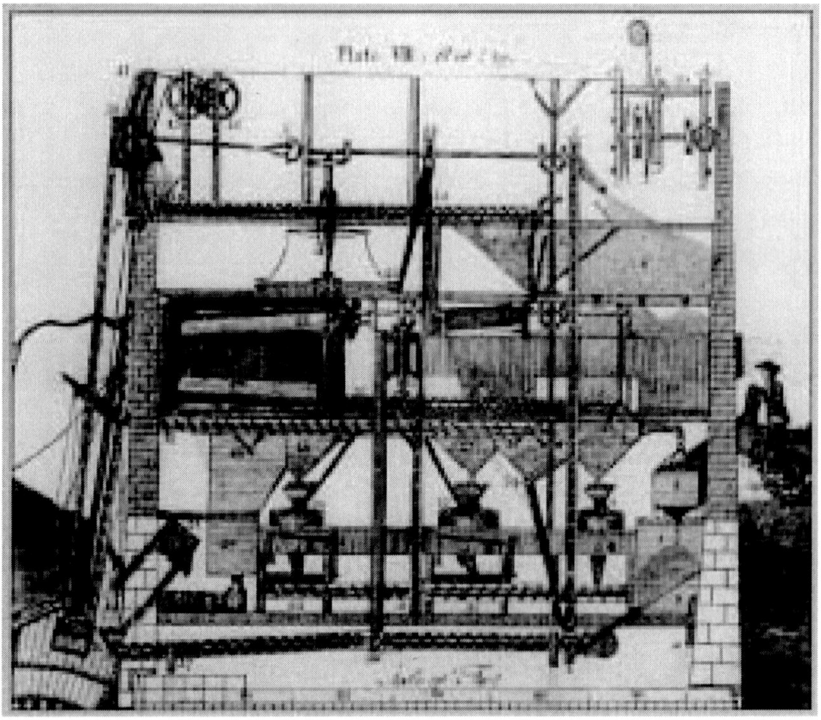

Figure 4.1: In 1795, an American engineer named Oliver Evans published a book titled The Young Millwright and Miller's Guide.

Evans is now regarded as one of America's most inventive mechanical pioneers. He applied his understanding of how water powered a mill wheel to create an efficient grain-milling system. His most significant contribution was the idea of an integrated and automated factory system. By removing human intervention through the use of machines, he addressed many of the challenges that would later be solved in the fully automated assembly line.

Although, this concept was not fully realized until the 1920s by Henry Ford, who developed a successful assembly line, Evans was the first to propose automation long before it became a reality.

- Before the grain is ground into flour, it must be cleaned of any foreign matter. This requires several cleaning processes. At each stage of cleaning, the grain is checked and cleaned again if necessary.
- The first device used to clean the grain is known as a separator. This machine passes the grain through a series of metal sieves. Grain and other small particles pass through the cut while larger objects such as sticks and stones are removed.

- The grain is then passed through a vacuum cleaner. This device works like a vacuum cleaner. The vacuum cleaner sucks in foreign materials lighter than the grain and removes them.
- Other foreign objects are removed in various ways. A device called a disc separator moves the grain over a series of toothed discs that collect objects the size of a grain of wheat. Smaller or larger objects pass over the discs and are removed.

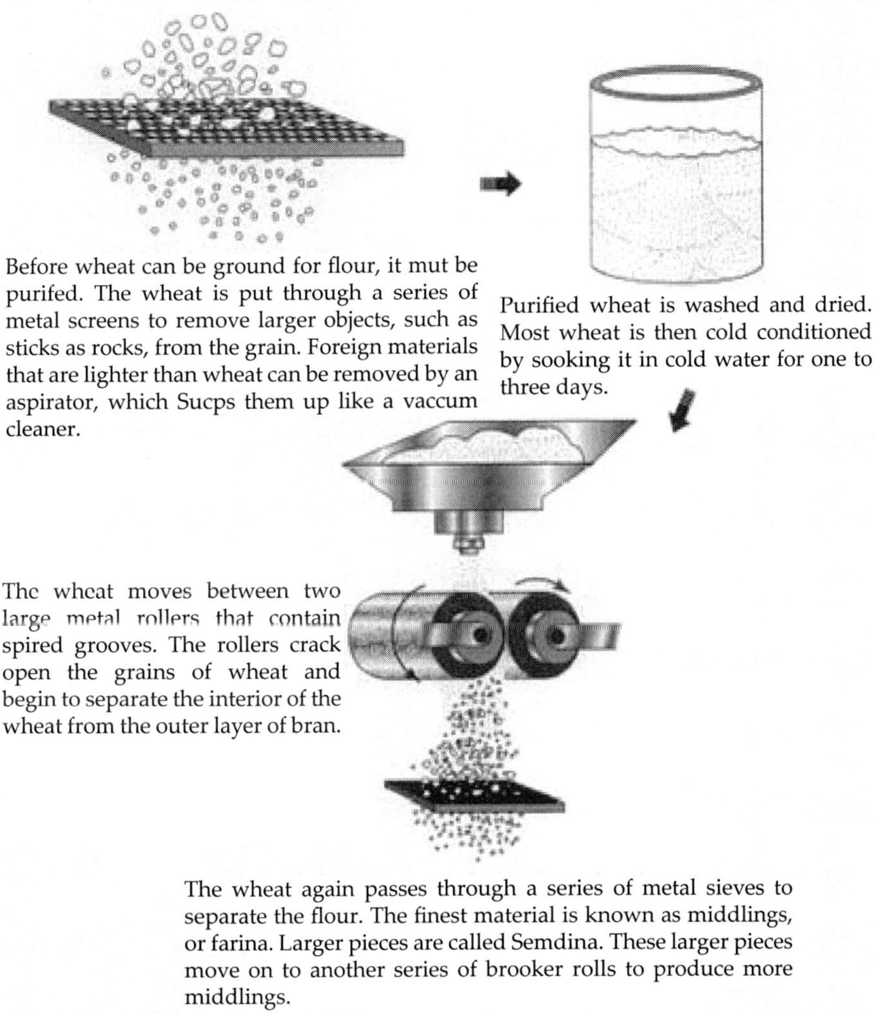

Figure 4.2: Ways to Removed the Other Foreign Objects.

- Another piece of equipment, the spiral seed separator, takes advantage of the fact that wheat grains are oval-shaped, whereas most other seeds are round. As the wheat moves down a fast-rotating cylinder, the oval-shaped wheat grains are drawn toward the center, while the round seeds move toward the edges, where they are then removed.

- Additional techniques used for purifying wheat include magnets to extract small metal pieces, scourers to remove dirt and debris, and electronic color sorting machines that eliminate materials that do not match the color of wheat.

Preparing the Wheat for Grinding

- The cleaned wheat is soaked in warm water and then placed in a centrifuge to be spun dry. This process helps to wash away any remaining impurities.
- To efficiently remove the outer bran layer during grinding, the moisture content of the wheat must be carefully controlled. This process, called conditioning or tempering, involves adjusting the moisture levels within each grain, typically by adding moisture rather than removing it.

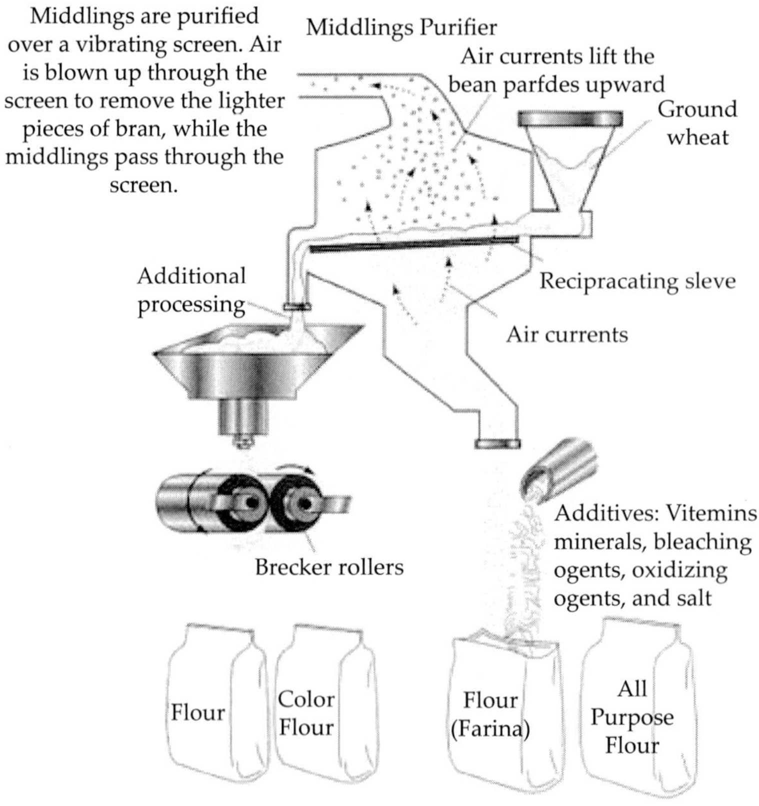

Figure 4.3: Cold conditioning involves immersing the wheat in cold water for a period ranging from one to three days. Warm conditioning requires soaking the wheat in water heated to 115°F (46°C) for 60 to 90 minutes, followed by a one-day resting period.

- Hot conditioning, which involves soaking the wheat in water at 140°F (60°C) for a brief period, is harder to control and is infrequently used. In some cases, steam conditioning at varying temperatures and pressures for specific durations is also applied. If excess moisture is introduced during conditioning or if the wheat remains too moist after purification, vacuum dryers can be used to remove the water.

Grinding the Wheat

- Wheat of varying grades and moisture content is blended to create a batch with the right characteristics required for the specific type of flour being produced. At this stage, the wheat may be processed through an Entoleter, a device that uses rapidly spinning disks to propel the wheat grains against small metal pins. Grains that crack in this process are deemed unsuitable for grinding and are removed.
- The wheat then moves through large metal rollers, known as breaker rolls. These rollers are of two different sizes and operate at different speeds. They also feature spiral grooves that help crack the wheat grains and begin separating the interior from the outer bran layer. The output from the breaker rolls passes through metal sieves, which sort the product into three categories: the finest material, resembling coarse flour, is called middlings or farina; larger pieces of the interior are referred to as semolina; and the third category consists of pieces where the interior is still attached to the bran. The middlings are sent to a purifier, while the other materials move to another set of breaker rolls. Typically, four to five pairs of breaker rolls are required to generate the necessary amount of middlings.
- The middlings purifier uses a vibrating screen to sift the middlings. Air is blown upward through the screen to remove lighter bran particles that are mixed with the middlings. The cleaned middlings pass through the screen and are further ground.
- The refined middlings are ground into flour by passing them through pairs of large, smooth metal rollers. After each grinding stage, the flour is sifted through sieves to separate it into different grades based on fineness. Coarse flour is sifted through metal wire sieves, while finer flour is sifted through nylon or silk sieves. By sifting, separating, and regrinding the flour, several different grades of flour are produced simultaneously. These are then combined as needed to create the final product.

Processing the Flour

- After milling, small quantities of bleaching agents and oxidizing agents are typically added to the flour. Vitamins and minerals are added as per regulatory requirements to create enriched flour. For self-rising flour, leavening agents and salt are included. The flour is then allowed to mature for one or two months.
- The flour is packaged into cloth bags, typically holding 2, 5, 10, 25, 50, or 100 lb (approximately 0.9, 2.3, 4.5, 11.3, 22.7, or 45.4 kg). For larger-scale consumers, it may be packed in metal tote bins that hold 3000 lb (1361 kg), truck bins holding 45,000 lb (20,412 kg), or railroad bins containing 100,000 lb (45,360 kg).

Quality Control

Quality control of flour starts when the wheat is received at the flour mill, where it is tested for its protein and ash content. The ash content refers to the minerals left after burning the wheat.

At each stage of the purification process, samples are taken to ensure no foreign matter is included in the flour. Since flour is intended for human consumption, all milling equipment is thoroughly cleaned and sterilized using hot steam and ultraviolet light. Additionally, antibacterial and antifungal agents are applied to eliminate any potential microscopic contaminants, with hot water used afterward to wash away any residual agents.

The final flour product undergoes baking tests in test kitchens to confirm its suitability for its intended uses. The vitamin and mineral content is measured to meet government standards, and the exact levels of additives are checked to ensure proper labeling.

MULTIPURPOSE FLOUR MILL UNIT

To boost the consumption of locally grown food crops among tribal families, a pilot initiative was launched with the establishment of 14 multipurpose processing mills in tribal gudems (villages), benefiting over 5,000 tribal households under the Tribal Sub Plan (TSP) activities of the Krishi Vigyan Kendra at Professor Jayashankar Telangana State Agricultural University in Adilabad.

Prior to the establishment of these mills, tribals had to travel to mandal headquarters or nearby towns to mill sorghum, wheat, and millets into flour (atta) and rawa for their daily food needs. With the help of the multipurpose flour mills, tribal communities are now able to process their locally grown food into various products, even during the ongoing COVID pandemic. These mills are also used for preparing condiments such as ginger-garlic paste, turmeric powder, and chili powder, providing added value to their daily food preparation.

Advantages of Multi Processing Units

- The primary goal is to process locally grown sorghum, millets, wheat, pulses, and other food crops for household consumption.
- Over 1,000 households, benefiting approximately 5,000 individuals, have been positively impacted.
- In each village, a farmer is responsible for managing the unit and earns between Rs. 2,800 to 3,500 per month in addition to their regular farm income.
- The initiative has helped bridge the gap in primary processing of sorghum, millets, soybean, red gram, Bengal gram, and spices for domestic consumption in tribal hamlets.
- Tribal families no longer need to travel to nearby mandal headquarters or major villages for flour milling or for acquiring spices like chili powder and turmeric powder.
- The ability to prepare diverse meals from locally grown foods has played a significant role in reducing nutritional deficiencies, especially among children and girls.
- Tribal women have been trained in producing malted foods, dhal milling, and spice powders, empowering them with income-generating opportunities.

5

Spice Processing and Acquaintance with Operation of Different Equipment

INTRODUCTION

To turn raw spices into usable products like ground powders, whole spices, or blended mixes, a number of processes are involved in spice processing. The procedure guarantees that the spices are safe to eat and appropriate for long-term storage in addition to preserving their flavor and aroma. When processing spices, it is essential to use specialized equipment for tasks like cleaning, grinding, blending, and packaging.

Since they add flavor, color, and aroma to any dish, spices have long been a useful addition to the kitchen. Spices like coriander, cumin, and turmeric are now more than just ingredients, they are a thriving industry. Anyone working in the food industry or just curious about how spices are transformed from unprocessed farm produce to the fine powders we use in recipes needs to understand the processing of spices. Establishing a productive, economical, and superior spice processing facility can have a significant impact on those in the industry. Spice processing might be the solution if you want to improve the quality of your spices. This guide explains the steps involved in processing spices, how it operates, and the advantages it provides.

SOURCING THE BEST RAW MATERIALS

Careful raw material selection is the first step in the processing of spices. To guarantee a consistent and superior supply of spices, Indian spice manufacturing companies form solid alliances with regional farmers and growers. Selecting the right raw material is crucial because it establishes the flavor and aroma that will characterize the finished product.

Second, Cleaning and Sorting

The raw spices are carefully cleaned and sorted once they arrive at the manufacturing facility. In order to eliminate contaminants, foreign materials, and impurities that might have been introduced during cultivation and transportation, this step is crucial. Making sure that only the purest spices are used in the production process is the aim.

Third, Grinding The Heart of Spice Processing

The core of the production of spices is the grinding process. The chosen spices are ground to the appropriate consistency, transforming them from their whole, raw state into a fine powder. The final product's texture and quality are significantly influenced by the type of grinding equipment used, such as a stone mill or hammer mill. To maintain its distinct qualities, each spice might need to be ground using a particular technique.

Here is an overview of spice processing and how the various equipment used works:

Selection and Cleaning of Spices

Spices grown in Indian fields offer the best aroma and flavor. It is of great importance to us that the quality control process begins in the fields (in the production centers). When it comes to producing high-quality spices, drying is an important step. The results of the other stages of the production process are greatly influenced by the level of perfection achieved during the drying process. Proper drying is essential to preserve the aroma and flavor of the material. The material dries naturally from sunlight, but is dried if necessary to maintain optimum moisture content.

All seeds are collected in a warehouse and dried in bulk before being shipped to various locations in small and large bags, as needed. Seed is often packaged in 25 kg bags, 625 kg bags, or 1000 kg bags. To maintain quality, proper transportation is necessary. Putting the supply chain in place is essential.

Before spices can be processed, they must be thoroughly cleaned to remove impurities such as dust, stones, foreign particles, and sometimes pesticide residues.

Cleaning Process

- **Pre-cleaning**: In this stage, coarse impurities are eliminated by hand sorting, sieving, or removing metal particles with a magnetic separator.
- **Washing**: To get rid of dust or grime, spices like coriander seeds or chilies may occasionally be cleaned.
- **Air Cleaning**: To ensure that whole spices are clean before additional processing, lighter particles like dust are blown off using air classifiers or blowers.

Equipment Used

- **Vibrating cleaners**: These machines use vibrations to separate soil from spices.
- **Air classifiers**: Machines that separate particles by weight using air flow, useful for removing dust and light debris.
- **Magnetic separators**: Used to remove metal particles from spice grains.

- **Rotating drum cleaners**: Spices pass through rotating drums that separate stones, dust, and other unwanted particles.

Cleaning of Dried Spices

- Prior to processing, it is essential to clean the crop. The first step involves using a winnowing basket to remove dust and impurities. This basket can be made from bamboo, palm, or other types of leaves. An experienced individual can efficiently and quickly remove dust, dirt, and stones. For spices and herbs, contaminants are typically removed by washing with mild alkaline cleaning solutions and neutralizing agents, followed by passing the materials through concentric zones with counter-current flow, spray rinsing, and drying.
- Once cleaned and dried, the material is stored in an intermediate silo, tank, or hopper located near the processing area. The stored material is then pneumatically transported to the grinding machine for further processing. Various pneumatic conveying systems may be used, depending on the material's characteristics and the desired output.

Cleaning and Maintenance of the Work Area

Keeping your food processing facility clean is more important than the product itself. Since cleaning and disinfection are perhaps the most important elements of a sanitation program, sufficient time should be spent determining the appropriate methods and parameters. All food contact surfaces should have detailed procedures and non-production features include non-production parts of equipment, overhead structures, screens, walls, ceilings, equipment lighting, refrigeration units, heaters, ventilation, air conditioning systems and anything that can affect food safety. Workplace hygiene is essential because it contributes to employee health, and a healthy workforce is a more productive and happier workforce. A strong workplace hygiene policy is the best way to ensure that staff maintains a clean workplace.

Maintenance of Workplace Hygiene

The four components of basic workplace hygiene are personal hygiene, a clean kitchen, a clean work area, and clean restrooms.

- **Establish a hygiene policy**: Establish a formal hygiene policy and share it with your employees. Clearly communicate your goals and expectations for maintaining a clean work environment. This demonstrates your commitment to workplace hygiene and shows your employees that their well-being is a priority.
- **Make sure the lavatory is clean**: A clean restroom is crucial for maintaining a hygienic workplace. Ensure that there is an ample supply of soap, toilet paper, and hand towels available in the restroom at all times.
- **Wipes, sanitizer, and Issues should all be readily available**: Such items can help your employees keep their workspace clean and hygienic. If these products are readily available, workers are more likely to use them.

- **Cleaning schedule**: Make sure your workplace is cleaned regularly. This helps prevent illness and a clean workplace also increases morale and professionalism.

Grinding Post-Cleaning

- In the routine grinding of spices, energy is applied to break down larger particles into smaller ones while preserving the product's flavor and color. This process generates heat as energy is expended in breaking down the particles further.
- Spices are ground using either low-temperature or cryogenic techniques. Cold air is used in low-temperature methods, while liquid nitrogen is employed in cryogenic methods. This ensures that heat is controlled within safe limits throughout the grinding chamber and milling system, resulting in spice powders that are more aromatic, vibrant, and flavorful.
- Various grinding techniques, including horizontal and vertical hammer mills and roller mills, are employed to reduce the size of spices to the desired particle size. After grinding, both coarse and fine particles are handled pneumatically and moved to the mixing process, where the ingredients are blended according to specific formulations.

Drying

To keep them from spoiling and to concentrate their flavor and aroma, many spices—especially those that are harvested fresh—need to be dried. The type of spice being processed determines the drying procedure.

Drying Process

- **Sun Drying**: This natural and economical technique is frequently used to dry spices like cumin, coriander, and chili peppers.
- **Mechanical Drying**: To guarantee even drying in inclement weather, mechanical dryers are utilized. To keep the spices' flavor and volatile oils intact, heat and airflow are regulated.

Equipment Used

- **Fluidized Bed Dryers**: These devices use hot air streams to evenly dry spices.
- **Tunnel Dryers**: Spices pass through a lengthy tunnel with regulated airflow and temperature.
- **Rotating Dryers**: These dryers use revolving drums to guarantee uniform drying and are used for larger quantities of spices.

Grinding and Milling

- One of the most important steps in the processing of spices is grinding. For convenient use in the food industry, it turns whole spices into powder or other desired forms. The spice's flavor is enhanced by the essential oils and fragrances that are released during the grinding process.

Grinding Process

- **Grinding whole spices**: Spices like pepper, cardamom, cloves, and cumin are ground into a powder. Depending on the desired fineness or coarseness, different grinders are used.
- **Blending**: After grinding, spices can be mixed with other spices to create specific blends such as curry powder, garam masala, or spice rubs.

Equipment Used

- **Hammer Mills**: Commonly used for grinding spices such as coriander, cumin, and pepper, hammer mills work by utilizing high-speed rotating hammers along with screens that control the size of the ground particles.
- **Ball Mills**: Typically used for very fine grinding, ball mills are employed when a very fine powder is required for spices.
- **Disc Mills**: These mills are employed for grinding dry spices like pepper and coriander, and they can produce both coarse and fine powder depending on the desired result.
- **Pin Mills**: Designed for fine grinding of spices like cardamom and nutmeg, pin mills use rotating pins to break down the spice material.
- **Roller Mills**: These mills crush spices between two rollers, making them ideal for processing larger quantities of spices.

Blending and Mixing

Blending or mixing spices is a crucial process in the preparation of spice powders or seasonings used in cooking. It ensures that the spices are uniformly mixed, achieving consistency and homogeneity in the final product.

By connecting grinding equipment to mixers through pneumatic systems, spice powders can be compressed and mixed according to customer specifications. Like the grinding process, this step is fully automated, requiring no manual operator involvement. The entire processing system is designed for continuous operation, even when the mixing process is done in batches. Once the mixing cycle is complete, the finished product is discharged into a small hopper, and the material is pneumatically transferred to the intermediate storage silo or tank.

Blending Process

- **Single Spices**: After grinding, individual spices are either packaged or stored for future use.
- **Blended Spices**: For ready-to-use spice mixes (such as curry powder or taco seasoning), various spices are combined together. These blends may also include additional ingredients like salt, sugar, or other additives to enhance flavor or preserve the mix.

Equipment Used

- **Ribbon Blenders**: These are large-scale machines used to blend spice powders, ensuring a uniform mix. The machine features a rotating ribbon inside a cylindrical container, which effectively mixes the powders.

- **V Blender**: A V-shaped blender used for the dry blending of spices or seasonings. It provides gentle mixing to avoid excessive heat generation and ensures an even blend.

Powder Mixers: These mixers are designed specifically to blend powdered spices evenly, ensuring consistency in the final product.

Post-Mixing

For efficient storage and easy integration into consumer packaging, 25 kg bags, jumbo bags, or Intermediate Bulk Containers (IBCs) are ideal for finished spice powders. After the final mixing, selecting the right automatic bagging machine is crucial to ensure that the material is accurately weighed and packed for consumer distribution. When choosing a bagging machine, you must first determine the type of product, the packaging material to be used, and the required throughput—i.e., the number of bags to be filled per minute. Once the bags are filled, they are sealed either through heat sealing or stitching before being sent for distribution.

Sieving and Screening

Sieving or screening is employed to separate fine powders from coarser particles, ensuring that the spice powder achieves the desired consistency and texture.

Sieving Process

- **Fine Powder Separation**: Following grinding or blending, spices are passed through mesh screens to filter out larger particles or any impurities that may have bypassed earlier stages of processing.
- **Quality Control**: Sieving ensures consistent particle size, which is essential for maintaining the desired product quality.

Equipment Used

- **Vibrating Screens**: Employed for screening spices to eliminate larger particles, ensuring the spice powder is uniformly fine.
- **Rotary Sieves**: Used to differentiate finer particles from coarser ones, ensuring the production of high-quality spice powders.

Packaging

Once grinding, blending, and sieving are complete, spices are prepared for packaging. Effective packaging is essential to maintain the spices' freshness, flavor, and aroma over time. Packaging is a critical element in spice processing as it preserves the quality and taste of the final product.

Indian spice manufacturers utilize packaging materials that shield the spices from moisture, light, and air, all of which can degrade the spice's quality. Airtight packaging further aids in prolonging the shelf life of spices, ensuring that they remain in optimal condition when they reach consumers.

Packaging Process

- **Weighing**: Spices are measured according to the designated packaging sizes.
- **Sealing**: After packaging, spices are sealed in bags or jars to ensure their freshness. This process can be done manually or with the help of automated packaging machines.
- **Labeling**: The final spice products are labeled with essential information, such as ingredients, shelf life, and nutritional details.

Equipment Used

- **Auger Fillers**: These machines are designed to fill spice powders into bags or containers by measuring the spices either by volume or weight.
- **Heat Sealers**: These machines are used to seal spice packets, ensuring the packaging is airtight and protecting the spices from moisture.
- **Vacuum Packing Machines**: For spices that need extended shelf life, these machines remove air from the packaging to prevent oxidation, thus preserving aroma and flavor.
- **Labeling Machines**: These machines automatically apply labels to the packaged products.

Various Factors Affecting the Packaging of Apices

- **Insect Infestation**: Spices are vulnerable to spoiling due to insect infestation, which is aggravated by high humidity, heat, and oxygen levels. Various insect species, such as drug store beetles, cigarette beetles, and coffee bean weevils, target spices and spice powders. These insects thrive in stable environments, making tropical conditions conducive to their activity, leading to losses in both quality and quantity. Inadequately protected warehouses also face damage from rodents, further contributing to spoilage.
- **Moisture Content**: Spices, particularly in powdered form, are hygroscopic, meaning they absorb moisture from the air. This results in sogginess, caking, or lumping of the powder, which disrupts the free-flowing quality. While whole spices do not face caking issues, high relative humidity can cause musty odors to develop.
- **Microbial Deterioration**: High humidity (above 65%) promotes moisture absorption, leading to microbial growth. Though the microorganisms commonly found in raw spices are usually not hazardous, they can pose risks when used in food preparation. Hence, proper inspection of spices is necessary to prevent contamination.
- **Loss of Aroma and Essence**: Spices contain volatile oils responsible for their distinct aroma and flavor. These properties can be lost through a reduction in volatile oil content or oxidation of aromatic components, diminishing the spice's characteristic scent and taste.
- **Colour Bleaching**: Spices with natural colors, like green and bell peppers, green cardamom, turmeric, red chilies, paprika, and saffron, are susceptible to

color fading. This degradation is accelerated by oxygen, light, humidity, and temperature, leading to the loss of their vibrant colors.

Storage

Once packaged, spices are stored in warehouses until they are distributed. Proper storage conditions are important to maintain the quality of the spices.

Storage Considerations

- **Temperature and Humidity Control**: To maintain the flavor and prevent mold growth, spices should be stored in cool and dry environments. Proper control of temperature and humidity ensures their preservation over time.
- **Shelf Life**: Spices should be consumed within the time frame indicated on the packaging to guarantee their freshness and potency. Using them within the recommended shelf life ensures the best quality and flavor.

Quality Assurance

Throughout the entire spice processing process, strict quality assurance protocols are consistently applied. Modern spice manufacturing companies allocate resources to advanced testing facilities and laboratories that conduct frequent tests to evaluate purity, flavor, and hygiene. These tests guarantee that the spices comply with the stringent standards established by regulatory authorities and meet the high expectations of consumers.

COMMON TYPES OF SPICES AND THEIR PROCESSING

- **Whole Spices**: These include items such as peppercorns, cinnamon sticks, cardamom pods, and cloves, which are typically cleaned, dried, and then either packaged or ground when required.
- **Ground Spices**: Spices like ground turmeric, cumin, and coriander are generally ground and processed into a powder form.
- **Blended Spices**: Spices that are mixed, such as curry powder, garam masala, or chili powder, require meticulous blending and, in some cases, the addition of other ingredients like salt or herbs.

Equipment in Spice Processing

- **Cleaning Equipment**: Includes vibratory cleaners, air classifiers, and magnetic separators.
- **Drying Equipment**: Consists of fluidized bed dryers, rotary dryers, and tunnel dryers.
- **Grinding Equipment**: Comprises hammer mills, ball mills, disc mills, pin mills, and roller mills.
- **Blending Equipment**: Features ribbon blenders, V blenders, and powder mixers.
- **Sieving and Screening Equipment**: Utilizes vibrating screens and rotary sieves.

- **Packaging Equipment**: Encompasses auger fillers, heat sealers, vacuum packing machines, and labeling machines.

Why is Spice Processing Important?

Spice processing plays a crucial role in improving the quality and making the spices ready for consumption or export. Here's why it's important:

- **Quality Control**: Effective spice processing ensures that the final product meets the necessary quality standards for both domestic and international markets.
- **Enhanced Shelf Life**: While spices can lose their potency over time, appropriate processing techniques help extend their shelf life.
- **Flavour Consistency**: Proper processing ensures that each batch of spices maintains a consistent flavour.
- **Market Value**: Processed spices generally have a higher market value and are often sold at a premium compared to raw spices.

Benefits of a Dedicated Spice Processing Unit

If you're thinking about establishing a spice processing plant, here are some advantages:

- **Control Over Quality**: Having your own processing unit gives you complete control over the quality of the spices you produce.
- **Cost Savings**: Processing spices internally can lead to long-term cost savings.
- **Customization Options**: You can tailor spice blends to suit specific markets or customer preferences.

In spice processing, every aspect is important—from selecting the right equipment to implementing stringent quality control measures. For more details on advanced spice processing solutions, explore spice processing for insights into the machinery and setups that can elevate your spice business.

Challenges of India's Spice Manufacturing Industry

India's spice manufacturing industry faces several challenges as follows:

Problems Related to Working Labour

Prolonged exposure to the intense odor of spices can have negative effects on health. This makes it challenging to find workers willing to work in the Indian spice industry.

Market Credit

Spices face significant credit market risks with distributors, which can create considerable challenges when it comes to securing financing for production.

There are Leaks in the Packaging

The poor quality of hand-made packaging in India leads to package leakage, largely due to financial limitations. The use of advanced machinery has also been challenging due to its high cost.

There are Many Competitors

The spice industry is highly competitive, with numerous vendors vying for market share. Competition mainly takes place at the regional level. Alongside numerous small local businesses, there is also a growing demand for organic spices, which adhere to strict quality standards.

Spices Wastage at Handling Level

At each stage of spice handling—whether for cleaning, storage, processing, or packaging—wastage occurs due to improper handling of the powders. This inefficiency leads to a reduction in profits for the manufacturer. Unfortunately, automation systems to prevent this issue are not implemented at all sites.

THE ROLE OF TECHNOLOGY IN THE MODERN SPICE MANUFACTURING PROCESS

In recent times, technology has transformed the spice manufacturing sector, optimizing processes and boosting efficiency. The use of advanced machinery and automation has drastically minimized human errors, leading to a notable increase in overall productivity. For example, computer-driven systems are now employed to monitor and control temperature, humidity, and other environmental factors during both drying and milling phases, guaranteeing a consistent quality of the final product. Additionally, innovative methods such as cryogenic grinding, which utilizes extremely low temperatures to grind spices, help preserve their natural flavors and aromas.

Step-by-Step Guide to Establish your Spices Manufacturing Unit

Establishing a spice factory can be a thrilling endeavor that enables you to transform your love of flavors into a successful company. The necessary steps to establish your own spice manufacturing facility will be outlined in this easy-to-follow guide.

Step 1 Research and Planning

Do extensive research on the Spices industry before starting your own business. Recognize the popular spice varieties, market demand, and possible rivals. Create a thorough business plan that includes your objectives, target market, and projected financials.

Step 2 Legal Requirements

It is essential to abide by the law. Get the required licenses, register your company, and follow safety and health regulations. To make sure you are fulfilling all legal requirements for running a spice factory in your area, speak with the local authorities.

Step 3 Location and Infrastructure

Select a good site for your spice factory. Take into account zoning compliance, accessibility for transportation, and closeness to suppliers of raw materials.

Provide a clean, orderly workstation with spaces set aside for processing, packing, and storing.

Step 4 Equipments and Machinery

Purchase high-quality tools and machinery to grind, clean, and package spices. You might require industrial grinders, mixers, and packaging machines, depending on the size of your business. Make sure that every piece of equipment is maintained on a regular basis and complies with safety regulations.

Step 5 Raw Material Sourcing

Build a rapport with trustworthy vendors to source raw materials. Collaborate closely with trustworthy growers and distributors to guarantee the quality and consistency of your spices. To ensure a steady supply chain, negotiate agreements for bulk purchases.

Step 6 Quality Control

Put in place a strong quality control system to guarantee your spices' freshness and purity. Test batches frequently for adulteration, microbial contamination, and general quality. Maintaining a high standard will distinguish your brand and gain the trust of your clients.

Step 7 Packaging and Branding

Invest in aesthetically pleasing and useful packaging to keep your spices fresh. Make a distinctive brand identity that includes a recognizable logo and packaging. To attract customers who care about the environment, take into account eco-friendly packaging options.

Step 8 Marketing and Distribution

Create a marketing plan to advertise your spices. Make use of online and offline resources, including websites, social media, and neighborhood stores. Create distribution channels to guarantee that a large audience sees your spices. Think about joint ventures with supermarkets, eateries, and internet sites.

Step 9 Compliance with Food Safety Standards

Respect food safety laws to win over customers' trust. Put in place traceability systems, appropriate labeling, and hygienic procedures. Stay up to date on any changes to regulations and regularly refresh your knowledge of food safety standards.

Step 10 Continuous Improvement

Assess your operations on a regular basis and look for methods to increase productivity and product quality. Keep up with consumer preferences and industry trends so you can modify your offerings appropriately. Utilize consumer feedback to improve your goods and services.

Features of Automatic Spice Powder Packing Machine

- **Efficiency**: By achieving high-speed, continuous packaging operations, the automatic spice powder packaging machine significantly increases both production capacity and packaging efficiency.
- **Accurate measurement**: To guarantee the correct amount of spice powder in every packaging bag and maintain product quality and consistency, the packaging machine employs a sophisticated measurement system.
- **Flexibility:** To accommodate spice powders with varying specifications and packaging needs, the automatic spice powder packaging machine can be modified and configured to meet specific needs.

Figure 5.1: Spice Powder Plant.

Spice processing consists of several essential stages, including cleaning, drying, grinding, blending, and packaging. Each step plays a crucial role in preserving the spices' natural essential oils, rich flavors, and aromatic properties. The effective operation of specialized equipment is key to maintaining efficiency and ensuring high-quality spice production. A thorough understanding of each machine's function and role in the process helps guarantee that the final spice products meet market standards and consumer expectations.

6

Operation and Management of Fruit and Vegetable Pack House

INTRODUCTION

A produce packing plant is a specialized facility designed to sort, package, and sometimes store fresh produce. These facilities are essential in the agricultural supply chain, helping to maintain the quality, safety, and freshness of fruits and vegetables as they are prepared for distribution to retailers or consumers. Packing plants are commonly used in commercial agricultural operations, especially for fruits and vegetables grown in large quantities.

Uses and Managing a fruit and vegetable packing plant involves overseeing all activities related to the handling, grading, packaging, and storage of fresh produce, ensuring that it meets quality standards and is ready for distribution. Effective operations and management are essential to maintaining product quality, optimizing efficiency, and ensuring profitability for producers and suppliers.

The operation includes several stages that require coordination, from the receipt of the harvested products until they are sent to markets or retailers. Management, on the other hand, refers to the processes, strategies and decisions that ensure the smooth operation of the packing plant.

Packing plants serve as a collection center for fruits and vegetables prior to their distribution and marketing. These can be simple packing sheds with limited equipment and minimal operations or a large, well-equipped complex with equipment for specialized operations. The types of operations performed vary depending on the different products and market demands. Products destined for export or supermarkets often undergo more elaborate operations than those in local markets. Some of these operations include the following:

OPERATION

The specific operations carried out in a packinghouse depend on the type of crop being processed and the target market. Some or all of the following steps may be involved:

- **Reception**: Unloading, inspection, and recording of incoming produce.
- **Sorting**: Separation based on quality, size, or other criteria.
- **Special Treatments (if required)**: Processes such as cleaning, washing, fungicide application, and size grading.
- **Packing**: Preparing the produce for storage or distribution.
- **Post-Packaging Treatments (if required)**: Additional measures such as fumigation, cooling, or storage to maintain freshness.
- **Assembly and Dispatch**: Organizing and sending out packed goods for distribution.

A well-organized packinghouse ensures efficiency by preventing clutter and disorder, which can lead to compromised hygiene and product quality. Ideally, tasks such as receiving, sorting, cleaning, fungicide dipping, packing, and dispatching should be conducted in separate designated areas rather than in a single, congested space covered with plant debris.

The packing process varies depending on the type of produce. Dumping may be performed using either dry or water-assisted methods. Cleaning can involve either washing with chlorinated water or dry brushing. If waxing is required, it is done after washing and drying. Grading ensures separation between processing-grade and fresh market produce, while sizing further classifies items, often reserving smaller produce for local markets or processing. Typically, the highest-quality produce is packaged and sold at regional or national levels.

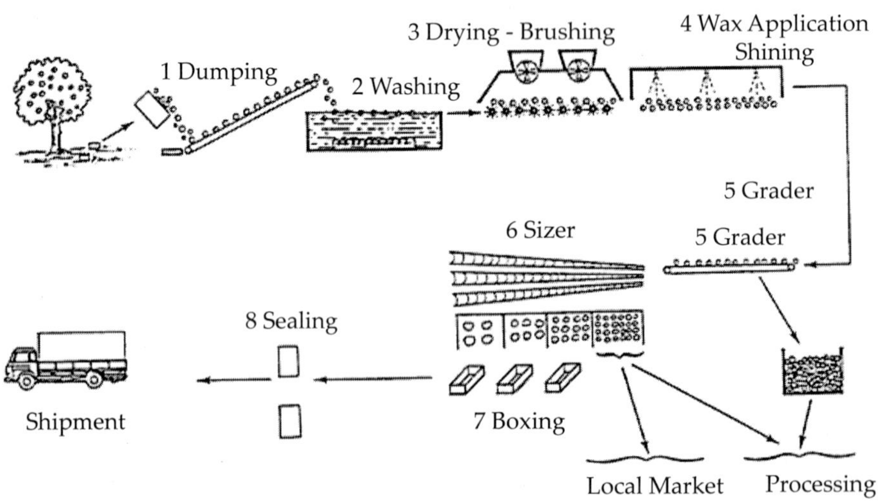

Figure 6.1: Improvement of Post-Harvest Fresh Fruits and Vegetables Handling.

Dumping

The product must be removed from the harvest silo or container in some way and transported to the packaging plant. This first step is known as "pouring." Pouring should be done gently, either by water-assisted methods or dry pouring. Wet pouring can reduce bruising and scratches by using portable chlorinated water (100-150 ppm) to transport delicate products. When dry pouring is used, full ramps, inclines, or moving conveyor belts can reduce product damage.

Whenever products are spilled from one container to another, care should be taken to minimize mechanical damage to the products. When unloading products from field silos or transport vehicles to the packaging plant, dry or wet dumping may be practiced. When dry dumping practices are used, the field container should be emptied slowly and gently onto a steep ramp with full sides. In the illustration below, a conveyor then transports the discarded dry goods to the packaging plant.

DRY DUMPING

Apples and other produce will float if their specific density is less than that of water. To boost the water's specific density and ensure fruit floatation, salts (like sodium lignin sulfonate, sodium silicate, or sodium sulfate) must be added to some produce, like pears.

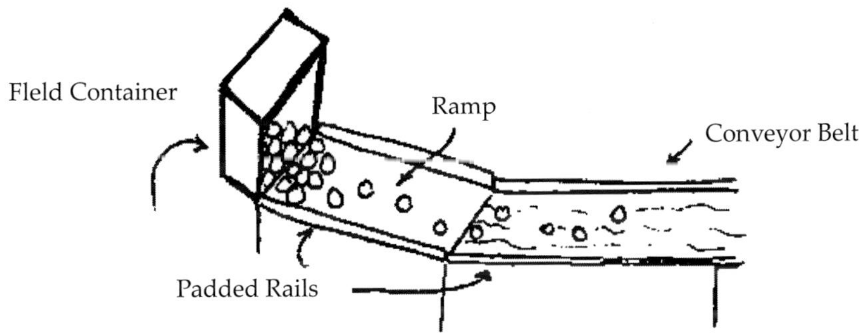

Figure 6.2: Wet Dumping, Which Involves Immersion and Floatation or Dumping into Water Instead of Onto a Dry Ramp, is Occasionally Used to Lessen Mechanical Damage.

When fruit is being moved from a conveyor into a bulk bin, the canvas curtain shown below is used to break up the fall.

Conveyor Equipment

To reduce bruising:

- Use foam-filled ramps;
- Slow down the speed of fruit on the ramps by installing screens, curtains, blankets or deceleration curtains;
- Use a flexible curtain to slow down fruit as it falls from a higher conveyor. high to a lower belt (use a light curtain for a short transition, a heavier curtain for a higher transition);
- A belt to prevent fruit from falling directly onto the roller sorter;
- Remove the support board under the mat in an area where fruit will fall onto a new mat.

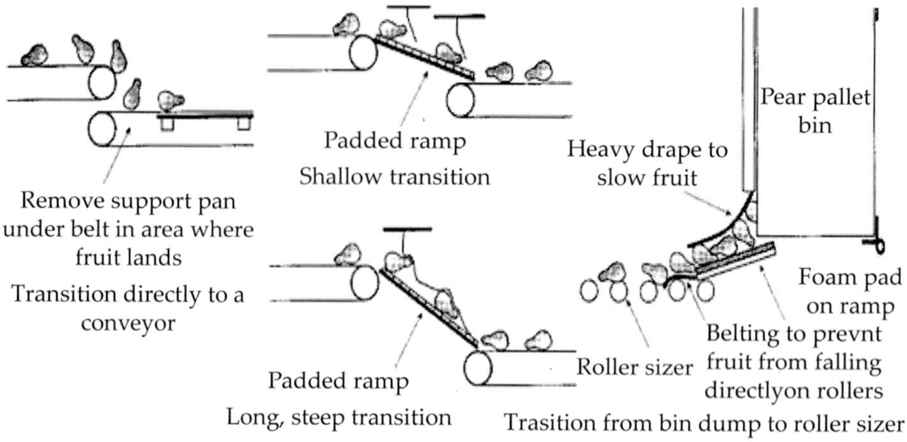

Figure 6.3: Postharvest Technology of Horticultural Crops.

Sorting and Trimming

In order to ensure consistency in size, shape, and varietal traits, freshly harvested fruits and vegetables are sorted. To improve the produce's appearance and stop infection from the diseased parts, damaged, discolored, and decayed parts are removed.

Washing

Washing is necessary to remove foreign materials from the field such as soil, chemicals, and latex. This is usually done before the product is stored or immediately sold. To reduce the incidence of rot, chlorine is often added to the wash water.

Steel drums can be used to make a simple washing station. The drums are cut into pieces and provided with drainage holes, and all metal ends are covered with split rubber or plastic tubing.

The barrels are then placed on an inclined wooden table. The table is constructed of wooden slats and serves as a drying rack before packaging.

Since steel drums are often used to store oil and chemicals, they must be thoroughly cleaned before being used as a washing medium.

This produce washing tank is constructed from sheet metal that has been galvanized. To help move water through the produce, a perforated sheet metal baffle is placed close to the drain pipe.

A perforated pipe allows fresh water to be added under pressure, which aids in moving floating produce toward the tank's drain end for removal following cleaning.

A detachable trash screen in front of the baffle and/or a recirculating system for the wash water (with chlorine added) are possible upgrades to the design below.

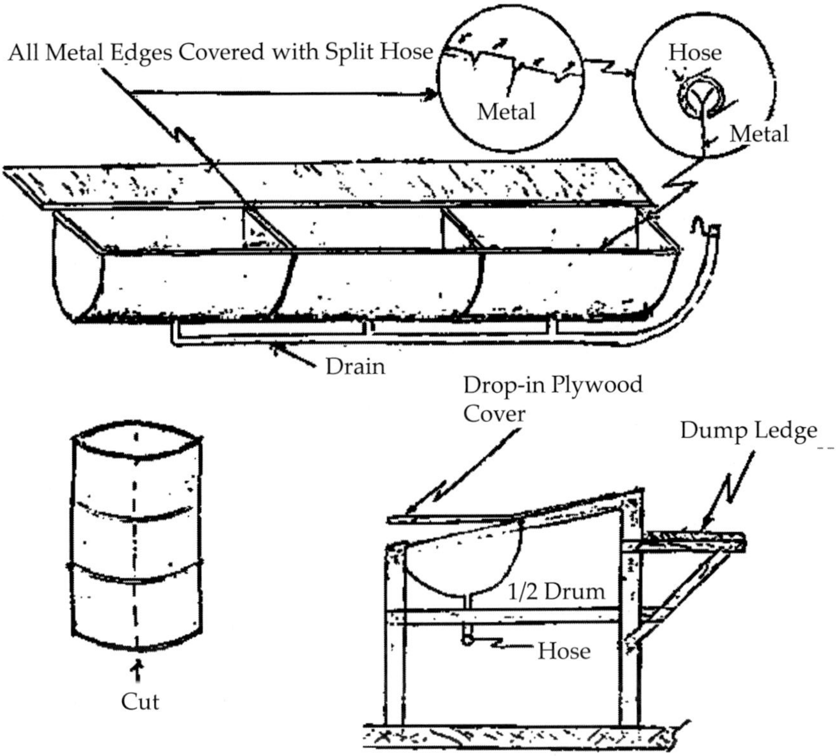

Figure 6.4: Postharvest Handling Manual.Commercialization of Alternative Crops Project.

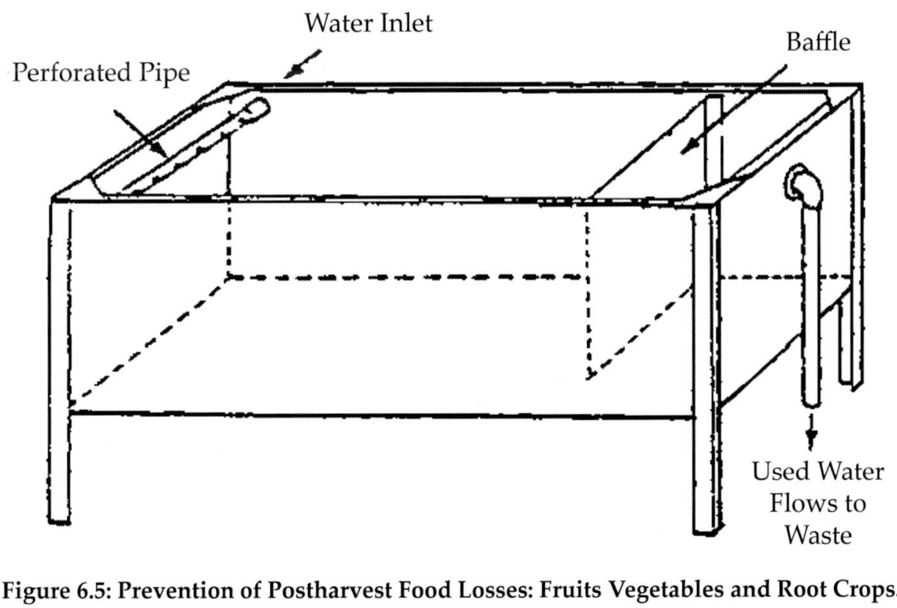

Figure 6.5: Prevention of Postharvest Food Losses: Fruits Vegetables and Root Crops.

Drying

Drying is carried out to eliminate excess moisture from the surface of the produce. However, over-drying should be avoided, as it can lead to wilting, shrinkage, and excessive water loss, which may negatively impact the quality and freshness of the produce.

Waxing

Waxing is applied to specific fruits and vegetables, such as ginger, tomatoes, citrus fruits, and melons, to minimize water loss and prevent shriveling. Additionally, the use of edible wax enhances the produce's appearance.

The waxing equipment shown here is intended for use after a sequence of dry brushes on a conveyor line. Industrial wool felt is utilized to evenly distribute the liquid wax onto the fruits or vegetables from a trough that matches the width of the belt. To minimize wax evaporation from the felt, a layer of heavy polyethylene sheeting is placed over it.

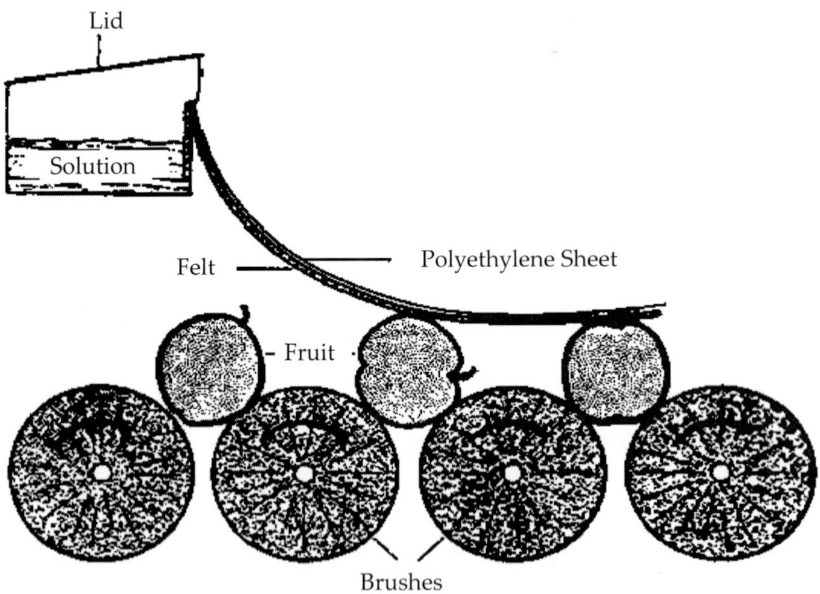

Figure 6.6: A wipe-on device for the application of materials to butts.

SIZING

Sorting produce by size is optional but can be beneficial if certain size categories command higher market prices. In many low-input packing facilities, manual sizing remains a common practice. Workers should be trained to identify the desired sizes and either pack the items directly into containers or carefully place them into bins for further packing along the processing line.

Sizing can be performed visually using standard size gauges. To assist operators, examples of the smallest and largest acceptable sizes for each product can be displayed for easy reference. Handheld sizers are also commonly used for various types of produce.

Examples of Grade Standards

Table 6.1: Grade Standards of Agricultural Products.

Garlic size designations	Diameter in inches
#11 Super-Colossal	2 15/16 and up
#10 Colossal	2 11/16 – 2 15/16
#9 Super-Jumbo	2 7/16 – 2 11/16
#8 Extra-Jumbo	2 3/16 – 2 7/16
#7 Jumbo	1 15/16 – 2 3/16
#6 Giant	1 13/16 – 1 15/16
#5 Tube	1 11/16 – 1 12/16
#4 Medium Tube	1 9/16 – 1 11/16

Several types of mechanical sizing are available for small-scale operations. One type consists of a long inclined plane with a series of converging openings (the largest at the top, the smallest at the bottom). This type of sizing works best with round products. Other sizing systems are designed as conveyors equipped with chains or plastic belts with openings of varying sizes and are useful for most product sizes. Another simple method of mechanical sizing is to use a set of diverging gauge rolls, where the smaller products fall through the rollers first onto a sorting belt or bin, and the larger products fall between increasingly different rollers.

Diverging Bar Rollers Sizer

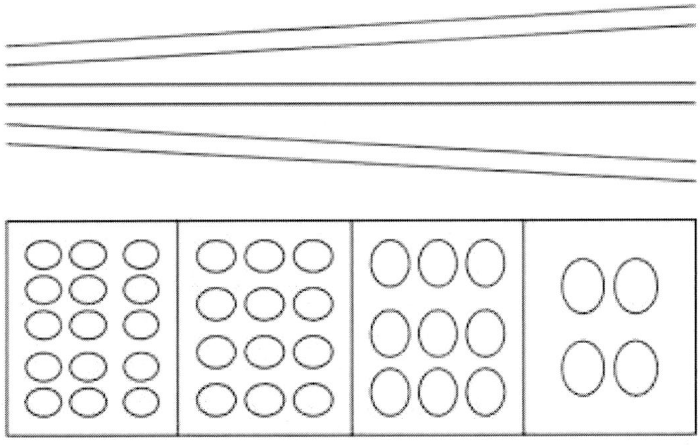

Figure 6.7: Diverging Bar Rollers Sizer.

Narrow Pallet System

The University of Wisconsin advocates for this produce handling system because it enhances efficiency, reduces costs, and improves worker safety. Using a hand pallet truck allows handlers to move up to 16 cartons simultaneously, significantly cutting down the time spent transporting boxes while minimizing physical strain.

Figure 6.8: Wisconsin Healthy Farmers, Healthy Profits Project, December Pallet System Second Edition.

A hand pallet truck functions similarly to a traditional dolly but features pivoting forks at the base instead of a fixed metal plate. When produce is stacked on a small plastic pallet (14 × 24 inches), the forks can be positioned underneath, enabling the entire stack to be moved at once. The truck can be tilted by releasing the forks for easy loading and unloading and locked into an upright position for transport.

CURING

Injured or bruised areas of root, rhizome, and tuber crops are allowed to heal by keeping them at ambient temperatures for several days. This curing process triggers the formation of periderm layers at the wounded spots, which helps minimize moisture loss and protect against microbial infections. Once adequately cured, the vegetables can be stored for extended periods.

Chemical Treatments

Fungicides and growth regulators are widely used to prevent decay and control unwanted growth, respectively. It is essential to closely monitor the use of these chemicals, ensuring they stay within the recommended limits for human consumption.

Fungicide Treatment

Decay caused by moulds or bacteria is a primary contributor to the loss of fresh produce during marketing. Infection can occur either before or after harvest, often through physical injuries or direct penetration of the intact skin of the produce. Pre-harvest infections may remain dormant until post-harvest, particularly in fruits, where they develop as the fruit ripens. Crops like mangoes, bananas, avocados, and sweet peppers are susceptible to latent anthracnose infections.

Post-harvest fungicide application is common for crops like apples, bananas, and citrus fruits that are stored for extended periods or transported over long distances. As mentioned, fungicides are typically applied only after produce has been washed and drained.

Most fungicides used for post-harvest decay control come in wettable powders or emulsifiable concentrations, which form suspensions in water rather than solutions. These suspensions need to be agitated constantly during application; otherwise, the concentration of fungicide can drop below the effective level due to settling.

In smaller-scale packing operations, fungicide can be applied through:

- **Dipping**: This method involves hand-dipping the produce in a fungicide suspension agitated manually. Wire-mesh baskets can hold several items at once. After dipping, the produce should be drained and dried in a shaded, well-ventilated area.
- **Spraying**: This method involves using a hand-operated knapsack sprayer while the produce remains on trays or racks. After washing and drying, the produce should be sprayed thoroughly until runoff occurs.

Larger-scale operations may use mechanized spray or drenching systems, including a mechanical mixer for the fungicide. Produce moves through the spray or drenching system, often on a conveyor. Other methods like smokes, dusts, or vapors are typically used only by large-scale operations, especially when produce is to be stored for extended periods.

GRADING

Fresh fruits and vegetables are categorized into various groups based on established quality and size criteria, with each category being assigned a standard name and size classification.

Packaging

Produce is placed in appropriate containers designed to safeguard against mechanical and biological damage during transit and handling. The packaging materials must meet recognized standards for durability, strength, and pressure resistance. Additionally, the containers should allow for sufficient ventilation to prevent the produce from overheating due to respiration. However, excessive ventilation can lead to wilting.

Fruit Packing Line

Small-scale packing equipment for produce is offered by various manufacturers and suppliers. This specific model features a receiving belt, a washer, and a sorting table.

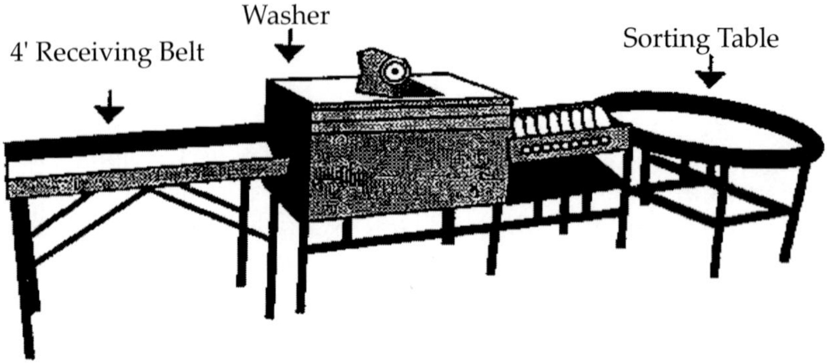

Figure 6.9: Catalog of TEW Manufacturing Corporation, P.O. Box 87, Penfield, NY 14526 USA

Palletising

In large-volume operations, packed shipping containers for most fruit and vegetables, such as rock melons, muskmelons, capsicums, and tomatoes, are palletized for shipment. However, for immature fruit vegetables like sweet corn, palletizing is less common in low-volume operations due to the absence of forklifts. In these cases, palletizing typically occurs either at a centralized cooling facility or during the loading process. The palletizing process generally happens after hydrocooling or package-ice cooling but before forced-air cooling. In field-pack operations, palletizing is usually carried out in the field itself.

Cooling

Different cooling methods are used for fruit and vegetables, with each tailored to the specific needs of the produce. Forced-air cooling is widely used for items like beans, rock melons, cucumbers, muskmelons, peas, capsicum, soft-rind squashes, and tomatoes. For chilling-sensitive products such as squashes, peppers, eggplants, and cherry tomatoes, forced-air evaporative cooling is applied selectively.

Hydrocooling is commonly done before grading, sizing, and packing for products like beans, cantaloupe, sweet corn, and okra. Sorting of defective products are takes place both before and after the cooling process. However, hydrocooling cycles may not be sufficient, particularly in hot weather. To address this, allowing sufficient time in cold rooms after packing and palletizing ensures that the product is adequately cooled before transport.

Package icing and liquid-icing techniques are used to cool rock melons and to complement hydrocooling for sweet corn. In large-volume operations, temporary cold storage is used, where fruit vegetables are placed in cold rooms for storage before shipment. In smaller farm operations, products are often sent to central facilities owned by cooperatives or distributors for cooling and short-term storage.

For transport, some tomatoes, rock melons, and other muskmelons are shipped in refrigerated railcars, but most fruit vegetables are transported in refrigerated trucks or container vans. While some items like cantaloupe and tomatoes may be shipped together, it's essential to separate ethylene-sensitive products. Immature fruit-type vegetables, such as cucumber, legumes, bitter melon, and eggplant, are sensitive to ethylene exposure. Among mature fruit types, watermelon is negatively affected by ethylene, causing softening, mealiness in the flesh, and rind separation.

Pre-Cooling

Pre-cooling is a critical step before storing produce at low temperatures. It involves the swift removal of field heat from the produce to lower the rate of respiration, reduce microbial activity, and ease the refrigeration load. This process can be achieved using chilled water, ice, or cool air (forced air cooling), cooling the produce down to its half cooling temperature.

Storage

Storing produce at low temperatures is an effective method for extending the shelf life of fresh fruits and vegetables. It also allows for better marketing and distribution of produce during peak production times. The temperature needs for different types of produce can vary based on factors such as variety, location, and stage of maturity. It is important to understand that cool storage helps preserve quality, but it does not enhance it.

Special Treatments

Ripening

Ethylene is commonly used to promote uniform and controlled ripening, especially for mature green tomatoes, and occasionally for melons like honeydew, casaba, and Crenshaw. This ethylene treatment can be applied either at the shipping point or the destination, although optimal fruit quality is generally achieved when the treatment is done soon after harvest at the shipping point.

The ideal temperature for ripening is between 12.5°C to 25°C (55°F to 77°F), with higher temperatures speeding up the ripening process. However, temperatures above 30°C (86°F) can inhibit the development of red color in tomatoes. A typical ethylene concentration of around 100 ppm is used. For honeydew melons, particularly class 12 melons, ethylene treatment may last up to 24 hours, while tomatoes are usually treated for up to three days at 20°C (68°F).

Ethylene treatments can be done either before or after packing tomatoes, but most tomatoes undergo treatment after packing. Treating before packing helps to identify and remove any decaying fruit before the final packout, while treating after packing ensures more uniform packing. Despite this, some "checkerboarding" may still occur, requiring repackaging.

Modified Atmospheres

Modified atmospheres are not commonly used for these commodities in commercial operations, although there are ongoing tests for shipping melons and tomatoes under modified atmospheres, particularly for long-distance markets. When packaging vine-ripe tomatoes for consumers, modified atmospheres are sometimes utilized. For tomatoes stored at recommended temperatures, maintaining oxygen levels between 3 to 5 per cent helps slow the ripening process, while ensuring carbon dioxide levels remain below 5 per cent to prevent injury to the fruit.

Though less research has been done on muskmelons, the ideal atmospheric conditions for their storage are 3 to 5 per cent oxygen and 10 to 20 per cent carbon dioxide. For mature fruit-type vegetables, temperature plays a crucial role in controlling the ripening rate. However, most mature-harvested fruit vegetables are susceptible to chilling injury when stored below the recommended temperature.

Chilling injury is cumulative, with its severity depending on both the temperature and duration of exposure. For example, tomatoes exposed to temperatures below 10°C (50°F) will experience a lack of color development, reduced flavor, and increased decay.

Transportation

Proper handling of produce during transportation is crucial to minimizing losses and preserving its quality from the farm to the packing house and from the packing house to the market. Using refrigerated trucks for transporting highly perishable and high-value produce helps maintain their quality for a longer period. In contrast, when fruits and vegetables are transported in non-ventilated vans, their temperature increases rapidly, leading to accelerated respiration and faster decay.

MANAGEMENT

The operation and management of a fruit and vegetable pack house encompass overseeing every aspect of handling, sorting, packaging, and storing fresh produce, ensuring it meets quality standards and is ready for distribution. Effective operation and management are essential to maintain the quality of the produce, enhance efficiency, and guarantee profitability for both producers and suppliers.

The operation consists of multiple stages requiring careful coordination, starting from receiving harvested produce and ending with shipping it to markets or retailers. Management, however, pertains to the strategies, processes, and decision-making that ensure the pack house operates smoothly.

Key components of operation and management in a fruit and vegetable pack house include the following:

Production Flow Management

- **Receiving and Handling:** The first step involves the efficient receipt of harvested produce. This process includes inspecting the quality, sorting out damaged or substandard produce, and ensuring the proper storage conditions are in place.
- **Sorting and Grading**: Sorting produce based on size, color, and quality ensures uniformity and meets market standards.
- **Packaging**: Packaging must be done with care to protect the produce and ensure it meets retail or consumer requirements.
- **Storage and Preservation**: Pack houses typically have cold storage or refrigeration systems to maintain freshness. Proper temperature and humidity control are critical to reducing spoilage and extending shelf life.

Quality Control

- Quality control ensures that the produce meets required standards for freshness, safety, and appearance. This includes inspecting for bruises, discoloration, and signs of spoilage, along with ensuring compliance with food safety regulations.
- Regular inspections, sampling, and testing help identify any quality issues before shipping.

Inventory and Supply Chain Management

- Efficient management of raw materials, packaging supplies, and finished goods is essential to reduce costs and ensure timely delivery.
- The pack house must maintain a streamlined inventory system, track goods movement, and coordinate logistics with suppliers, transport companies, and retailers.

Workforce Management

- Managing the workforce is vital to maintaining productivity, especially during peak harvest times. This includes training workers in handling, sorting, and packaging processes, ensuring safety standards are met, and minimizing human error.
- Labor management also involves scheduling shifts, managing payroll, and addressing worker welfare.

Technology and Automation

- Many modern pack houses use automated sorting, grading, and packing technologies. These systems boost efficiency, reduce human error, and ensure product consistency.
- Information management systems track inventory, manage orders, and provide real-time data to aid decision-making.

Health, Safety, and Regulatory Compliance

- Fruit and vegetable pack houses must comply with health and safety regulations, along with food safety standards such as HACCP (Hazard Analysis and Critical Control Points) and other certifications.
- Ensuring worker safety, environmental protection, and adherence to local and international food standards is crucial for operational efficiency and legal compliance.

Logistics and Distribution

- Managing logistics and transportation is essential to ensure that products reach the market or customers on time and in optimal condition.
- This includes coordinating shipment timing, handling transportation to maintain cold chains, and managing relationships with logistics providers.

Cost and Financial Management

- Managing the financial side of the pack house involves budgeting, cost analysis, and tracking profit margins. It's essential to control overheads like labor costs, utility expenses, and packaging materials to maintain profitability.

Effective operation and management of a fruit and vegetable pack house require meticulous attention to detail across various processes. It involves applying best practices in food handling, workforce management, technology use, and quality control, all of which contribute to delivering high-quality produce to the market.

SPECIAL TREATMENTS AFTER PACKING

Certain post-packing treatments are applied to specific crops, with such practices being more common in large-scale operations aimed at urban and export markets. The key treatments include:

- **Fumigation**: This treatment is used to control insect pests, such as fruit flies, and is often a mandatory requirement for importing produce into many countries. It requires specialized equipment and skilled operators to perform effectively.
- **Initiation of Fruit Ripening**: This process involves treating the packed fruit with ethylene gas within insulated, temperature-controlled storage for several days to initiate ripening. Due to the high costs, this method is generally limited to larger operations.
- **Degreening of Citrus Fruit**: In tropical regions, citrus fruits may remain green even when ripe unless exposed to low night temperatures. However, they will develop their natural color when subjected to artificial degreening, which typically involves an ethylene treatment similar to that used for ripening. This process is not often carried out in small packing houses.

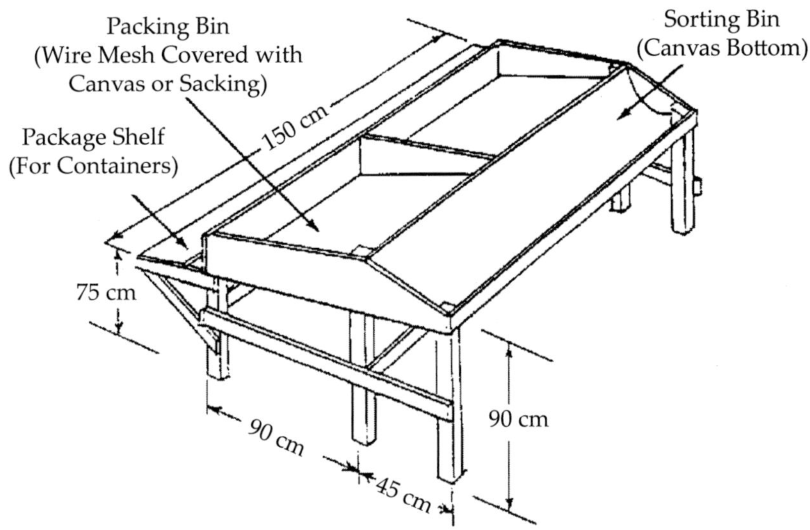

Figure 6.10: Sorting and packing stand is simply made for small-scale operations and gets work off the floor Incoming produce goes into the sorting bin, then into the packing bin and finally into containers held on shelf.

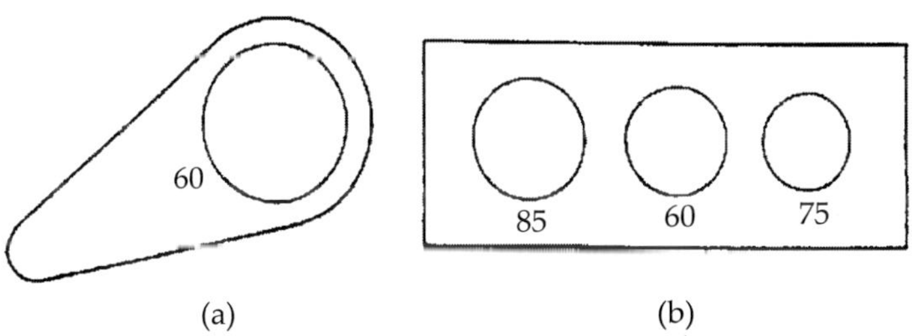

Figure 6.11: Sizing rings are used for grading round produce. The hand-held model (a) comes in various sizes. The multi-size model (b) can be fixed to a packing stand

Assembly of packed produce for dispatch. Time plays a crucial role in the marketing of fresh produce, as delays contribute to increased losses. Once the produce is packed, it should be dispatched to the market promptly. As such, transportation arrangements should be prioritized by the packing-house management.

In small-scale operations, however, it may take time to assemble a full load. Therefore, when packed produce takes longer to accumulate, it is vital to take steps to prevent its deterioration. The following precautions should be observed:

- Packed containers should be shielded from the sun and rain, as heat and moisture cause rapid degradation of produce and can compromise the integrity of cardboard boxes.
- Careful handling of packed boxes during stacking is necessary to avoid damaging the contents. Any damage to the produce accelerates water loss and decay.

- When waiting for transport, packed containers should be stacked in a way that allows for adequate ventilation to prevent overheating, which can lead to rapid spoilage.

To minimize losses of fresh produce during packing operations, the following practices should be followed:

- Keep the produce as cool as possible.
- Ensure the produce remains dry.
- Protect the produce from injury.
- Ensure rapid movement of the produce to market.

Planning a Packing House

When selecting a site for a packing house, several key factors must be taken into account:

- Is the location easily accessible from the production areas, the intended markets, and major transportation routes?
- Is there a sufficient labor force available in the area to support packing operations?
- Are essential services such as electricity, water supply, and telephone connectivity readily available?

Before finalizing the location, it is crucial to assess the quality of the water that will be used for washing the produce. If the water source is a river, stream, or stagnant body, it must be tested to confirm that it is free from contaminants such as sewage, industrial waste, pesticides, herbicides, or fertilizers. Ensuring clean water is essential for maintaining hygiene and preventing contamination of fresh produce.

Site characteristics. Once the general location has been selected, the following considerations should be taken into account:

- The site should be flat and, if possible, positioned to minimize exposure to strong winds.
- If the packing operation is intended to be permanent, there should be sufficient space available for future expansion.
- There must be ample space to accommodate vehicle movement and parking, ensuring that the largest expected number and size of trucks can be managed efficiently. Roadways should be at least 3.5 meters wide to facilitate smooth traffic flow.
- Proper drainage systems must be in place to handle both rainwater runoff and the water used in packing operations.
- The site should allow for effective security measures, such as fencing and the presence of watchmen, to ensure the safety of produce, equipment, and workers.

LAYOUT, CONSTRUCTION AND EQUIPMENT

Small-scale packing houses typically handle multiple crops simultaneously or throughout different periods. Given the relatively small volumes of produce managed, the layout of buildings and equipment should be kept simple yet adaptable to accommodate varying needs.

Layout Considerations

The design of the packing house is influenced by the available space. Generally, a single-level structure with a designated receiving area at one end and a dispatching area at the opposite end provides the most efficient workflow. This arrangement helps maintain separation between the reception zone, which is often contaminated with dirt and debris, and the packing and dispatching sections, thereby reducing the risk of contamination. Additionally, such a setup minimizes congestion and prevents operational confusion between incoming and outgoing vehicles.

If space limitations require an alternative approach, a U-shaped layout—where the reception and dispatch areas are adjacent—may be an option. However, this configuration is not ideal, as it increases the likelihood of cross-contamination, congestion, and complications in future expansions.

Functional Areas of the Packing House

To ensure efficient operations, the packing house should allow for smooth movement of produce through three essential stages:

Reception Area

- This is the entry point where harvested produce is received, sorted, and cleaned, including washing if necessary.
- The area tends to accumulate soil, dust, and decaying plant material, making it one of the dirtiest sections.
- To prevent contamination of sorted and packed produce, the reception area should ideally be physically separated from the other sections—such as through doors or partitions.

Preparation and Packing Section

- This section includes facilities for any special treatments, such as drying stations for washed or chemically treated produce.
- The primary activity here is packing the cleaned produce, with provisions for selection and grading if required.
- Adequate space should be allocated for the storage and organized assembly of packing materials, ensuring they remain dry and readily accessible.
- The entire area must be sheltered from weather conditions while maintaining good ventilation and lighting.
- It is essential to keep the selection, grading, and packing sections clean and dry to uphold quality standards.

Streamlining Packing Operations

Disorganized packing processes can lead to unnecessary delays, increased costs, and compromised product quality. Implementing a structured, step-by-step layout for the packing shed can optimize time, enhance efficiency, and reduce expenses while ensuring that the produce retains its quality.

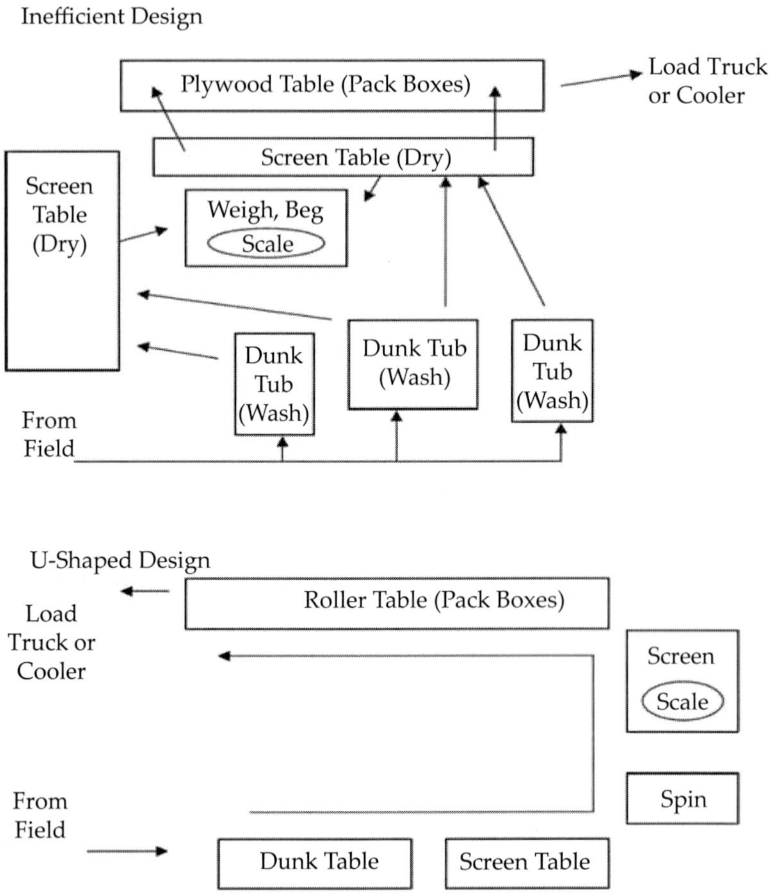

Figure 6.12: Inefficient Design.

Dispatch

The dispatch section should be positioned adjacent to the packing operation while remaining free from permanent equipment to allow for flexibility. It must be spacious enough to accommodate the temporary storage of packed produce while ensuring smooth and unhindered movement of both workers and produce.

Maintaining cleanliness and proper ventilation in this area is essential to preserve the quality of packed goods. Additionally, if there is a dedicated office or quality control unit, it is most likely to be situated within or near the dispatch area to facilitate oversight and coordination of final shipments.

CONSTRUCTION

The choice of building materials and construction methods for a packing house depends on factors such as the type of crops to be handled, the expected volume of produce, target markets, and available financial resources. Small-scale operations can function effectively with simple and cost-efficient structures.

Requirements

- **Overhead Protection**: Adequate shielding from sun and rain is essential. A roof with a wide overhang (at least one meter on all sides) helps provide this protection.
- **Ventilation & Weather Protection**: Proper ventilation is necessary while also safeguarding against wind-driven rain and dust. This can be achieved by constructing walls that leave an open ventilation space beneath the extended roof.
- **Durable Flooring**: A hard, level surface ensures safe and easy movement of workers and produce.

Types of Construction for Small-Scale Packing Houses

- **Basic Structures**: On-farm packing sheds can be made using inexpensive, locally available materials such as bamboo, bush poles, dried grass, or thatch. While these structures may have a shorter lifespan, their affordability and ease of repair make them practical. If water supply is available, soaking the plant-based walls and roof periodically can help cool the interior.
- **Moderately Durable Structures**: A more robust option is a wooden frame structure with a corrugated metal sheet roof and walls, built over a concrete floor. However, in regions with intense sunlight, metal buildings can trap excessive heat, affecting both workers and produce. To mitigate this, a ventilation gap between the walls and roof is recommended, along with an extended roof overhang. In some cases, walls may not be necessary if the roof alone provides sufficient shade and rain protection.

Permanent Packing Houses

For long-term facilities, non-slip concrete floors with a drainage system should be installed to allow easy cleaning. Applying an anti-dusting surface treatment to the concrete can further improve hygiene.

Except for large-scale commercial operations, permanent packing houses should avoid fixed equipment installations. This flexibility allows the interior layout to be adjusted as needed to accommodate different crop volumes and processing requirements.

EQUIPMENT

The equipment required for a packing house depends on the scale of operations and the types of crops handled. The setup should be simple, cost-effective, and locally sourced where possible. Additionally, mobility is key, so fixed concrete washing tanks should be avoided.

Equipment and Tools

- **Bins or Trays**: Easily manageable by a single worker, these containers are ideal for transporting produce up to the packing stage. They can be made from wood or high-density polyethylene (HDPE) plastic. While plastic containers are more expensive than wooden ones, they are easier to clean and more durable. Multiple containers can be moved simultaneously.
- **Push-Carts**: Various types of two- or four-wheeled carts, similar to those used in markets or factories, are useful for transporting produce within the packing house.
- **Roller Conveyors**: Mounted on stands approximately 75 cm high, these conveyors facilitate the smooth movement of bins or trays through different processing stages. They are also helpful for loading and unloading produce when containers are handled individually.
- **Mechanized Moving-Belt Conveyors**: Although effective, these conveyors are costly and more suitable for large-scale operations.
- **Hand-Pushed Lift Trucks**: These are particularly useful in larger packing houses where unit loads are handled on pallets . However, they cannot lift loaded pallets onto vehicles unless the loading bay is elevated to match truck bed height or a mechanical hoist is available .
- **Motorized Forklift Trucks**: In large packing houses, forklifts are essential for efficiently moving palletized loads across the facility .

By selecting the right combination of equipment, packing houses can enhance productivity, reduce manual labor, and improve the overall efficiency of handling and transporting fresh produce.

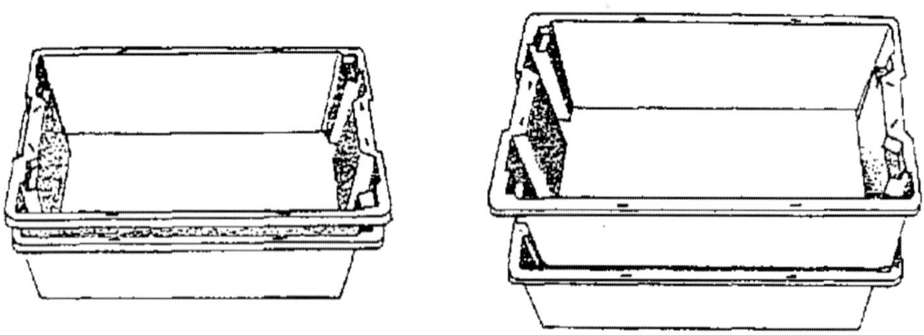

(a) (b)

Figure 6.13: Polythene crates are costly but durable

They nest and conserve space in transit or storage when empty (a). In order to prevent crates from nesting and crushing their contents, they stack neatly and firmly when filled (b) if every other crate is turned in the opposite direction from the one below.

Selection, grading and packing. Any unmarketable pieces of produce that may have passed previous sorting should be removed during a final selection just before packing. A basic stand can be used for selection, grading, and packing when handling small amounts of produce by hand. If handling larger quantities of produce, the stand shown can be duplicated or made to any convenient length. Produce can be chosen and frequently sized by skilled workers using their eyes or basic hand-held or fixed gauges. Produce that has been chosen and graded is put in the packing bin before being packed into shelf-mounted containers. After being packed, the containers proceed to the dispatch assembly area.

Additional Equipment

Since a significant portion of produce is traded based on weight, packing houses must have reliable weighing systems. Various types of weighing scales are available, and selecting the most appropriate option requires careful consideration of the specific needs of the operation. It is advisable to assess both the weighing requirements and the range of scales available before making a decision.

Figure 6.14: Hand-operated pallet truck can be used on level concrete floors

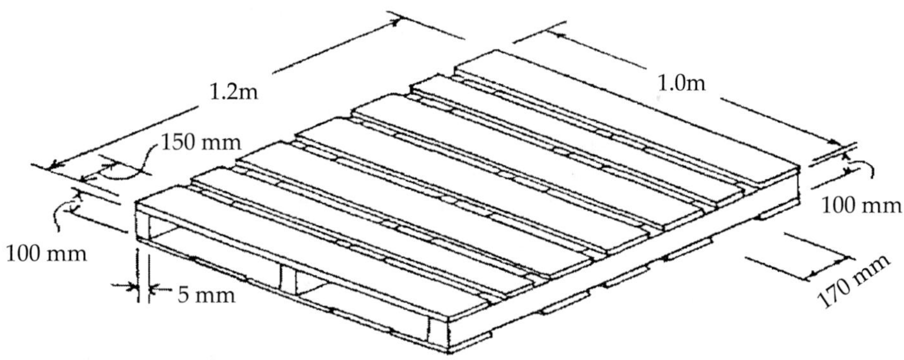

Figure 6.15: Wooden pallets of standard size can support several boxes or sacks of produce

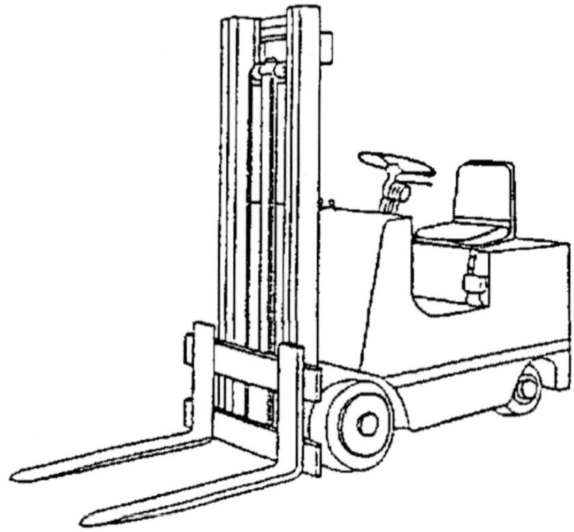

Figure 6.16: Mechanized forklift truck can carry palletized produce in packing house and load transport vehicles

- **Washing**: Produce can be washed using fresh running water in a galvanized tank. For floating produce, water from an inlet pipe with perforations on one side moves the items along the tank. A vertical baffle near the outlet end ensures thorough washing of all produce in the tank.
- **Drying**: After washing or fungicide treatment, produce must be dried before packing. In small packing houses, drying can be done on a rack or table made of wooden slats or plastic-covered wire mesh. For on-the-farm packing, drying tables can be constructed from bamboo or bush poles.

If fungicide is applied using a knapsack sprayer after washing, the drying rack serves as a convenient platform for application. The produce is then left to dry before being packed.

Figure 6.17: Tank for washing produce made of galvanized sheet steel

Water flows under pressure through a perforated pipe, guiding floating produce along the tank. A baffle positioned near the drain pipe aids in circulating water effectively through the produce, ensuring thorough washing.

Packing-House Management

Effective management of packing houses demands a high degree of efficiency in coordinating the technical, organizational, and commercial aspects of the operations. Any errors or delays in any part of the process will directly impact the returns for growers. Operations should be maintained year-round if it is financially viable.

Meeting market requirements. The management should be capable of guiding and directing both growers and packing-house staff to ensure the most efficient operations and the highest quality output, ultimately leading to the best possible returns.

Procurement and control. A thorough understanding of the size and timing of produce arrivals at the packing house is crucial for its smooth operation. The packing house may coordinate the pickup of harvested produce. Growers supplying produce to a central packing house must be informed about the quality control measures and standards in place. Additionally, the quality of packed produce must be monitored to minimize the potential for disputes during marketing.

Supplies of packing materials. Forecasts for the upcoming year's requirements should be prepared ahead of time. Early discussions with suppliers should be conducted to secure the best prices and delivery schedules. It is crucial to maintain accurate stock control to ensure that supplies are always available during packing operations.

Disposal of low-grade produce. There will always be some inferior produce when it is chosen and graded for the market. Even though they might have some value, the packing house should get the most out of how they are disposed of. The amount of produce that is a complete loss must also be known by management. It is necessary to keep track of how the low-quality and total-loss produce are disposed of.

Staffing. The packing house needs a sufficient number of employees to run effectively, but labor costs must be taken into consideration. This calls for effective labor deployment as well as sufficient supervision. A manager, clerks, mechanics, maintenance personnel, drivers, and some proficient packers are examples of permanent staff. Temporary workers will be needed during peak times.

Staff training. The manager must be technically qualified and capable of training his foremen because he is in charge of all packing-house operations. Additionally, he has to make sure that the packing employees receive in-service training.

Grower training. When multiple growers supply a packing house, management should make sure they are aware of how to meet the market's quality requirements. It is preferred to collaborate with post-harvest extension personnel. This could involve official training during off-season hours, but it will work best if farm visits are conducted during harvesting and packing-house operations.

Accounting and costing of operations. Agreements should be made with producers regarding payment for products, taking into account quality control requirements. The operating cost of a packaging plant should be calculated per kg of product processed to minimize costs and maximize producers' profits.

Documentation and accounting. The manager is in charge of making sure that correct accounts are prepared and that accurate records are kept. This is essential to the packing house's commercial success.

BENEFITS OF PACK HOUSES

The model of pack houses, as shown in Figure below, demonstrates how a pack house functions as a critical link between growers and the market. It serves as a central platform for aggregating products, cleaning, and processing them under the supervision of plant quarantine authorities. The process also includes examination/testing of export consignments and certification.

The primary goal of a pack house is to help exporters of horticultural produce meet international standards, particularly in terms of produce quality and quarantine safety.

A pack house is designed to accommodate all necessary operations, including material handling, holding, pre-inspection, sorting, grading, washing, standard treatments, packaging, stacking, pre-cooling, cold storage, and quarantine checks.

This setup is essential for handling and processing all types of horticultural produce, such as fresh fruits and vegetables, for export purposes.

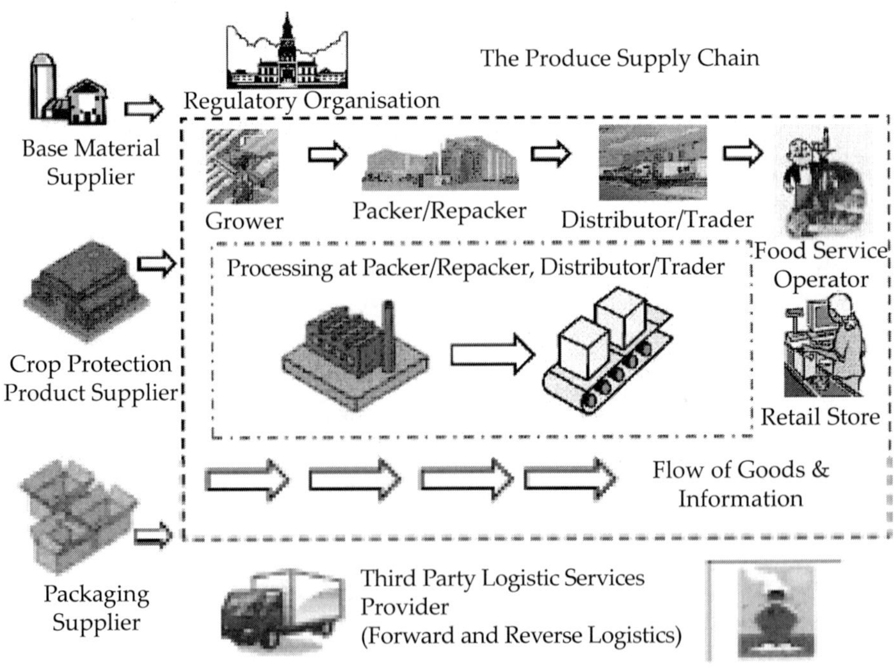

Figure 6.18: The produce supply chain and the pack house

A state-of-the-art pack house is dedicated to continuous innovation and process improvement to ensure high quality and compliance with market standards. Numerous private entities have emerged, offering auditable certification for world-class safety standards in fruits and vegetables. Some notable certifications include:

- **Global G.A.P**: This certification spans all production stages, from pre-harvest activities like soil management and plant protection product application to post-harvest handling, packaging, and storage. It is recognized in over 100 countries and is a minimum requirement for EU markets.
- **British Retail Consortium (BRC) Global Food Safety Standards**: This standard ensures the consistency of quality, food safety, and operational procedures throughout facilities, guaranteeing legal compliance and consumer protection.
- **TESCO Produce Pack House Standards (TPPS)**: This is a manufacturing standard exclusive to Tesco, ensuring quality and safety in their supply chain.
- **TESCO Nurture**: A quality standard exclusive to Tesco, implemented by farms and pack houses to maintain high quality.
- **Walmart Supply Chain Security Audit Standard**: This certification ensures facilities have the necessary systems to protect products from tampering during production, transportation, and shipping.
- **M&S Field to Fork**: An audit program exclusive to Marks & Spencer, covering all aspects of quality and food safety within their fresh and frozen produce supply chain.

A cutting-edge pack house can be certified for one or more of these safety standards, enabling it to enter various value chains and reduce costs. Such certification helps farmers meet industry standards more cost-effectively, promotes innovation, and minimizes the risk of product rejection by meeting quality requirements. Moreover, a well-certified pack house ensures compliance with customer and legal food safety regulations, offering traceability services and robust supply chain management. This helps minimize contamination risks during transportation, further reducing the likelihood of product rejection.

The impact of these dynamics within a pack house can significantly upgrade production processes (due to substantial returns), enhance distribution channels, improve employment quality, and increase human capital in rural areas. It generates demand for workforce development to meet standards, align skills with industry needs, and foster innovation in packing systems. This not only offers job diversification but also contributes to the growth of human capital in rural communities.

7

Preparation of Different Fruit-based Products

INTRODUCTION

Depending on the product being made, different methods are used to prepare fruit-based products, including smoothies, jams, sauces, dried fruits, fruit preserves, and fruit juices. Specialized equipment is usually needed for each process in order to attain the required consistency and quality. Here is a summary of how various fruit-based products are made and an introduction to the standard tools used in their production.

SQUASH

This kind of fruit beverage has 40–50% commercially available total soluble solids and at least 25% fruit juice or pulp. Approximately 1.0 per cent acid and 350 ppm sulfur dioxide or 600 ppm sodium benzoate are also present. To serve, it is diluted. Commercial squash is made with mango, orange, and pineapple. Another way to make it is to use potassium metabisulphite (KMS) as a preservative for lemon, bael, papaya, *etc.*, or sodium benzoate as a preservative for jamun, passion fruit, peach, plum, raspberry, strawberry, grapefruit, *etc.*

In India, people want cold beverages almost all year round. Acid squashes hold a significant position among these fruit juices. Due to their abundance of vital vitamins, minerals, and other nutrients, these are highly well-liked. Squash is a fruit beverage that has at least 25% fruit juice or pulp and at least 40% total soluble solids (sugar). Additionally, it includes 1-2 percent edible acid. Since squash has a relatively low sugar content, it should be preserved by adding an approved chemical preservative, such as sodium or potassium metabisulphite or sodium benzoate, along with flavour and colour. Fruits like mango, orange, pineapple, litchi, lemon, and so on can be used to make squash.

Flowchart For Processing of Squash

Fruits

↓

Washing

↓

Trimming

↓

Cutting or Grating

↓

Juice Extraction

↓

Straining

↓

Juice Measuring

↓

Preparation of Syrup
(Sugar + Water + Acid, Heating
Just to Dissolve)

↓

Straining

↓

Mixing with Juice

↓

Addition of Preservative
(0.6g KMS or 1.0g Sodium
Benzoate/Litre Squash)

↓

Bottling

↓

Capping

↓

Storage

Figure 7.1: Flow Chart for Processing of Squash.

This particular kind of fruit drink has at least 10% fruit juice and 10% total soluble solids in addition to roughly 0.3% acid. It is referred to as ready-to-serve (RTS) because it is not diluted before serving.

Flow-Sheet for Processing of RTS Beverages

It is a clear, sparkling, sweetened fruit juice that has been entirely stripped of pulp and other insoluble materials. At least twenty-five per cent juice and thirty per cent TSS are present. Additionally, it has 350 parts per million of sulfur dioxide and 1.5% acid. This works well for mixing with wines. You can make cordial with lemon and lime.

Fruits
(Pulp/Juice)
↓
Mixing with Strained Syrup Solution
(Sugar + Water + Acid, Heated Just to Dissolve) According to Recipe
↓
Homegenization
↓
Bottling
↓
Crown Corking
↓
Pasteurization
(At About 90°c) for 25 Minutes
↓
Cooling
↓
Storage

Figure 7.2: Flow Sheet for Processing of RTS Beverages.

NECTAR

At least 20% fruit juice or pulp, 15% total soluble solids, and roughly 0.3% acid are all present in this kind of fruit beverage. It is served without diluting it.

Table 7.1: Component of NECTAR.

<table>
<tr><th>S. No.</th><th>Fruit</th><th>Juice / Pulp (%)</th><th>Quantity of water required (litre)</th></tr>
<tr><td>1.</td><td>Mango</td><td>20</td><td rowspan="6">Quantity of finished product (litre) – Quantity of (juice (litre) + sugar (kg) + acid (kg) used</td></tr>
<tr><td>2.</td><td>Papaya</td><td>20</td></tr>
<tr><td>3.</td><td>Guava</td><td>20</td></tr>
<tr><td>4.</td><td>Bael</td><td>20</td></tr>
<tr><td>5.</td><td>Jamun</td><td>20</td></tr>
<tr><td>6.</td><td>Aonla (blend)</td><td>Aonla pulp 20
Lime juice 2
Ginger juice 1</td></tr>
</table>

Before adding the necessary amounts of sugar and citric acid dissolved in water to adjust the total soluble solids (TSS) and acidity, the total soluble solids and total acid content of the pulp or juice are measured.

FERMENTED BEVERAGES

Certain fruit juices, such as wine, champaigne, port, sherry, tokay, muscat, perry, orange wine, berry wine, nira, and cider, have undergone alcoholic fermentation by yeasts.

Ripe Grapes
↓
Removal of Stems
↓
Crushing (Basket Press)
↓
Filling Jar Up to Three - Fourths
↓
Addition of Sugar (20-24% TSS)
↓
Adjustment of pH (0.6 to 0.8% Acid)
↓
Addition of Preservative (KMS 1.5g/10kg Grapes)
↓
Keeping for an Hour
↓
Addition of Wine Yeast (S.E. 20ml/5kg Grapes)
↓
Fermentation (for 2 Days)
↓
Filtration
↓
Fermentation (for 10 Days)
↓
Racking (Syphoning off Clear Liquid)
↓
Fining and Filtration (Bentonite)
↓
Aging (Maturation) (6-8 Months)
↓
Pasteurization at 82°c (for 2 min.)
↓
Bottling
↓
Crown Corking
↓
Pasteurization at 82°c (for 20 min.)
↓
Cooling
↓
Storage

Figure 7.3: Flow Chart for Processing of Wine.

PROCESSING OF PICKLES

Pickling is the process of preserving food using common salt, and it is one of the oldest methods of vegetable preservation. Pickles not only enhance the flavor of meals but also serve as delicious appetizers. The most commonly enjoyed pickles include mango, followed by turnip, cauliflower, onion, and lime. A brine solution with 10 to 12 per cent salt content effectively prevents the growth of most spoilage organisms. Lactic acid bacteria, which are typically abundant on the surface of fresh fruits and vegetables, ferment the produce, leading to the pickling process. Class I preservatives play a key role in regulating fermentation while also improving the flavor and texture of the vegetable tissues.

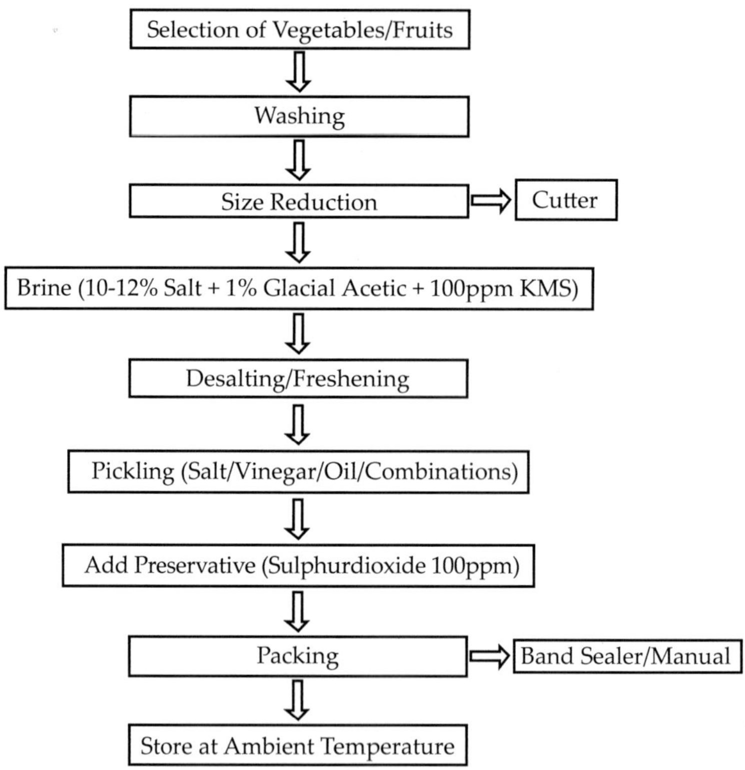

Figure 7.4: Flow Chart of Pickling Process from Fruits and Vegetables.

PROCESSING OF CHUTNEYS

High-quality chutney should be flavorful and appetizing. Mango chutney is a key food product that India exports to various countries, and apple and apricot chutneys are also quite popular in the nation. The preparation method for chutney closely resembles that of jam, with the addition of spices, vinegar, and salt. Fruits and vegetables are peeled, sliced, grated, or cut into small pieces, and then cooked in water until they become tender. The quality of chutney largely depends on the cooking process, which should be done slowly at a temperature just below boiling point. To ensure proper thickening, cooking is performed without a lid, although this may cause some loss of volatile oils from the spices. Chopped onions and garlic are added at the beginning to soften their sharp flavors, and spices are coarsely ground before being added. Instead of whole spices, a vinegar extract may also be used. Spices and vinegar are added just before the final cooking stage to prevent the loss of essential oils and vinegar, which can evaporate with prolonged boiling.

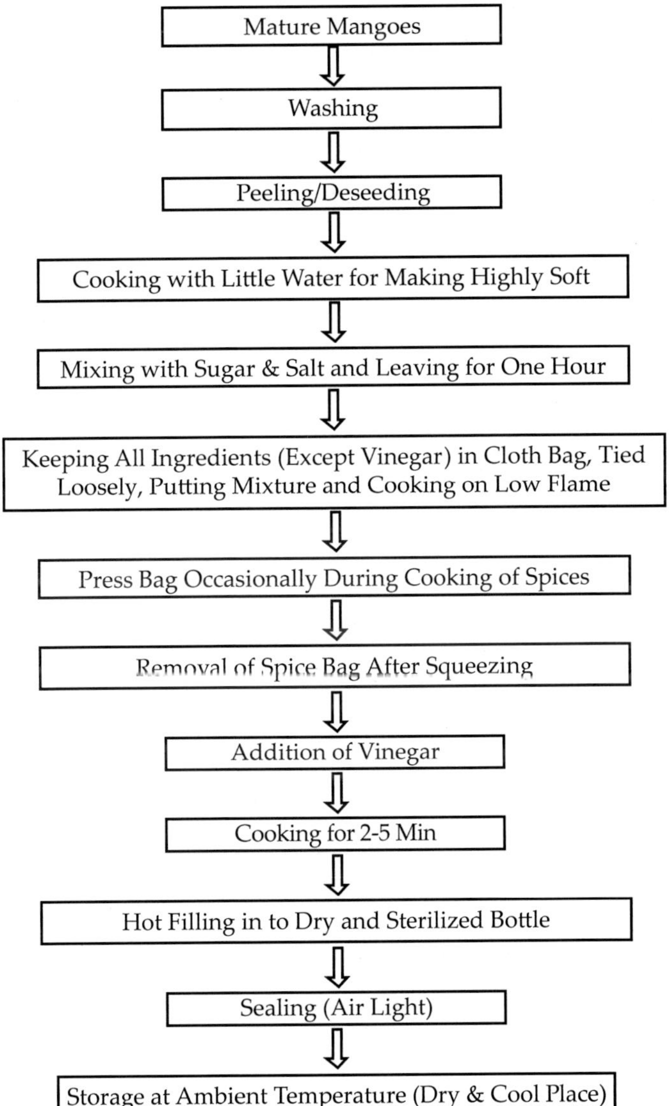

Figure 7.5: Processing Sheet of Sweet Mango Chutney.

PROCESSING OF JAM

Jam is a product made by cooking fruit pulp with sugar and acid until it reaches the desired consistency. Typically, jam contains 0.5-0.6 per cent acidity and 68 per cent total solids. Various fruits, such as apple, pear, tomato, sapota, apricot, loquat, peach, papaya, karonda, carrot, plum, strawberry, raspberry, mango, tomato, grape, and muskmelon, are used to make jam, either individually or as a blend of different fruits.

- Stainless steel machines and equipment are ideal for processing and preserving fruits and vegetables.
- Steam jacketed kettles are used for cooking and concentrating the fruit mixture.
- Fruit pulpers equipped with brushes and stainless steel sieves of various sizes are used to extract pulp completely from the fruits.

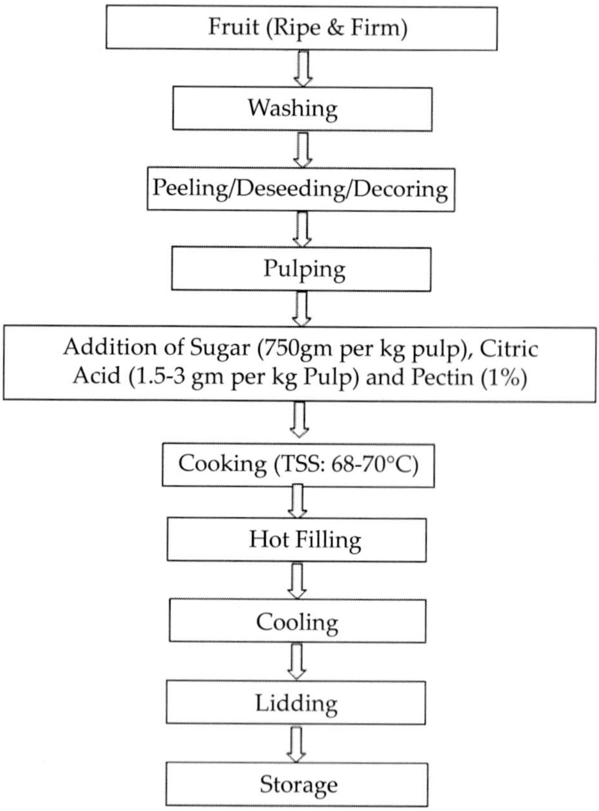

Figure 7.6: Process Flow Chart for Processing Jam.

PROCESSING OF JELLY

Jelly is a semi-solid product created by boiling clear, strained fruit juice with sugar and acid until it thickens. The final product has a total soluble solids content of no less than 65% and an acidity level ranging from 0.5 to 0.7 per cent.

Qualities of Jelly

- Clear
- Transparent

- Sparkling
- Attractivecolour
- Keep its shape in which it is cut not breaking.

Fruit (Firm & Mature)
⇓
Washing
⇓
Cutting
⇓
Boiling (Fruit: Water - 1:1.5 to 2.5
⇓
Addition of Citric Acid (2g/kg Fruit
⇓
Cooking
⇓
Judging the End Point by Temperature (105°C) & TSS 98°B
⇓
Removal of Bucm Foam
⇓
Add Additives (Colour and Flavour)
⇓
Hot Filling and Cooling
⇓
Lidding
⇓
Storage

Figure 7.7: Process Flow Chart for Processing Jelly.

PROCESSING OF MARMALADE

Fruit peels are suspended in a fruit jelly called marmalade. Citrus fruits are typically used to make marmalades. The marmalade has a slightly higher protein content. The FPO requirements for the marmalade region are the same as those for the jelly.

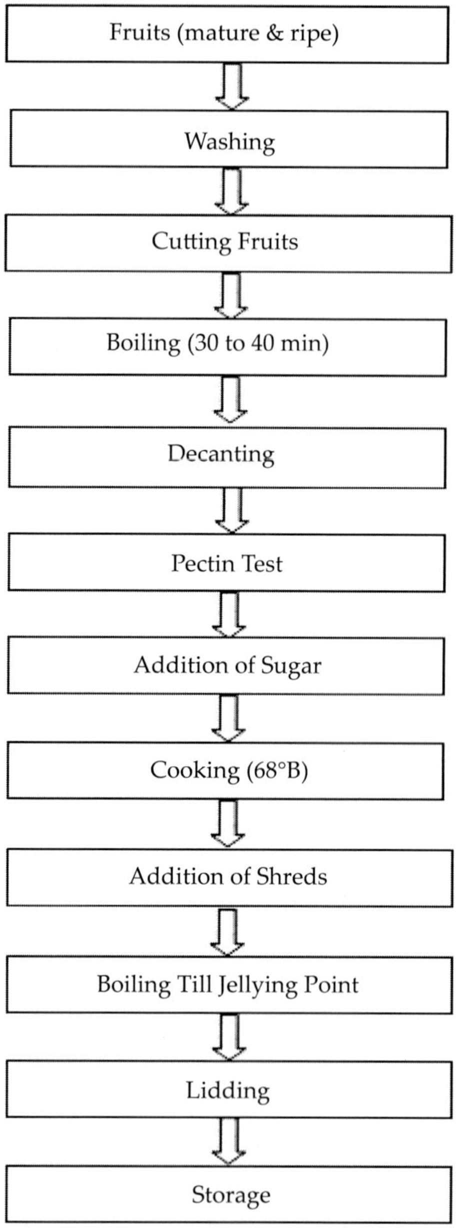

Figure 7.8: Process Flow Chart of Marmalade

PROCESSING OF MURABBA AND CANDY

The term "preserve" or "murabba" refers to a mature fruit or vegetable or its parts that have been impregnated with a thick sugar syrup until they become tends and are transported.

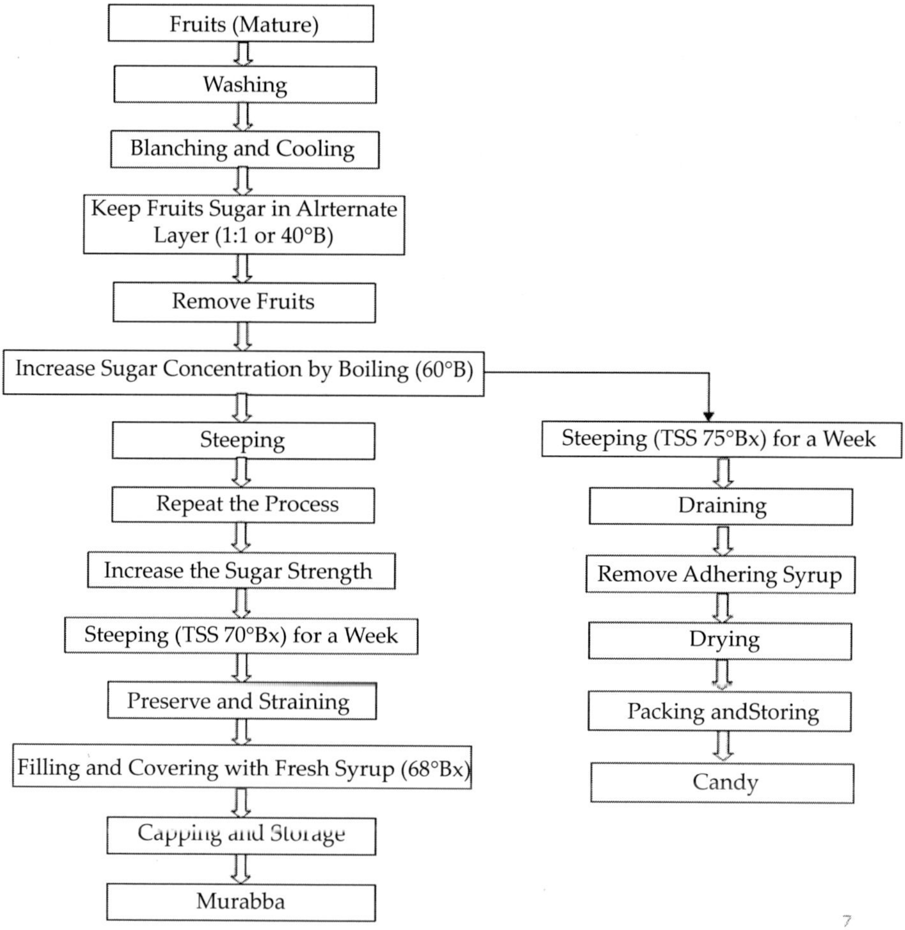

Figure 7.9: Process Flow Chart of Hurabba and Candy.

SAUCES AND KETCHUPS

Sauces and ketchup are essentially similar, but sauces are generally thinner and contain a higher per centage of total solids (at least 30%) compared to ketchups (at least 28%). Various fruits and vegetables such as tomato, apple, papaya, walnut, soybean, and mushroom are used to make sauces.

Sauces can be classified into two types: (i) Thin sauces, which are low in viscosity and mainly consist of vinegar extracts flavored with herbs and spices, and (ii) Thick sauces, which have a high viscosity.

The process of making sauces or ketchups is similar to that of chutney, with the key difference being that the pulp or juice of the fruit or vegetable is sieved after cooking to remove skins, seeds, and stalks, ensuring a smooth final product. Since fine pulp or juice is used, the cooking process for sauces and ketchups tends to take longer.

TOMATO PUREE AND PASTE

Medium tomato puree is made from tomato pulp, which is free of skins and seeds, and may or may not have added salt. It contains at least 9.0% salt-free tomato solids. This puree can be further concentrated to make heavy tomato puree, which contains no less than 12% solids. When concentrated even further to contain at least 25% tomato solids, it is referred to as tomato paste. If the concentration reaches 33% or more of solids, it is called concentrated tomato paste. Tomato pulp is produced from ripe tomatoes in a manner similar to tomato juice.

The pulp is cooked for concentration, either in an open cooker or a vacuum pan. In the open cooker, most vitamins are destroyed, and the product may turn brown. However, using a vacuum pan—although more expensive—helps retain nutrients and reduces browning significantly. In vacuum pans, the juice is boiled at around 71°C. Typically, tomato juice can be concentrated to 14-15% solids in an open cooker, but higher concentrations require a vacuum pan. Additionally, sterilization of the product is possible in a vacuum pan.

During the cooking process in an open cooker, a small amount of butter or edible oil is added to prevent foaming, burning, and sticking. If the solid content exceeds the required amount, additional juice is added to adjust the concentration. If the solids are too low, cooking continues until the desired consistency is reached. The final concentration of puree and paste is measured using a hand refractometer or by measuring the volume.

TOMATO SAUCE/KETCHUP

It has at least 12% tomato solids and 25% total solids, and is made from strained tomato juice or pulp, spices, salt, sugar, and vinegar, with or without onion and garlic.

Process of Canning

Selection of Fruits and Vegetables

- Vegetables and fruits must be completely fresh.
- Fruits ought to be uniformly mature and ripe but firm. Overripe fruits should be thrown out since they contain microorganisms and produce subpar goods. Since unripe fruits typically shrivel and toughen when canned, they should be discarded.
- Every vegetable—aside from tomatoes—should be soft.
- Tomatoes ought to be deep red, firm, and fully ripe.
- Dirt should not be present on fruits or vegetables.
- They ought to be devoid of imperfections, insect damage, or mechanical harm.

Grading

To achieve consistent quality, the chosen fruits and vegetables are graded based on size and color. This can be done manually or with the aid of devices like roller and screw graders. While peaches, pears, apricots, mangoes, pineapples, and other fruits are typically graded after being cut into pieces or slices, berries, plums, and cherries are graded whole.

Washing

Fruits and vegetables should have any dust and residue from pesticide sprays removed. There are 1012 microorganism spores per gram of soil. Consequently, it is crucial to wash with water to get rid of microorganisms. There are various methods for washing fruits and vegetables. Soaking in water with 25 to 50 parts per million chlorine (as detergent) is how root crops that become loose in soil are cleaned. Additional washing techniques include steaming, spraying, and so forth.

Peeling

Peeling is done to get rid of the outer layer. Peeling can be accomplished in a number of ways. (As lye peeling, flame peeling, steam peeling, mechanical peeling, and hand peeling).

Cutting

The pieces are cut to the size needed for canning. The core, stone, and seed are taken out. Some fruits, like plums, are canned whole because the seeds are difficult to remove.

Blanching

Blanching, also known as scalding, parboiling, or precooking, is a process where fruits and vegetables are briefly exposed to hot water or steam to prepare them for further processing. While fruits typically aren't blanched to preserve their active oxidizing enzymes, some fruits may be plunged into water heated between 180°F and 200°F for a short duration, typically ranging from half a minute to five minutes, depending on the variety. After this brief heat treatment, they are quickly cooled by immersion in cold water. This process helps to soften the texture of the fruit, allowing for a higher quantity to be packed into containers without causing damage to the individual pieces.

Blanching is commonly done for vegetables by immersing them in boiling water or steam for 2 to 5 minutes, followed by a cooling stage. The duration and intensity of blanching depend on the type of vegetable. This short heat treatment serves multiple purposes:

- It inactivates enzymes in plants that contribute to undesirable characteristics such as toughness, discoloration (due to polyphenol oxidase), off-flavors (due to peroxidase), softness, and loss of nutrients.
- It reduces the volume of leafy vegetables like spinach by causing shrinkage or wilting, making them easier to pack.
- It eliminates tissue gases that lead to the production of sulphides.
- It kills up to 99% of microorganisms, enhancing food safety.
- It improves the green color of vegetables like peas, broccoli, and spinach.
- It removes saponin from peas.
- It neutralizes acids and reduces the astringent taste of the peel, thus improving the flavor.

- It helps remove the skin from vegetables like beetroots and tomatoes, making peeling easier.

Cooling

For easier handling and preservation, the vegetables are dipped in cold water after blanching.

Filling

Cans are sterilized and cleaned with hot water before being filled, but in developing nations, they are also exposed to a steam jet to get rid of dust and other foreign objects. Large, automatic can-filling machines are used in developed nations, but in India, premium fruit grades are typically filled by hand to avoid bruising. The standard procedure is to fill by hand. Syruping or brining is the process of covering with syrup or brine after filling.

Exhausting

Exhausting is the process of removing air from cans, and it is a crucial step after filling and sealing the cans. This process offers several significant advantages, including:

- Prevention of corrosion on the tinplate and the formation of pinholes during storage.
- Minimization of discoloration by inhibiting oxidation.
- Enhanced retention of vitamins, especially vitamin C.
- Avoidance of can bulging when stored in hot climates or at high altitudes.
- Reduction of chemical reactions between the container and its contents.
- Prevention of excessive pressure buildup and strain during sterilization.

Exhausting can be done through heating or mechanically, with the heat treatment method being the most commonly used. In this method, cans are passed through a tank of hot water at temperatures between 82°C and 87°C or moved along a belt in a covered steam box. In the water exhaust box, the cans are arranged so that the water level is 4-5 cm below the tops of the cans. The box is heated until the water temperature reaches between 82°C and 100°C, ensuring that the center of the can reaches about 79°C. The duration of exhausting varies between 6 to 10 minutes depending on the product type. For glass jars or bottles, vacuum sealing machines are typically used, where the containers are placed in a closed chamber and a high vacuum is applied.

It is preferable to exhaust the cans at lower temperatures for longer periods to ensure uniform heating of the contents without turning them into pulp. High-temperature exhausting should be avoided, as the higher the temperature, the more water vapor is produced, leading to a greater vacuum inside the can.

Sealing

Using a can sealer, the cans are sealed airtight as soon as they are empty. To ensure an airtight seal, a rubber ring should be positioned between the glass jar's mouth and the lid. The temperature shouldn't drop below 74°C while sealing.

Processing

The process of heating foods for preservation is referred to as processing. In canning, however, processing specifically refers to heating or cooling canned foods to eliminate bacteria. Many bacterial spores can be destroyed by either high or very low temperatures. However, such extreme treatments can negatively impact the food's quality. It is essential to adjust the processing time and temperature to effectively kill all bacteria without over-cooking the product, as this can spoil both the flavor and appearance. Most fruits and vegetables can be processed at a temperature of 100°C, which is equivalent to boiling water.

Acid content slows down bacterial growth, and bacteria do not thrive in heavy sugar syrup, which is typically used for canning fruits. Non-acid vegetables, such as those that are harder in texture or close to the soil, require processing at higher temperatures between 115°C to 121°C. Some acidic vegetables like tomatoes and rhubarb are an exception and are processed at lower temperatures.

The acidity of fruits and vegetables, measured in pH, significantly impacts the ease of sterilization. The lower the pH, the easier it is to process and sterilize the product. For example, bacterial spores are more easily destroyed at a pH of 3.0 (fruits) than at pH 5.0 to 6.0 (vegetables, except for tomato and rhubarb). Bacterial spores do not germinate at pH values below 4.5. Therefore, products with a pH below 4.5 can be processed in boiling water, while products with a pH above 4.5 need higher temperatures of 115°C to 121°C and pressure of 0.70 to 1.05 kg/cm2 (10 to 15 lb/sq inch).

The time and temperature for processing depend on both the size of the can and the type of food. Larger cans require longer processing times. The canning of fruits and vegetables is typically done in open cookers or continuous cookers, while non-acid vegetables are processed in steam pressure under closed retorts, also known as automatic pressure cookers. In India, small vertical stationary retorts are commonly used for processing canned vegetables. The sealed cans are placed in cookers with water levels 2.5 to 5.0 cm above the can tops, the cover is sealed, and the cooker is heated to the desired temperature. The sterilization (processing) period begins once the water starts boiling. After the required time, the cooker is removed from heat, the pressure is released, and the cans are removed once the pressure reaches zero.

Cooling

After processing, it is crucial to rapidly cool the cans to around 39°C to halt the cooking process and prevent stack-burning. There are several methods used for cooling:

- Immersing the hot cans in tanks filled with cold water;
- Introducing cold water into the pressure cooker, especially for vegetables;
- Spraying the cans with jets of cold water; and
- Exposing the cans to air.

Typically, the first method, which involves dipping the cans in cold water, is the preferred technique. If the cans are not cooled promptly after processing, various changes in the product may occur. For instance, peaches and pears may darken, tomatoes can become brownish and acquire a bitter taste, peas may turn pulpy and develop a cooked flavor, and many vegetables may develop a flat sour taste, which results from fermentation.

Storage

Once labeled, the cans should be packed into sturdy wooden cases or corrugated cardboard cartons and kept in a cool, dry location. It's important that the outer surface of the cans is dry, as even small amounts of moisture can sometimes lead to rusting. Cans should be stored away from high temperatures, as heat accelerates the degradation of the product and may cause hydrogen swell. The shelf life of canned goods varies depending on the raw materials used. For example, canned peaches, grapefruit, pineapple, beans, spinach, and peas can be stored for up to two years, while products like pears, apricots, carrots, beets, and tomatoes have a shorter storage life.

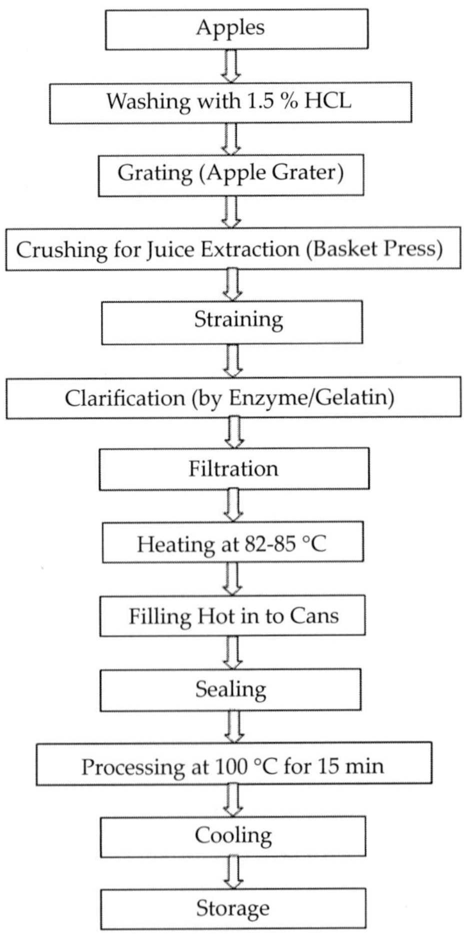

Fugure 7.10: Flow Sheet for Processing of Apple Juice.

Major Challenges, Constraints and Concerns

Despite significant achievements and policy initiatives, the industry is still facing several concerning trends, including:

- In India, food fortification contributes only 7% to the total value added, while countries like China (23%), the Philippines (45%), and the UK (188%) far surpass this figure. Moreover, the small-scale and unorganized sectors make up 75% of the total industry.
- A major issue within the industry is the consistent availability of suitable raw materials for processing. Additionally, productivity in India is comparatively low, and the cost of raw materials for processing is 3 to 4 times higher than the global market prices.
- External liberalization presents threats in the form of heightened competition due to the new world trade order. The WTO agreements have relaxed quantitative restrictions and non-tariff/sanitary barriers for importing countries, exposing Indian farmers to global market forces. This new trade regime introduces challenges related to trade-related Intellectual Property Rights, including patent laws, copyrights, and trade links.
- The strengths of high raw material production and a large domestic market need to be supported by operating processing units at optimal capacity, following economies of scale. This will help achieve a competitive advantage over imported products.
- As international trade competition increases, the availability of high-quality imported products in developing countries will grow. To compete effectively, these countries need improved post-harvest management, distribution, and processing chains, along with enhanced human resource capabilities in technology, management, and marketing.
- Advances in biotechnology have led to the production of Genetically Modified (GM) foods, which are already being introduced in certain countries. The impact of GM foods, both positive and negative, on human health must be critically examined.
- India has some of the highest taxes on processed food in the world. Unlike other countries, India imposes excise duty on processed foods, distinguishing between branded and unbranded sectors for taxation. With excise duty (CENVAT) at 16%, along with sales tax, octroi, entry tax, and customs duty on materials levied by various government bodies, the total tax burden ranges from 21% to 30% on food items.
- Policies like private sector participation through contract farming and land leasing arrangements can help ensure a steady supply of quality raw materials to the fruit and vegetable processing industry.
- It is crucial to educate consumers about processed fruit and vegetable products and their nutritional benefits.
- Backward and forward integration from farms to processors and consumers is essential, not only for improving supply chains but also for creating more employment opportunities and reducing poverty.

- The industry should have greater control over taxation with other nations, especially during the export and import of processed fruit and vegetable products.
- Commercial R&D activities in the food industry have been limited to only a few areas, and there has been little transition from laboratory findings to widespread field adoption.
- Indian brands are still struggling to establish a strong presence in international markets due to poor global marketing efforts.
- Many financial institutions lack the capacity to appraise high-tech export-oriented projects, especially those dealing with the export of perishables. There are also no suitable insurance schemes for such projects, which leads to high credit risks for banks. With new technologies, risk perception is higher than for existing projects.

The sector faces poor marketing, transport, and communication infrastructure, with limited market access for fruits and vegetables. Storage and cold chain facilities in rural areas are insufficient, and erratic power supply, poor roads, inadequate access to quality water, and a lack of education, health facilities, and rural industrialization compound these challenges.

8

Preparation of Different Vegetable-based Products

INTRODUCTION

The process of preparing vegetable-based products involves several essential steps, such as cleaning, chopping, cooking, and adding seasoning. Initially, vegetables are thoroughly washed to eliminate dirt and chemicals. Depending on the specific product, vegetables are then either peeled or chopped. Some vegetables undergo blanching to maintain their color and texture before they are frozen or subjected to additional processing. For products like vegetable soups, stews, or purees, the vegetables are simmered in water or broth to enhance their flavors.

The preparation process is supported by a range of equipment, including blenders for pureeing, steamers for gentle cooking, and slicers to ensure uniform cuts. Pressure cookers are used to speed up cooking times for items like stews, while dehydrators are employed to produce vegetable chips or dried snacks. Grinders and mills are used to create pastes or powders from vegetables. It is crucial that all equipment is handled carefully to ensure it operates effectively and safely, which is necessary for achieving the highest product quality. Regular maintenance of the equipment is vital for achieving consistent and reliable results.

VALUE ADDITION CONCEPT

Value addition is a strategic approach in post-harvest management aimed at enhancing the quality, market value, and economic potential of agricultural products such as fruits and vegetables. This process focuses on transforming raw produce into value-added products that are more desirable and useful for consumers and markets. It plays a critical role in modern agriculture, food processing, and marketing. Let's take a closer look at the concept of value addition in post-harvest management:

- **Product Diversification**: Value addition involves creating a variety of products from raw fruits and vegetables. For example, fresh fruits can be turned into juices, jams, or dried snacks, while vegetables can be processed into pickles, canned goods, or frozen products. These value-added items provide consumers with more options, boosting demand and marketability for agricultural produce.

- **Quality Enhancement**: One key focus of value addition is improving the quality of agricultural products. Through proper post-harvest handling, processing, and packaging, the nutritional content, appearance, taste, and shelf life of fruits and vegetables can be enhanced. Improving quality enhances consumer satisfaction and builds brand loyalty.
- **Market Value and Price Increase**: Value-added products generally fetch higher prices compared to raw produce. By processing and packaging fruits and vegetables into ready-to-use forms, their perceived value increases. As a result, farmers and producers enjoy better returns on their investments, improving their economic viability.
- **Waste Reduction and Profit Generation**: Value addition helps reduce post-harvest losses by making use of surplus or less visually appealing produce that would otherwise be discarded. By converting such produce into processed goods or by-products, farmers can generate extra income and minimize overall waste.
- **Extended Shelf Life**: Value-added products often have a much longer shelf life compared to raw fruits and vegetables. Techniques such as drying, freezing, canning, or pickling significantly reduce spoilage, allowing products to remain available for a longer time, even in the off-season.
- **New Market Opportunities**: Value addition creates opportunities for accessing new markets and consumer segments. Processed fruits and vegetables cater to different tastes, preferences, and dietary needs, attracting a broader audience and expanding market reach.
- **Promotion of Food Security**: Value addition helps preserve the nutritional content of fruits and vegetables. By processing and storing them in different forms, vital nutrients are retained and available throughout the year, contributing to food security, particularly during periods of scarcity or adverse weather.
- **Employment Generation**: Value-addition processes require skilled labor for tasks such as processing, packaging, marketing, and distribution. This creates job opportunities, particularly in rural areas, fostering economic growth and improving livelihoods.

PRINCIPLES OF PRESERVATION

- **Temperature Control**: Preservation techniques involve maintaining lower temperatures to slow down enzymatic and microbial activity. Reducing the temperature helps inhibit the growth of spoilage microorganisms and prolongs the freshness of fruits and vegetables.
- **Removal of Air and Moisture**: Both air and moisture contribute to faster deterioration and spoilage. Preservation methods like vacuum sealing or drying are used to eliminate air and reduce moisture levels, helping to extend shelf life.

- **pH Regulation**: Altering the pH level of the product can prevent microbial growth. Acidic environments are hostile to many spoilage-causing bacteria and fungi, thus improving the shelf life of preserved fruits and vegetables.
- **Use of Preservatives**: Natural or synthetic preservatives are employed to prevent spoilage and microbial activity. These substances work by inhibiting the function of microorganisms and enzymes that cause deterioration.
- **Packaging**: Effective packaging plays a vital role in preserving fruits and vegetables. Packaging materials should be resistant to air and moisture to help maintain the product's quality, safety, and freshness.

METHODS OF PRESERVATION

- **Refrigeration**: A common short-term preservation method, refrigeration helps maintain freshness by slowing down respiration and minimizing spoilage. However, it is not suitable for all produce, as certain fruits and vegetables may be sensitive to low temperatures.
- **Freezing**: Freezing is an efficient long-term preservation technique that rapidly lowers the temperature of fruits and vegetables to freezing levels. This process halts enzymatic and microbial activity, preserving the produce's quality and nutrients.
- **Drying**: Drying, or dehydration, removes moisture from fruits and vegetables, preventing microbial growth by reducing available water. This method extends shelf life, and dried products are compact and durable for long-term storage.
- **Canning**: Canning involves sealing fruits and vegetables in airtight containers and heating them to eliminate microorganisms. This heat treatment ensures safety and allows produce to be stored for an extended period.
- **Pickling**: Pickling preserves fruits and vegetables by immersing them in acidic solutions such as vinegar or brine. The acidic environment helps preserve the produce while enhancing its flavor.
- **Jam and Jelly Making**: The process of making jams and jellies involves cooking fruits with sugar and pectin. The high sugar content inhibits microbial growth, thereby prolonging the shelf life of the final product.
- **Fermentation**: A traditional preservation technique, fermentation involves microorganisms breaking down sugars in produce. The by-products, such as alcohol and acids, help prevent spoilage, making fermented items more shelf-stable.
- **High-Pressure Processing (HPP)**: This technique exposes packaged fruits and vegetables to high hydrostatic pressure, inactivating harmful microorganisms while preserving the produce's nutritional content and sensory characteristics.

The choice of preservation method depends on factors such as the type of produce, the desired shelf life, available resources, and the intended use of the preserved products. Proper preservation practices help reduce post-harvest losses, ensure year-round food availability, and add value to agricultural products.

VARIOUS TYPES OF TOMATO PRODUCTS

Tomato products are various food items created by processing and preserving tomatoes. Tomatoes are cherished for their rich flavor, nutritional benefits, and versatility in cooking. By transforming tomatoes into different products, their shelf life is extended, taste is enhanced, and they become available throughout the year.

- **Tomato Paste**: Tomato paste is a concentrated, thickened product made by cooking tomatoes to remove excess water. It has a deep red hue and a strong tomato flavor, commonly used as a base for sauces, soups, and stews, adding richness to dishes.
- **Tomato Sauce**: Tomato sauce is a smooth and pourable product made by blending or straining cooked tomatoes. It is often seasoned with herbs, spices, and sometimes other vegetables. This sauce is commonly used for pasta, pizzas, and many savory dishes.
- **Tomato Ketchup**: Tomato ketchup is a sweet, tangy condiment made from tomatoes, sugar, vinegar, and a mix of spices. It is cooked and blended to achieve the desired consistency and is a popular topping for burgers, hot dogs, and fries.
- **Crushed Tomatoes**: Crushed tomatoes are roughly chopped tomatoes preserved in their own juice. Offering a chunkier texture, they are typically used as a base for pasta sauces, chili, and other hearty dishes.
- **Tomato Puree**: Tomato puree is a smooth, thick liquid made by blending and straining tomatoes. Its velvety texture makes it perfect for use in soups, curries, gravies, and other sauces.
- **Diced Tomatoes**: Diced tomatoes are cut into small pieces and preserved in their juice. These are often used in recipes where texture is important, such as in salsas, vegetable blends, or as an ingredient in stews and soups.

These tomato products offer a wide range of uses, making tomatoes an indispensable ingredient in many culinary creations.

STANDARDS FOR TOMATO PRODUCTS

- **Quality Parameters**: Tomato products must adhere to specific quality standards, such as appropriate color, flavor, and texture. The tomatoes used should be ripe, free from defects, and not overly ripe.
- **Processing and Packaging**: The processing and packaging of tomato products should follow hygienic and standardized practices to ensure safety and avoid contamination.
- **Additives and Preservatives**: Any additives and preservatives used in tomato products must comply with relevant regulations, and their presence must be clearly stated on the product label.

- **Nutritional Information**: The nutritional content of tomato products, including calories, fats, carbohydrates, vitamins, and minerals, should be clearly displayed on the packaging.
- **Labeling and Storage**: Proper labeling is crucial, including an ingredient list, product name, manufacturing date, and storage instructions. Consumers should follow storage recommendations to preserve the quality of the product.
- **Packaging Material**: Tomato products should be packaged in appropriate containers that protect them from exposure to light, moisture, and air. This prevents spoilage and helps maintain the product's freshness.

9

Manufacturing of Snack Foods

INTRODUCTION

Snacks manufacturing involves transforming various ingredients into chips or other types of snacks. These snacks are often enhanced with added flavors, boosting their taste and appealing to buyers seeking a quick and satisfying bite. Ready-to-eat snacks come in a wide array of flavors and varieties, with snack manufacturers in India constantly introducing new options.

As per the India Snacks Market Forecast, based on surveys of snack companies and consumer preferences, the Indian snack market is projected to surpass Rs 1 billion by 2024, creating more opportunities for newcomers in the industry. The food sector has become a highly profitable industry, fostering the growth of innovative food processing units. Snack manufacturing companies like Kiwi Foods are leading the way by offering new, exciting products that are quickly gaining popularity.

Food is essential for energy, but sometimes, heavy meals aren't the best option, and snacks serve as a perfect alternative. Whether it's during tea time or a quick bite during a hectic workday, snacks are a versatile food choice for any occasion. The market offers a diverse range of options, from classic salted chips to unique varieties like pop pasta and masala corn. Snack manufacturers in India cater to the evolving tastes and preferences of consumers, providing a wide range of delicious snack choices.

PROCESSING SNACK FOODS

Snack foods can also be grouped according to the food processing method used to produce them, even though people typically divide them into two categories: sweet and salty. Simple extrusion is used to create the first-generation snacks; no additional processing is required. This category includes snacks like popcorn, dried fruit, potato chips, and nuts.

Snacks are mostly second-generation products, though. This indicates that they are high-protein, high-fiber snack foods made from extruded ingredients, such as corn chips, balls, curls, and puffed corn products. Breakfast cereal and other fried and flavored snacks made from extruded pellets are referred to as third-generation snacks. Snack pellets are non-expanded and composed of vegetable powder, potatoes, and cereals. These semi-finished goods are further processed by manufacturers to produce snacks that are ready to eat.

Figure 9.1: There are a Few Categories of Snacks Foods.

SNACK FOOD PROCESSING TECHNOLOGIES

The product must be designed and tested before any production technologies are used. This requires a great deal of preparation and thought. Production comes after the product's viability has been established. Consistency is crucial, and the precise mixture of ingredients must be kept constant from the start. Let's now discuss the key technologies used in the processing of snack foods.

Extrusion Process

Extrusion is a production process carried out in an extrusion cooker, which functions as a high-temperature, short-time, plug-flow bioreactor that integrates several operations into one system. The extrusion process consists of several key steps:

- Continuous mixing of raw ingredients (such as various grains with water),
- Shearing or kneading,
- Heating and cooking, utilizing the heat generated in the extruder,
- Puffing, which is the final stage involving the rapid expansion of plasticized and gelatinized starch from a pressure chamber.

Among all snack categories, extruded snacks show the most significant growth potential. The versatility of the extrusion process allows for creative snack designs that captivate consumers. Notable examples of extruded snacks include three-dimensional shapes such as alphabets, cartoon characters, or animal forms.

Producing a successful extruded snack involves a delicate balance of the manufacturer's production capabilities, quality control, cost management, and meeting consumer preferences (including tastes and trends). One of the key factors influencing the product's selling price is the cost of raw materials. Therefore, from a financial standpoint, it's more cost-effective to use low-cost materials while maintaining the quality of the snack.

Co-Extrusion Process

Co-extrusion was first introduced to the food processing industry in 1984. In this process, two different materials are extruded from a single die. These materials may be fed from a single extruder and pump or from two separate extruders. This technique allows snack food manufacturers to produce snacks with two distinct textures, colors, or flavors.

A typical example of a product created using co-extrusion is a cereal-based outer tube with a cheese filling. On the market, you can find three main types of co-extruded snack foods:

- Cereal-based tubes filled with a water-based filling,
- Cereal-based tubes with a fat-based filling,
- Cereal-based tubes with a cereal-based filling.

However, it's important to note that these snacks have a limited shelf life due to the migration of oil and moisture from the filling into the outer shell.

Figure 9.2: Co-Extrusion Processes in Snacks Process (Such as Cereals).

Expansion Process

This snack category is often referred to as second-generation snacks or collets. Expanded snacks are high in protein and fiber while being low in calories, and they are produced using high-shear extruders. Examples of such snacks include potato sticks, onion rings, corn curls, and three-dimensional snacks. These snacks can be seasoned with a variety of flavors, including sugars, salt, and oil.

The quality of expanded snack foods is influenced by the raw materials used in the formulation and the operational conditions of the extruder. Other factors that can impact the degree of puffing during production include the size of cereal particles, the dough's residence time in the extruder barrel, and the moisture content of the feed material.

Baking Process

An additional type of extruded expanded snack foods is baked collet. Examples include potato sticks, onion rings, and baked corn curls, which can be made from various tuber flours and cereal grains. To create healthier snack options, bran, fibers, protein, and cellulose can be incorporated with cereal grains, making up to 20% of the material.

For potato sticks, a common approach is mixing potato flour with rice or corn flour. The baking process itself involves cooking the snacks by transferring heat through the air using methods such as convection, conduction, or radiation. The efficiency of each heating method depends on factors like the type of oven used and the design of the product.

Frying Process

The most widely recognized extruded snacks in the current snack market are fried collets, which obtain their characteristic twisted puffed shape through a unique die arrangement. These fried collets are made using collet extruders, fried in vegetable oil, and then coated with various flavors. During the frying process, the moisture content decreases from 8% to 2%.

For large-scale production (over 5000 lb/hour throughput), snack manufacturers typically use continuous fryers, whereas smaller-scale producers (under 200 lb/hour) often prefer batch fryers. Corn meal is the most common material used for producing fried collet snacks.

Drying Process

Certain products, such as puffed snacks, achieve their crispiness through the drying process. After extrusion, these snacks must be dried until the moisture content falls below 4%. This ensures that the puffed snacks attain the desired texture and stability for storage. Effective control of the drying process is crucial to maintaining the proper moisture level, preventing it from exceeding or falling below the target amount.

THE NECESSARY EQUIPMENT FOR SNACK FOOD PRODUCTION

To produce high-quality snacks, specialized equipment is essential for flavoring and preservation. Granule, powder, or oil applicators, along with electrostatic salters, coating tumblers, cheese sprayers, and powder dispensers, are crucial for the flavoring process. These tools enable manufacturers to create a wide variety of snacks using the same base ingredients.

For preserving the quality of raw materials, proper moving and storage equipment is critical. Improper storage of natural ingredients, such as potatoes or corn, can significantly affect their quality. For instance, if potatoes are not stored correctly, dark spots may appear on products like chips or french fries.

Packaging plays a key role in extending the shelf life of the finished product. Additionally, process control must ensure that the weight of the packaged snacks aligns with the specified value on the package. Furthermore, nut processing systems, including sorters, blanchers, roasters, and coolers, are essential for maintaining product quality during processing.

Figure 9.3: Maintaining the Long Shelf Life of Snacks.

NEW PACKAGING TECHNOLOGIES

More investment and innovation are being made to produce new products with a variety of shapes, flavors, and tastes in response to the growing demand for more nutrient-dense food items. In order to satisfy these demands, snack food manufacturers frequently adopt new technologies. A brief overview of some contemporary technologies that will help snack companies accomplish these objectives is provided here.

Vacuum Frying Technology

The nutritional value of packaged and processed snacks has increased thanks to advancements in frying technology. For instance, a method called batch frying creates snack foods with minimal amounts of fat and acrylamide. When starchy raw materials are cooked at high temperatures for an extended period of time, acrylamide, a potentially cancer-causing chemical, is produced.

The frying vessel is enclosed during the vacuum frying process, and because of the lower pressure, the water temperature is lower than 100°C. This produces a nutritious final product by continuously frying ingredients at low temperatures, avoiding the formation of acrylamide and oil saturation.

Flexible Packaging Machines and Systems

Single-portion packaging has replaced share-size bags in snack packaging. Advanced packaging machines that use flexible packaging materials, sizes, high speeds, and reduced reject rates are necessary for this shift. Snack food manufacturers will be able to use better packaging materials and create smaller products that meet WHO standards by putting these creative systems into place.

Tubular Cable Drag Conveying Systems

Reducing packaging size requires modifications to other parts of the processing technology to ensure that the packaging line can accommodate the produced quantities. To manage this effectively, snack producers should consider investing in advanced conveyor systems, like Cablevey Conveyors, which provide gentle and sanitary movement of specific loads through various stages of production.

Figure 9.4: A Custom Conveyor Belt.

This high-tech conveyor belt system and bulk material handling equipment offer a wide range of capacities, ensuring safe material handling and maintaining a secure environment throughout different snack production stages. High-capacity tube conveyors with small 2-inch diameters are ideal for moving ingredients such as cookie crumbs or various seeds, while larger 8-inch diameter conveyors can safely handle bulk materials like peanuts, in-shell walnuts, or puffed rice cereals.

Once the product has been developed, tested, and proven successful, it's crucial for snack food manufacturers to consistently maintain the exact blend of materials from the outset. Recipe developers, food designers, and engineers follow a stringent set of standards to build, design, refine, and preserve specific ingredient blends and ratios.

Industrial Conveyor Belt for Food Processing

Modern conveyor systems like Cablevey's can help snack food manufacturers distribute materials throughout the processing facility in a sustainable, safe, and quick manner. Our conveyors will significantly lower waste and product damage at the same time.

Snack Production Process

The cutting-edge baking equipment from Reading Bakery Systems is made to satisfy your needs when your snack production process demands the highest level of quality and accuracy. For the baked snack, pretzel, cookie, cracker, bread and bun, pizza, sweet goods, and pet treat industries, Reading Bakery Systems is a top producer of commercial bakery equipment.

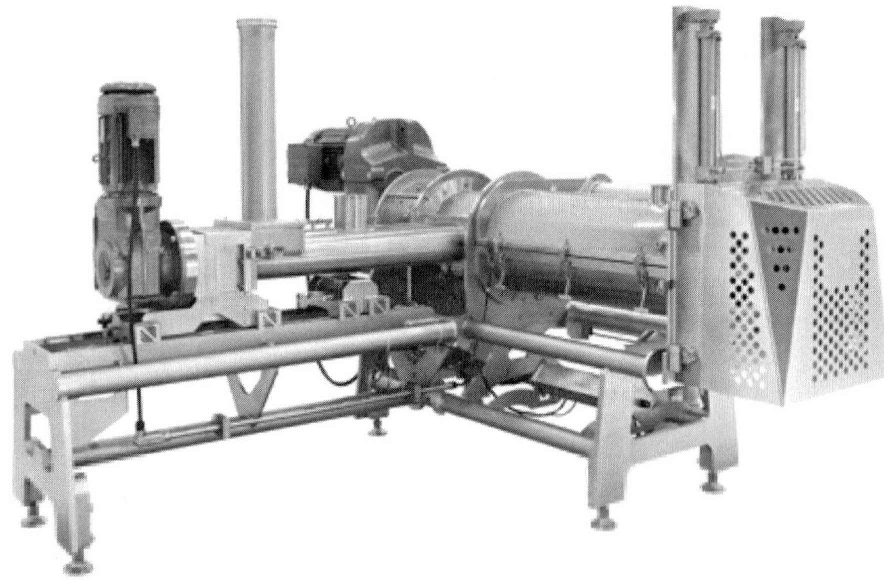

Figure 9.5: Snack Production (Cutting-Edge Baking) Equipment.

Mixing Equipment

Take into consideration the Exact EX Continuous Mixer for a consistent dough and final product. It is perfect for crackers, pretzels, pizza, pie crusts, sweets, pet treats, and many other wheat-based snacks because it evenly blends products with different dough moisture levels.

The Exact FX Continuous Mixer is the ideal tool for creating fake potato chips because it is made to evenly mix small amounts of moisture into large amounts of powder.

Test the Equipment and Techniques

If you're new to the snack industry or looking to explore innovative options to enhance your production volumes or processes, consider partnering with our team at the Reading Bakery Systems Science & Innovation Center.

The Innovation Center offers a wide range of dough mixing and forming processes, along with complete process lines for producing baked snacks, crackers, biscuits, cookies, pet treats, and other food products. It also features an Expanded Snack System for creating items like corn curls, balls, popcorn, and more.

The Center provides customers with access to our unparalleled expertise in manufacturing, research and development, quality assurance, equipment design, production management, and process development. Additionally, we offer support in die design and custom equipment creation.

SNACK FOOD PRODUCTION LINE'S

The snack food production line provides manufacturers with a high level of assurance, as its extrusion technology has been effectively applied in practice and is highly appreciated by food consumers.

Snack food is widely enjoyed by people of all ages and backgrounds, making it the go-to choice for daily entertainment. The Snack Food Production Line is considered the best equipment for producing a wide variety of snack foods, offering excellent cost performance.

This production line utilizes corn, rice, wheat, oats, and barley as raw materials to produce various snack foods through advanced extrusion technology. The resulting products are crisp in texture while retaining the nutritional value of the raw ingredients, making it a top-tier food processing machine in the industry.

The Snack Food Production Line consists of several components, including mixers, extruders, dryers, flavoring machines, cooling lines, and packaging machines, each serving a vital function. Manufacturers have the flexibility to customize the entire line or individual pieces of equipment, providing adaptability and versatility in production.

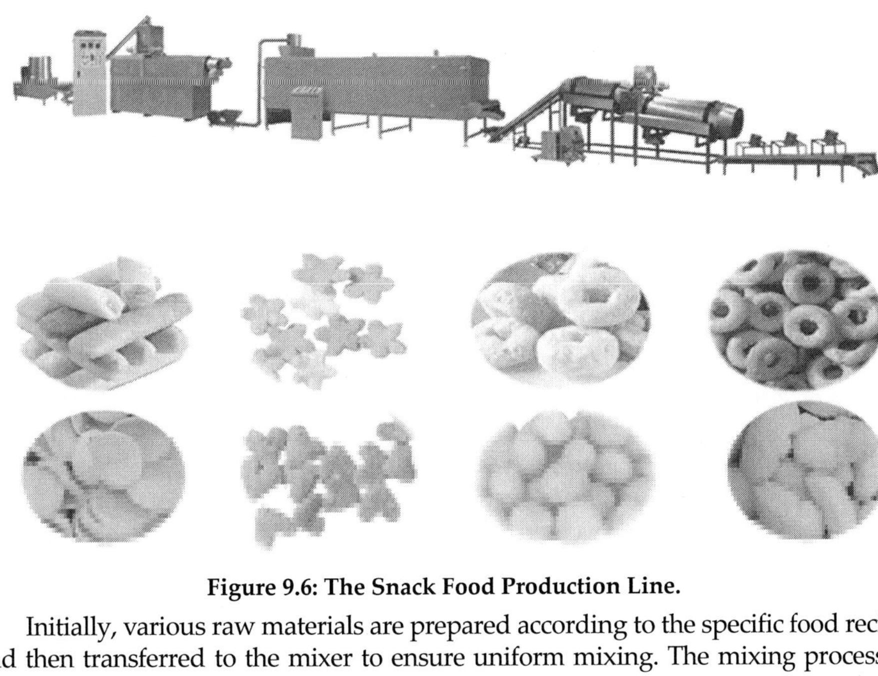

Figure 9.6: The Snack Food Production Line.

Initially, various raw materials are prepared according to the specific food recipe and then transferred to the mixer to ensure uniform mixing. The mixing process is designed to be leak-free, pollution-free, and efficient in utilizing the raw materials.

Next, the evenly mixed materials are fed into the extruder, where they are subjected to high temperature and pressure to extrude and shape the food. During this stage, the tissue structure of the grains is altered, creating a crisp texture. The shape of the food can be adjusted by changing the extruder die, with common shapes including spheres, tubes, fruit loops, stars, and hearts.

Once shaped, the food is further dried in a dryer, enhancing its crispiness and extending its shelf life.

After drying, the food undergoes seasoning, where salt, flavorings, pepper, and other seasonings are added in the seasoning barrel. This step allows for the creation of different flavor profiles that appeal to a variety of consumer tastes.

Finally, the finished snack food is cooled to prevent it from becoming soft after packaging, ensuring that it maintains its high quality and crispness.

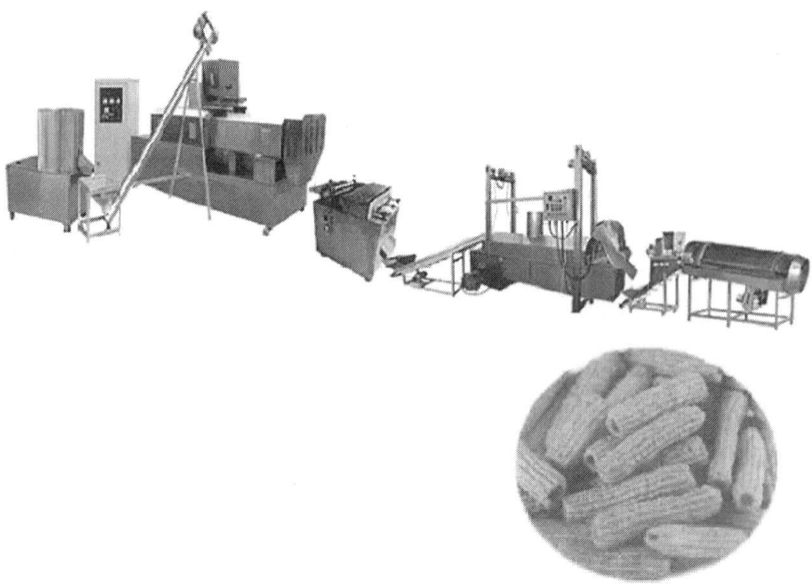

Figure 9.7: Broad Range of the Snack Food Production Line.

The Snack Food Production Line offers a broad range of applications and is capable of processing and producing various types of food products. It boasts a high level of automation, making it easy to operate, affordable, and highly efficient, which makes it an excellent choice for manufacturers aiming to improve both production efficiency and product quality.

One of its key advantages is that the technology used in this production line is at a world-leading level, with extrusion technology being the most widely adopted method in the food processing industry. The quality of this technology plays a significant role in determining the final quality of the food produced. This makes the Snack Food Production Line a reliable choice for manufacturers, as its extrusion technology has been extensively tested and proven in practice, and the food produced is highly favored by consumers.

10

Acquaintance with Food Safety Hygiene, and Certifications

INTRODUCTION

In order to guarantee that the food products produced are safe for consumption, free of contaminants, and prepared in a clean and controlled environment, food safety and hygiene are essential steps in the food production process. Maintaining consumer confidence and preventing foodborne illnesses require following food safety procedures and earning the appropriate certifications.

FOOD SAFETY SYSTEMS AND STANDARDS

HACCP (Hazard Analysis and Critical Control Points)

The HACCP method is a methodical approach to food safety that finds, assesses, and manages risks that are important to food safety. This covers biological, chemical, and physical risks.

Principles of HACCP

- Perform an analysis of the hazards.
- Determine the production process's critical control points (CCPs).
- Determine critical limits, such as food temperature limits.
- Keep a regular eye on CCPs.
- When boundaries are crossed, set up corrective measures.
- Maintain documentation of observations and actions.
- Regularly review and revise the HACCP plan.

Good Manufacturing Practices (GMP)

GMP includes all of the procedures and standards that guarantee food products are produced in a controlled and hygienic setting. GMP emphasizes operational procedures, equipment cleanliness, and making sure ingredients are handled and stored correctly.

ISO 22000 (Food Safety Management Systems)

An international standard called ISO 22000 describes what a food safety management system must have. It focuses on controlling food safety hazards at each step of the food production process by combining the concepts of HACCP and GMP.

Codex Alimentarius

A set of globally accepted standards, recommendations, and codes of conduct pertaining to food safety and quality is known as the Codex Alimentarius. It was created by the World Health Organization (WHO) and the Food and Agriculture Organization (FAO) to guarantee consumer safety and equitable food trade practices.

WHAT IS FOOD HYGIENE AND SAFETY TRAINING?

Food hygiene and safety training involves educating individuals on how to handle food in a safe manner to ensure it remains safe for consumption. Anyone working with food is considered a food handler, which includes tasks related to food storage, preparation, and service.

Food handlers must be aware of the risks linked to food handling and understand the necessary steps to prevent cross-contamination. They play a key role in ensuring the food is safe to eat and will not cause harm to customers. Practicing good hygiene is crucial in this process.

Food hygiene and safety training covers:

- The fundamental principles of personal hygiene.
- Best practices for maintaining a clean and safe work environment.

Furthermore, this training will:

- Assist food businesses in demonstrating compliance with legal requirements.
- Instill confidence in customers regarding the safety of the food being served.

Food Hygiene & Safety for Your Business

Proper food hygiene practices are essential in all types of food establishments, including but not limited to:

- Restaurants
- Cafés
- Pubs
- Takeaways
- Bakeries
- Supermarkets
- Hotels

- Schools
- Nurseries
- Hospitals

These practices ensure that food is prepared, handled, and served safely, regardless of the type of establishment.

Effective food hygiene practices are crucial in any food-related business, and they include:

- Proper cleaning and disinfection
- Maintaining food at safe temperatures
- Ensuring personal hygiene
- Controlling pests

According to the Food Standards Agency (FSA), anyone involved in food preparation or handling, such as:

- Chefs
- Cooks
- Bakers
- Kitchen assistants
- Baristas
- Sandwich makers ...must follow these hygiene practices.

Understanding food hygiene principles is essential for both the success of a food business and compliance with legal obligations. As a food business operator, it's crucial to train your staff in food safety and hygiene to ensure they serve safe food that meets customer expectations. Staff without proper training may not possess the necessary knowledge to handle food safely.

Having high standards of food hygiene benefits the business in many ways, including:

- Satisfied and repeat customers
- A strong reputation
- A good food hygiene rating
- Compliance with food safety laws
- Improved staff morale
- Reduced staff turnover

On the other hand, poor hygiene standards can lead to serious consequences such as:

- Damage to reputation
- Loss of customers
- Lower profits
- Decreased staff morale and higher turnover
- Foodborne illness outbreaks

- Legal issues and penalties
- Increased food wastage
- More customer complaints
- A poor food hygiene rating

FOOD HANDLER

The term "food handler" refers to individuals who directly handle open food as part of their job. It also includes anyone who may touch surfaces that come into contact with food or other areas where open food is handled. This includes roles such as chefs, cooks, bakers, waiters/waitresses, and kitchen porters.

Food hygiene training must cover essential food safety topics to ensure that each job role is performed safely and in compliance with food safety standards.

What the Law Says

The law mandates that food businesses provide food handlers with appropriate food hygiene training. This requirement is outlined in EC Regulation 852/2004, which states:

"Food business operators must ensure that food handlers are supervised, instructed, and/or trained in food hygiene matters appropriate to their work activities."

The most effective way to communicate food hygiene information is through staff training. New employees must receive sufficient training before handling food.

A reputable food hygiene training provider will issue certificates to employees after training. These certificates serve as proof of compliance with legal requirements.

It is recommended that food hygiene and safety training be updated every three years to ensure that food handlers and businesses stay informed about best practices and any legal changes.

Anyone involved in creating and maintaining HACCP procedures must be legally trained in the principles of HACCP.

What Level of Food Hygiene & Safety Training is Needed?

A Level 1 certificate in food hygiene and safety provides foundational knowledge on maintaining food safety. It focuses on general hygiene principles but does not delve deeply into food preparation and cooking specifics.

Roles that may require Level 1 food hygiene and safety training include:

- Front-of-house staff
- Checkout staff/cashiers
- Waiters/waitresses
- Bar workers

- Kitchen porters
- Food delivery drivers

A Level 2 food hygiene and safety certificate offers more detailed information about food safety, including preparation and cooking. Job roles in the catering industry that involve direct food handling, such as chefs or cooks working in various establishments (restaurants, cafes, takeaways, pubs, hotels, B&Bs, hospitals, care homes, nurseries, food vans, schools, universities, or colleges), may require Level 2 training.

Level 3 food hygiene and safety training is essential for those in managerial or supervisory positions who need to communicate food safety practices to staff and for those involved in developing food safety management systems. Job roles such as supervisors or managers require Level 3 training to ensure proper implementation of food safety protocols.

FOOD SAFETY CERTIFICATION

Food safety certification is a comprehensive process in which a food business—whether it's a restaurant, processing plant, or packaging facility—is assessed according to recognized food safety standards. These standards ensure that food is managed, prepared, and stored safely to minimize the risk of foodborne illnesses. Certification is generally carried out by independent third-party organizations and involves ongoing audits to ensure continued compliance and quality.

The exam typically consists of multiple-choice questions with a required passing score. Upon passing, the individual receives either a physical or digital certificate. Digital certificates are often available for immediate download after successful completion of the exam.

When a food business undergoes a hygiene inspection by the local authority, it is often required to present food hygiene certificates for its staff. These certificates should prominently display the name of the food handler who completed the course. Some food businesses also choose to showcase their food hygiene certificates to demonstrate their commitment to safety.

Why Does Food Safety Certification Matter?

- **Public Health Protection**: The primary goal of food safety certification is to safeguard public health. By adhering to stringent safety protocols, businesses minimize the risk of foodborne illnesses, which can have serious or even fatal consequences.
- **Consumer Confidence**: In today's world, where consumers are increasingly conscious of their food choices, a food safety certification acts as a mark of trust. It assures customers that the food they are consuming adheres to high safety standards.
- **Compliance with Regulations**: In many regions, food businesses must meet specific safety requirements. Certification acts as proof of compliance with these regulations, helping businesses avoid costly fines and potential legal complications.

- **Business Reputation and Marketability**: Obtaining food safety certification can improve a company's reputation, demonstrating its commitment to quality and safety. This can differentiate the business in a competitive market.
- **Risk Management**: The certification process encourages businesses to identify and address potential hazards, reducing the chances of food safety incidents and enhancing operational efficiency.
- **Global Trade Opportunities**: For businesses seeking to expand globally, a recognized food safety certification can be crucial. It often serves as a requirement for entering international markets, allowing businesses to tap into global trade opportunities.

Types of Food Safety Certifications

There are several food safety certifications, each focusing on specific aspects of food safety. Some of the most widely recognized include Hazard Analysis Critical Control Point (HACCP), ISO 22000, and SQF (Safe Quality Food). Each of these programs has its own set of standards and objectives, targeting different segments within the food industry.

Food safety certification goes beyond mere regulatory compliance; it represents a commitment to quality, safety, and building consumer trust. As food production and distribution become more globalized, these certifications are essential in ensuring public health and strengthening business credibility. With consumer demand for higher standards continuing to rise, the role of food safety certification will only increase in importance. For businesses within the food sector, investing in these certifications is not only beneficial but crucial for long-term success and sustainability.

FOOD HYGIENE CERTIFICATE RENEWAL TIMELINE

Although there is no expiration date on a food hygiene certificate, it is advised to undergo refresher training every three years. This is the best way to do it.

Why is the Renewal of Food Hygiene and Safety Training Important?

Renewing food hygiene and safety training is highly recommended as people tend to forget information or become complacent over time. There are aspects that food handlers may need to be reminded of to ensure they continue to follow safe practices and serve food that is safe for customers. Renewal of training also ensures that food handlers feel more confident in their food safety knowledge, especially if they are asked questions by an Environmental Health Officer (EHO) during a food hygiene inspection.

Legislation, guidance, and best practices evolve over time, and without refresher training, food handlers may be operating with outdated knowledge. This could result in actions that do not comply with the law or, worse, are unsafe.

Refresher food hygiene and safety training helps remind food handlers about:

- The hazards associated with food safety and how to manage them.
- Proper methods for food preparation, including chilling, freezing, defrosting, cooling, cooking, reheating, and hot holding foods safely.
- The critical temperatures to be monitored and maintained.
- Safe food storage practices.
- Controlling cross-contamination.
- Effective stock control.
- The distinctions between Best Before and Use By dates.
- Their legal obligations related to food handling.
- Proper cleaning and disinfection methods.
- Food safety management systems.
- The most recent food safety legislation.

11

Record Keeping, Finance and HRM for Agro-Processing

INTRODUCTION

Efficient management of record-keeping, inventory, finance, and human resources is crucial to the success of any agro-processing business. Proper record-keeping ensures accurate documentation of transactions, operations, and adherence to legal and regulatory standards, promoting transparency and accountability. Effective inventory management is vital for maintaining appropriate stock levels of raw materials, work-in-progress, and finished products, which directly affect production efficiency, cost management, and product availability. In financial management, sound practices allow businesses to monitor cash flow, manage costs, evaluate profitability, and secure necessary capital for growth and day-to-day operations.

Moreover, human resource management plays a significant role in building a skilled, motivated workforce by ensuring proper staffing, providing employee training, and adhering to labor regulations. Collectively, these components are essential for the smooth functioning of an agro-processing business, contributing to enhanced operational efficiency, financial health, and sustained growth.

RECORD KEEPING FOR AGRO-PROCESSING

Record-keeping in agro-processing is a fundamental aspect of the food production and manufacturing sector. It ensures traceability, adherence to food safety regulations, operational efficiency, and transparency in converting raw materials into finished goods. Well-maintained records are crucial for managing quality control, inventory, and ensuring compliance with health and safety standards.

Key Areas and Types of Records Kept in Agro-Processing

Below are the key areas and types of records that should be kept in agro-processing:

Raw Material and Ingredient Records

- **Supplier Information**: Keep detailed records of all suppliers, including their contact information, certification details, and the raw materials they supply.
- **Quality Control of Raw Materials**: Maintain records of inspections and test results for raw materials such as fruits, vegetables, grains, and other ingredients. This includes information on sourcing, quality standards, and any testing conducted (e.g., pesticide residue analysis, moisture content).
- **Purchase Orders and Invoices**: Track purchase orders and invoices for raw materials, documenting quantities, costs, and delivery schedules.
- **Storage Conditions**: Log temperatures and humidity levels in storage areas for perishable items (such as refrigerated storage logs for fruits).
- **Purpose:** These records facilitate traceability in the event of quality or safety concerns and help guarantee that only premium ingredients are used.

Production Process Records

- **Production Logs**: Keep track of every production batch's specifics, such as the date, time, and amount of raw materials and equipment used, as well as any deviations or problems that may arise.
- **Recipes and Formulations**: Keep thorough recipes and formulas for every product, including batch sizes, processing guidelines, and ingredient specifications.
- **Processing Times and Temperatures**: To guarantee ideal conditions for food safety and product quality, note the times and temperatures utilized during different processing stages, such as cooking, pasteurization, fermentation, drying, or freezing.
- **Equipment Maintenance and Calibration**: To make sure that machines (such as temperature sensors and weighing scales) are operating correctly, keep a record of cleaning schedules, equipment maintenance plans, and machine calibrations.

Purpose: These records aid in keeping an eye on the production process's efficiency, consistency, and quality. In the event that problems occur during processing, they also permit remedial measures.

Quality Control and Testing Records

- **Raw Material Testing**: Document the findings of tests conducted on raw materials, such as moisture content, pesticide residue testing, and microbiological testing.
- **In-Process Testing**: For quality assurance, record test results for pH levels, acidity, moisture, viscosity, color, and other pertinent quality attributes during production.
- **Testing of the Final Product**: Document the results of tests conducted on the final product for safety and quality parameters, including shelf life, taste, texture, and sensory assessment.

- **Batch Testing**: To confirm that the product satisfies quality and safety standards, record the batch number, test results, and certification (if applicable) for each batch.
- **Non-Conformance and Corrective Actions:** Keep track of any quality problems, specification deviations, and remedial measures (such as product disposal, reprocessing, or rework).

Purpose: These records, which are crucial for product recalls or audits, show that the product satisfies safety and quality standards.

Inventory and Storage Records

- **Raw Material Inventory:** Keep tabs on the amounts of raw materials available, along with usage patterns, stock levels, and reorder points.
- **Finished Goods Inventory:** Keep track of the stock of completed goods, including its quantities, shelf life, and storage settings (such as ambient or refrigeration).
- **Goods Movement:** Keep track of the flow of both raw materials and completed goods, including incoming shipments, storage, and distribution or delivery.
- **FIFO (First In, First Out):** To avoid spoiling or waste, use the FIFO method and maintain track of inventory expiration dates to ensure appropriate inventory rotation.

Purpose: These records aid in effective inventory management, guarantee that there is neither an excess nor a shortage, and minimize waste by means of appropriate stock rotation.

Health and Safety Records

- **Employee Health and Hygiene Records:** Keep track of staff education on food safety, personal hygiene, and the use of personal protective equipment (PPE).
- **Sanitation and Cleaning Schedules:** Keep track of the cleaning procedures for equipment, storage facilities, and production areas. This includes sanitation inspections and the kinds of cleaning solutions that are used.
- **Pest Control Logs:** Maintain a record of all inspections, contamination prevention measures, and pest control activities.
- **Inspections for safety:** To guarantee adherence to occupational health and safety regulations, document safety inspections of the workspace, equipment, and storage spaces.

Purpose: These records serve to safeguard both workers and customers by proving adherence to worker health and food safety laws.

Compliance and Regulatory Records

- **Licenses and Certifications**: Keep copies of all pertinent licenses and certifications (such as health permits, food safety certifications, ISO 22000, organic, or halal certifications) that are necessary for the business to operate lawfully.

- **Inspection Reports**: Document any audits or inspections conducted by regulatory agencies (such as health departments or food safety authorities) and any responses to suggestions made.
- **Traceability Records:** In the event of a product recall or contamination problem, keep track of the traceability of ingredients and products at every stage of manufacturing, packaging, and distribution.

Purpose: To make sure the company satisfies industry and legal standards and passes audits by the appropriate authorities, compliance and regulatory records are crucial.

Packaging and Labeling Records

- **Packaging Materials:** Keep track of the supplier details, material specifications, and certifications (such as those for food-grade materials) for the packaging materials that are used.
- **Labeling Compliance:** Verify that the labeling and packaging contain the ingredients, allergens, nutritional information, expiration dates, and certification marks that are required by law.
- **Batch/Production Numbers:** For traceability purposes, note the labels applied to each product, the production dates, and the batch numbers.

Purpose: These records aid in making sure that labeling and packaging meet legal requirements and are in line with the caliber of the product.

Distribution and Shipping Records

- **Shipping Logs:** Keep track of outgoing shipments, including product specifications, client data, dates of shipment, and modes of transportation.
- **Records of temperature control (for perishable goods):** Keep an eye on temperatures while they are being transported and stored, particularly for products that are sensitive to temperature changes.
- **Receiving Records:** Maintain track of all shipments that arrive and check them for damage or deviations from the order specifications.

Purpose: These records aid in tracking the flow of goods through the supply chain and guarantee that goods are shipped and received in accordance with storage requirements.

Financial and Operational Records

- **Cost of Goods Sold (COGS):** Maintain track of production costs, such as labor, energy, raw material costs, and overhead.
- **Sales and Revenue Records:** Keep tabs on customer orders, sales transactions, and revenue.
- **Production Efficiency Metrics:** Keep track of key performance indicators (KPIs) for waste levels, downtime, and production output.

Purpose: Budgeting, operational effectiveness, and financial transparency all depend on these records.

METHODS OF RECORD KEEPING

Paper Methods

Nowadays, a lot of records are maintained using the conventional paper method. A ledger book for financial records that contains a list of all daily debits and credits may be used for this. It's okay if this is your current approach and it works well for you. The two most crucial things are consistency and record keeping. Pen and paper record keeping is still used by many very successful businesses.

Electronic Methods

Record-keeping software is becoming as sector-specific as production agriculture. It appears that software programs have been created to help with record keeping in the majority of industries. In the program crop area, this is clearly visible. Numerous businesses have created software programs to help with record keeping, ranging from mapping to profit and loss statements for every industry. Data entry will take a significant amount of your time when you first start using the package, but once it is set up, using a smartphone or tablet computer can make it much easier.

Combination

Another option is to use both electronic and paper methods. Keeping a daily log of events on paper and then entering them into a computer could be an option if you are uneasy using a computer. Another employee or family member may use the computer as well (children or grandchildren may find this entertaining). Although, it is ideal to keep daily records of all transactions and events, smaller businesses without a dedicated bookkeeper may not be able to do so during the hectic planting or harvesting season. As mentioned earlier, be consistent and diligent in your approach.

Advice for Enhancing Inventory Control in the Food Industry

Below pointers will help you get started on the path to improving your inventory management in the food industry:

Know What you have on Hand

The first crucial step in effective inventory management is maintaining accurate records of all food items in stock, along with their quantities. There are numerous reasons why knowing your stock levels is vital in the food industry. The most obvious reason is that it enables you to plan production and sales more effectively. Without an accurate inventory count, it becomes difficult to forecast how much you need to produce or purchase to meet customer demand.

Additionally, inventory management is essential for food safety and quality control. Without proper knowledge of available ingredients, it becomes challenging to ensure their correct usage and freshness. This can lead to food spoilage or products that fail to meet customer expectations.

Moreover, effective inventory management can help save money. By understanding your inventory, you can avoid overstocking items that may expire before being used, thus minimizing food waste and reducing costs.

Keeping a close eye on your stock levels is beneficial in several ways and is a key factor in maintaining smooth operations and financial efficiency.

Keep Track of Expiration Dates

Tracking expiration dates for all food items in your inventory is crucial for several reasons. It ensures that you're using and selling the freshest products available. One of the primary reasons to track expiration dates in perishable goods is to guarantee food safety. Expired items may no longer be safe to eat and could potentially cause illness.

Additionally, expired products contribute to waste, as they must be discarded if not consumed in time. By monitoring expiration dates, you can avoid wasting money on items that go unsold or unused.

Another key reason for tracking expiration dates is quality control. Over time, some foods may lose their flavor or freshness. If customers don't enjoy the product, it can negatively impact satisfaction. Expired items can also pose health risks for those with allergies or specific dietary needs.

From a financial perspective, managing expiration dates is essential. Expired goods turn into dead stock, which can result in lost products and incur carrying costs. Furthermore, many insurance policies require businesses to track expiration dates for coverage to remain valid.

Keeping track of expiration dates helps ensure food safety, maintain product quality, and support the financial health of a business.

Rotate Stock Regularly

One effective strategy for maintaining freshness and minimizing waste is regularly rotating your stock. This involves using the oldest items first and then moving on to the newer ones. Stock rotation offers several benefits:

- It helps ensure that food remains fresh and makes it easier to monitor shelf life.
- It prevents spoilage and waste, which in turn optimizes inventory costs.
- It allows you to keep an accurate record of inventory levels and restock as necessary.
- It ensures that customers have the best possible experience when purchasing from you.

Store Food Properly

Proper storage is crucial for maintaining the freshness of food and preventing spoilage. Effective inventory control plays a key role in any food business, ensuring that food remains fresh and safe for consumption. Food items should always be stored in cool, dry, and dark conditions. There are several reasons why proper storage is important:

- It helps reduce food waste. Improper storage can cause food to spoil quickly, rendering it unusable. This not only costs businesses money but also contributes to environmental pollution and greenhouse gas emissions, which are detrimental to sustainable inventory management practices.
- It helps preserve the nutritional value of food. Mishandling or spoilage of food can lead to a reduction in its nutritional content, potentially causing health problems for consumers. Proper storage ensures that the food retains its value and benefits people's health.

Don't Over Order

It's essential to maintain a balance when auditing inventory with barcode scanning, placing orders for new stock, and managing other related processes. Failing to order enough inventory could lead to shortages, causing disruptions in your operations. Efficient inventory and purchase order management is one of the core pillars of business success.

If you lose track of your inventory, you won't know when to restock, leading to delays and bottlenecks in production and sales. However, many businesses overlook the risks of overordering. While it's crucial to have enough stock to meet customer demand, excessive inventory can result in significant costs.

Here are a few reasons why overordering can be problematic:

- **Tied-up capital**: Overbuying leads to increased carrying costs, tying up money in inventory that could otherwise be invested in growing other parts of the business.
- **Reduced profit margins**: Ordering in excess adds to shipping and handling costs, eroding your profit margins.
- **Risk of spoilage**: Excess food increases the likelihood of spoilage before it can be used, resulting in wasted money and potential health hazards.
- **Storage issues**: An overcrowded storage area makes it harder to move around and locate needed items, which can lead to inefficiencies and accidents.
- **Inventory tracking difficulties**: Too much stock can make it difficult to manage inventory effectively, leading to ordering errors and other complications.

By being mindful of your ordering practices, you can save money and avoid unnecessary headaches in the long term.

Use a Just-in-Time Inventory System

A Just-in-Time (JIT) inventory system helps businesses avoid both overordering and underordering by only purchasing the inventory needed for a specific period. This system offers several key advantages, particularly in the food industry.

One of the primary benefits of JIT inventory is its ability to reduce spoilage and waste. Since businesses only order the amount of food they need, they can minimize the chances of having surplus products that may spoil before being used.

Another significant advantage is cost savings. With JIT inventory management, businesses avoid spending money on excess stock that might eventually go to waste. This system also helps streamline the inventory process, making it more efficient and effective.

Lastly, JIT inventory systems can improve customer service. By maintaining the right amount of stock, businesses are better able to meet customer demand, resulting in greater customer satisfaction and repeat business.

Overall, implementing a JIT inventory system is crucial for effective inventory management in the food industry, helping businesses optimize their operations and improve their bottom line.

Review Your Inventory Regularly

Regularly reviewing your inventory is essential to ensure that your records are accurate and up-to-date. This practice allows you to address issues promptly and make necessary adjustments.

Conducting regular inventory reviews helps you to:

- **Maintain accurate stock records:** Accurate inventory records are crucial for financial management, operational efficiency, and providing good customer service.
- **Identify customer trends and anticipate future inventory needs:** Analyzing trends can help you adjust your ordering and stocking strategies to better meet demand.
- **Perform regular audits of inventory processes:** Routine audits help you identify potential issues and inefficiencies early, preventing them from becoming larger problems.

By conducting regular inventory audits, you can ensure that your records are correct, identify emerging trends, and catch potential problems before they escalate.

THE BEST WAYS TO KEEP RECORDS OF AGRO-PROCESSING

- **Digitization**: Implement electronic systems to streamline record storage and management, making it easier to access, retrieve, and analyze data. Using software such as Enterprise Resource Planning (ERP) or Manufacturing Execution Systems (MES) can centralize your record-keeping process.
- **Regular Audits**: Carry out frequent internal and external audits to verify the accuracy, completeness, and compliance of all records with industry standards and regulatory requirements.
- **Data Retention Policies**: Establish a clear data retention policy that outlines how long various types of records should be kept. For example, raw material records may be stored for a year, while financial records could be kept for seven years.
- **Security and Confidentiality**: Protect sensitive records, such as financial information or employee health data, by ensuring they are securely stored and accessible only to authorized personnel, maintaining confidentiality.
- **Training**: Continuously train staff responsible for record-keeping to emphasize the importance of accuracy, compliance, and proper documentation practices.

Efficient record-keeping in agro-processing is not only essential for complying with food safety regulations but also for improving operational efficiency, reducing risks, and enhancing traceability throughout the production process. Well-organized and thorough records help maintain high-quality standards, ensure safe consumer products, manage inventory effectively, and pass regulatory audits or certifications.

TYPICAL RECORDS MAINTAINED ON FARMS

Farm record keeping involves tracking a wide array of essential data for effective farm management, analysis, and strategic planning. Here are some common types of records maintained on farms:

Financial Records

- Income and expenditure documentation
- Receipts and invoices for sales and purchases
- Loan and credit records
- Asset inventory and depreciation schedules
- Tax-related documents

Crop Production Records

- Planting dates, varieties used, and field locations
- Input records (e.g., seeds, fertilizers, pesticides, water usage)
- Harvest dates and yields
- Crop rotation plans and field histories
- Pest and disease management logs

Livestock Records

- Birth, death, and purchase documentation
- Health and vaccination records
- Breeding and production records (e.g., milk yield, egg production)
- Feed consumption and feed conversion rates
- Weight and growth tracking

Labor Records

- Employee details, job roles, and hours worked
- Training records
- Payroll and compensation records

Equipment and Machinery Records

- Purchase, repair, and maintenance logs
- Usage tracking (hours of operation)
- Depreciation schedules

Inventory Records

- Supplies inventory (e.g., seeds, feed, fertilizers, pesticides)
- Product inventory (stored crops, livestock products)
- Tools and equipment inventory

Environmental and Compliance Records

- Soil test and health records
- Water usage and irrigation schedules
- Compliance with agricultural and environmental regulations
- Certifications (e.g., organic, animal welfare)

Field and Farm Maps

- Field layouts, crop locations, and rotations
- Infrastructure locations (e.g., buildings, irrigation systems)

These records are crucial for ensuring operational efficiency, maintaining farm productivity, meeting legal and regulatory standards, and making informed decisions for future planning and growth.

FINANCE FOR AGRO-PROCESSING

Finance in agro-processing pertains to managing the financial aspects of producing, processing, and distributing agricultural products. Sound financial management is essential for the growth and sustainability of agro-processing businesses, as it influences key factors like investment choices, cost control, profitability, and cash flow.

These businesses, which transform raw agricultural products into finished or semi-finished goods, encounter distinctive financial challenges, including the seasonality of raw materials, perishability, inventory management issues, and the need for compliance with industry regulations. Effective financial strategies are crucial to navigating these challenges and ensuring long-term success.

Agro-Processing Financial Components

Capital Requirements and Financing Options

Agro-processing businesses require capital at different stages, from establishing facilities and acquiring machinery to purchasing raw materials and covering operational costs. Key sources of financing include:

- **Equity Financing:** Raising funds by offering shares in the business to investors. This provides long-term capital but results in ownership dilution.
- **Debt Financing:** Loans or credit lines from banks or financial institutions, providing short-term or long-term funding for working capital or capital expenditures. It's important to assess interest rates and repayment terms.
- **Government Grants and Subsidies:** Many governments offer grants, subsidies, or low-interest loans to support agro-processing businesses, particularly those involved in sustainable or export-focused production.

- **Venture Capital:** High-growth agro-processing businesses may attract venture capital investments in exchange for equity, providing the necessary capital for expansion or scaling.
- **Trade Credit:** Suppliers may extend trade credit, allowing businesses to purchase raw materials on credit and pay later, helping to maintain smoother cash flow during procurement.
- **Crowdfunding:** For smaller agro-processing startups, crowdfunding platforms offer an opportunity to raise funds from a diverse pool of small investors.

Purpose: Securing sufficient capital enables agro-processing businesses to address their investment requirements, finance operations, and ensure long-term viability.

Cost Management and Control

Cost management is vital in agro-processing due to the significant expenses involved in raw materials, labor, and specialized equipment. The main cost categories include:

- **Raw Material Costs:** Agro-processing businesses rely on agricultural products, which often experience price fluctuations due to seasonal changes and weather conditions. Effective procurement strategies and long-term supplier contracts can help stabilize raw material prices.
- **Labor Costs:** Agro-processing facilities require both skilled and unskilled labor, with costs varying based on seasonality, overtime, and training needs. Managing workforce productivity and optimizing staffing levels can help control labor expenses.
- **Energy and Utilities:** The energy-intensive nature of agro-processing, especially in activities like drying, freezing, cooking, or packaging, makes energy management essential. Investing in energy-efficient equipment can significantly reduce utility expenses.
- **Maintenance and Repairs:** Regular maintenance of machinery is crucial to prevent downtime and avoid costly repairs. Allocating a budget for preventative maintenance helps minimize unexpected costs and prolong the life of equipment.
- **Packaging Costs:** Packaging represents a major cost in agro-processing. Efficient packaging design, bulk purchasing of materials, and optimizing packaging processes can help reduce packaging expenses.
- **Logistics and Distribution:** The cost of transporting finished goods to customers, which includes transportation, warehousing, and distribution, is a key part of the supply chain. Optimizing delivery routes and utilizing various distribution methods can help cut logistics costs.

Purpose: Effective cost control minimizes waste, boosts operational effectiveness, and maximizes resource utilization to guarantee profitability.

Cash Flow Management

Agro-processing businesses often encounter cash flow issues due to the timing of raw material purchases, production cycles, and delayed customer payments. Proper cash flow management is essential for maintaining smooth operations. Key practices include:

- **Cash Flow Forecasting:** Regular forecasting of cash inflows and outflows ensures that the business maintains adequate liquidity to cover operational costs and investment requirements. This includes predicting seasonal variations in demand and fluctuations in raw material prices.
- **Accounts Receivable Management:** Agro-processing businesses often operate with credit terms for customers. Effective management of accounts receivable—such as prompt invoicing and follow-ups on overdue payments—helps maintain a consistent cash flow.
- **Working Capital Management:** Proper management of working capital (current assets minus current liabilities) is essential to cover everyday expenses like wages, utility bills, and raw material costs. This involves optimizing inventory turnover and negotiating favorable supplier payment terms.
- **Cash Reserves:** Keeping a cash reserve is important to handle unforeseen expenses or cash flow gaps, particularly during off-peak production periods.

Purpose: By controlling cash flow, a company can maintain its financial stability by making sure it can pay its employees, suppliers, and other operating expenses on schedule.

Profitability Analysis

Profitability analysis is essential for agro-processing businesses to determine if they are earning enough income to cover expenses and generate a return on investment. Key profitability measures include:

- **Gross Profit Margin:** This ratio calculates the difference between sales revenue and the cost of goods sold (COGS), then divides that by sales revenue. It provides insight into the basic profitability of the production process.
- **Formula:** Gross Profit Margin = (Revenue - COGS)/Revenue × 100
- **Operating Profit Margin:** This ratio shows the business's profitability after accounting for operating expenses like administrative, marketing, and research costs.
- **Formula:** Operating Profit Margin = Operating Income/Revenue × 100
- **Net Profit Margin:** This measure takes into account all expenses, including interest, taxes, and depreciation, to determine the business's overall profitability.
- **Formula:** Net Profit Margin = Net Income/Revenue × 100
- **Break-Even Analysis:** This analysis determines the point where total revenue equals total costs, indicating when the business begins making a profit. It's crucial for setting pricing strategies, controlling costs, and setting sales goals.

Purpose: Profitability analysis helps businesses evaluate their financial health, identify key cost drivers, and make informed decisions on pricing, improving production efficiency, and making strategic investments.

Financial Reporting and Compliance

Agro-processing businesses must maintain precise and up-to-date financial records to ensure compliance with legal obligations and industry standards. Key financial reports include:

- **Income Statement (Profit and Loss Statement):** This document details the company's revenue, expenses, and profits over a designated period, enabling stakeholders to evaluate financial performance.
- **Balance Sheet:** The balance sheet presents the company's assets, liabilities, and equity, offering a snapshot of financial health and solvency.
- **Cash Flow Statement:** This report tracks cash inflows and outflows, helping assess the company's ability to generate cash and manage short-term liquidity needs.
- **Cost of Goods Sold (COGS) Statement:** This statement outlines direct costs related to the production of goods, such as raw materials, labor, and manufacturing expenses.
- **Tax Compliance:** Ensure timely and accurate tax reporting, including sales tax, payroll tax, and corporate income tax. Agro-processing businesses should collaborate with accountants to stay in compliance with local tax regulations.

Purpose: Accurate financial reporting ensures legal compliance, provides transparency for investors and lenders, and supports informed decision-making based on financial performance.

Financial Risk Management

Agro-processing businesses face various financial risks, including:

- **Commodity Price Volatility:** The prices of raw agricultural materials can vary greatly due to factors such as climate conditions, geopolitical events, or changes in market demand. To mitigate this risk, businesses can use hedging strategies or establish long-term supply agreements with suppliers.
- **Currency Exchange Risks:** For businesses involved in international trade, fluctuations in exchange rates can affect profitability. Hedging strategies or operating in local currencies can help reduce exposure to currency risk.
- **Interest Rate Risks:** Fluctuations in interest rates can impact borrowing costs. Businesses can manage this risk by locking in fixed interest rates or using financial instruments to hedge against rate changes.
- **Operational Risks:** These include risks related to supply chain disruptions, equipment breakdowns, or food safety issues. Businesses can mitigate operational risks by maintaining adequate insurance coverage and implementing strong internal controls.

Purpose: Effective financial risk management protects the business from unforeseen events that could adversely affect profitability or disrupt operations, ensuring long-term financial stability.

Strategies for Investment and Growth

Agro-processing businesses often need to make strategic investments to stay competitive or foster growth. Key strategies for investment include:

- **Capital Expenditure (CapEx):** Investing in machinery, facilities, and technology can help increase production capacity, enhance efficiency, and reduce costs over time.
- **Research and Development (R&D):** Investing in R&D enables businesses to develop new products or improve existing ones, which can open up new revenue streams. Additionally, R&D helps businesses adapt to changing consumer preferences and meet regulatory requirements.
- **Market Expansion:** Expanding into new markets, either domestically or internationally, may require adjustments to production lines, obtaining certifications, or enhancing distribution channels to reach a broader customer base.
- **Sustainability Investments:** Investing in sustainable practices such as waste reduction, energy efficiency, and water conservation helps businesses appeal to environmentally-conscious consumers and comply with sustainability regulations.

Purpose: Strategic investments support business growth, increase profitability, and maintain competitiveness in the market.

Finance plays a crucial role in agro-processing, covering activities such as securing capital, managing costs, monitoring cash flow, and assessing profitability. By managing these financial aspects effectively, agro-processing businesses can optimize operations, increase profitability, mitigate financial risks, and ensure long-term sustainability. Moreover, understanding the unique financial challenges of agro-processing — such as commodity price fluctuations and seasonality — is vital for making informed financial decisions and staying ahead of market trends.

HUMAN RESOURCE MANAGEMENT FOR AGRO-PROCESSING

Human Resource Management (HRM) in the agro-processing industry is vital for recruiting, attracting, and retaining skilled employees who are key to achieving the company's objectives. HRM plays a strategic role in supporting employees and fostering a positive work environment, ensuring that food production and manufacturing processes run smoothly.

In the agro-processing sector, HRM is particularly focused on hiring, training, and developing a skilled workforce that is essential for maintaining high productivity, quality standards, and safety protocols. Effective workforce management also helps minimize risks, enhances employee satisfaction, and ensures compliance with regulatory requirements. By managing human resources effectively, businesses in the agro-processing industry can maintain operational efficiency, meet customer demands, and contribute to overall business growth and success.

Recruitment and Staffing in the Field of Agro-Processing

- **Identifying Staffing Needs:** Assess the workforce requirements based on factors such as production schedules, the types of products being produced, and the operational capacity of the business. This includes determining the number of production workers, quality control inspectors, maintenance technicians, supervisors, and other support staff needed.

- **Job Descriptions and Specifications:** Develop clear and comprehensive job descriptions for each position within the company. These descriptions should outline the job responsibilities, necessary skills, qualifications, experience, and working conditions to ensure clarity for both employees and management.
- **Recruitment Strategies:** Employ suitable recruitment techniques to attract skilled workers, including online job portals, recruitment agencies, and internal advertisements. In rural areas, working with local communities can be an effective strategy for sourcing qualified candidates.
- **Selection Process:** Use a structured selection process that includes interviews, technical skill assessments (for example, testing machine operators), and reference checks. This ensures that the best-suited candidates are selected for each role.

Purpose: Efficient recruitment ensures that the workforce is competent, productive, and able to meet the needs of agro-processing production, contributing to the overall success of the business.

Training and Development in the Field of Agro-Processing

- **Orientation and Induction:** New employees should undergo a comprehensive orientation program that introduces them to the company's culture, policies, safety protocols, and standard operating procedures (SOPs). In agro-processing, it is especially important to familiarize workers with food safety standards such as HACCP and GMP to ensure compliance and maintain product quality.
- **Job-Specific Training:** Offer tailored training programs based on the specific tasks that employees will be responsible for. This could include operating machinery, implementing quality control measures, or adhering to food safety standards, ensuring they are fully equipped to perform their roles efficiently.
- **Cross-Training:** Promote cross-training initiatives so employees can learn different roles within the organization. This enhances workforce flexibility, ensuring smooth operations during employee absences or peak production times, reducing downtime and improving overall productivity.
- **Ongoing Skill Development:** Establish continuous learning programs that focus on enhancing technical competencies, such as machine maintenance, troubleshooting, or familiarity with new production technologies. This could involve in-house training sessions or external certifications, such as ISO certifications or HACCP training, to further develop employee skills.

Purpose: Effective training and development ensure that employees stay informed about industry standards, improve their job performance, and reduce operational errors and safety risks, ultimately supporting the success and efficiency of the agro-processing business.

Performance Management in the Field of Agro-Processing

- **Setting Clear Expectations:** Establish clear performance goals and key performance indicators (KPIs) for employees, which should include specific production targets, quality benchmarks, and safety protocols to guide their work and performance.
- **Regular Performance Appraisals:** Schedule periodic performance reviews, whether quarterly or annually, to assess employee contributions, acknowledge strengths, pinpoint areas for development, and set fresh objectives for growth. Incorporating 360-degree feedback can provide a more comprehensive evaluation from different perspectives.
- **Recognition and Rewards:** Create a reward system that celebrates exceptional performance, such as offering bonuses, promotions, or non-financial incentives like "Employee of the Month" awards to foster motivation and loyalty.
- **Corrective Action:** If performance falls short of expectations, provide constructive feedback, and implement improvement plans that may involve additional training, mentoring, or role adjustments to help employees meet their potential.

Purpose: Effective performance management ensures that employee goals are aligned with organizational objectives, enhances productivity, fosters continuous improvement, and boosts employee motivation and engagement, ultimately benefiting both individuals and the company.

Workplace Safety and Health in the Field of Agro-Processing

- **Health and Safety Training:** Provide comprehensive safety training to all employees, covering areas such as the correct handling of machinery, equipment, chemicals, and personal protective equipment (PPE) to ensure they are well-prepared for their roles.
- **Safety Protocols:** Develop and enforce clear safety procedures, including safe operation protocols for machines, emergency response plans, and protocols for handling hazardous materials, in accordance with occupational health and safety regulations.
- **Ergonomics:** Focus on ergonomics in the workplace to prevent repetitive stress injuries, especially in agro-processing environments where employees may be required to perform manual tasks or stand for extended periods.
- **Health Monitoring:** Conduct regular health assessments and medical checkups for employees who may be exposed to biological or chemical hazards, ensuring that potential risks are identified and addressed proactively.

Purpose: A safe and healthy work environment helps minimize accidents, boosts employee morale, enhances productivity, and ensures compliance with health and safety regulations, ultimately fostering a positive workplace culture.

Compensation and Benefits of Agro-processing employes

- **Salary Structure:** Design a salary structure that is competitive and reflective of industry standards, local labor market conditions, and the experience level of employees. Ensure compensation is equitable, transparent, and consistent with the company's financial capacity.

- **Overtime and Incentives:** Establish clear policies regarding overtime pay, particularly during peak production periods, ensuring employees are compensated fairly for extended working hours. Offer incentives to motivate employees to achieve production targets or maintain high-quality standards.
- **Benefits Package:** Provide a comprehensive benefits package, including health insurance, retirement plans, paid time off, and performance-based bonuses. In some cases, consider offering housing or transportation allowances, particularly for employees working in remote areas.
- **Bonuses and Profit Sharing:** Implement financial incentives tied to the company's performance, such as profit-sharing schemes, to encourage employees to contribute to the business's overall success.

Purpose: A well-structured compensation and benefits system helps attract, retain, and motivate talent, ensuring employees remain engaged and committed to achieving the company's goals.

Employee Relations in the Industries of Agro-Processing

- **Communication Channels:** Implement clear and open communication channels between management and staff. Regular meetings, structured feedback systems, and suggestion boxes can provide employees with opportunities to express their concerns, ideas, and suggestions.
- **Conflict Resolution:** Establish protocols for effectively handling conflicts, whether they occur among employees, between employees and management, or concerning work conditions. A well-organized conflict resolution process helps maintain a harmonious work atmosphere and can prevent potential legal disputes.
- **Employee Engagement:** Actively engage employees through methods such as surveys, team-building exercises, and employee recognition events. Making employees feel valued and appreciated contributes to increased job satisfaction and higher retention rates.

Purpose: Fostering positive employee relations enhances workplace culture, reduces turnover, and promotes a more cooperative and efficient work environment.

Compliance with Labor Laws

- **Legal Compliance:** Make sure the business complies with regional labor regulations, such as those pertaining to minimum wages, working hours, overtime, and benefits. Keep abreast of modifications to laws that impact the food processing sector.
- **Employment Contracts:** Give workers explicit written agreements that specify their duties, pay, working conditions, and dispute resolution

protocols. Contracts give both parties legal protection and aid in avoiding misunderstandings.

- **Union Relations, if relevant:** Workers in agro-processing facilities may be represented by unions in some areas. Reducing labor disputes and preserving operational stability can be achieved by fostering good relations with unions and negotiating just agreements.

Purpose: Adherence to labor laws enhances a company's standing as a conscientious employer and helps avoid legal problems and penalties.

Succession Planning and Career Development

- **Identifying Future Leaders:** Create a comprehensive strategy to identify and cultivate potential leaders within the organization. This can be achieved through mentoring, leadership development programs, and providing opportunities for career progression.
- **Retention of Key Employees:** Establish effective strategies to retain highly experienced employees by offering opportunities for career advancement, access to professional development initiatives, and attractive compensation packages.
- **Job Rotation:** Implement job rotation schemes to help employees gain a broad range of skills and prepare them for higher responsibilities within the organization.

Purpose: Succession planning is essential for building a robust talent pool to fill important roles, reducing employee turnover, and fostering personal and professional growth within the company.

Challenges in HRM for Agro-Processing Fields

- **Seasonal Workforce:** Agro-processing businesses often face fluctuations in production levels due to seasonal variations. Managing the varying demands for labor while maintaining consistent quality and safety standards can present significant challenges.
- **Labor Shortages in Rural Areas:** Finding skilled workers in rural areas can be challenging due to a limited pool of trained labor. Addressing this issue through training programs and community outreach initiatives can help attract and develop local talent.
- **Employee Turnover:** The agro-processing sector often experiences high turnover, particularly in lower-skilled or manual labor roles. To reduce turnover, businesses can implement strategies to enhance employee retention and improve workplace conditions.
- **Cultural and Language Barriers:** In areas with a diverse workforce, language differences and cultural diversity may create communication and teamwork challenges. Offering language training and promoting an inclusive work culture can help bridge these gaps and foster better collaboration.

Efficient Human Resource Management (HRM) in agro-processing is crucial for ensuring seamless operations, upholding product quality, and meeting regulatory requirements. By emphasizing recruitment, training, performance management, safety, compensation, and employee relations, agro-processing businesses can cultivate a highly skilled and motivated workforce. Implementing sound HRM practices also helps mitigate operational risks, boosts productivity, and creates a positive work environment, ultimately improving employee satisfaction and retention.

Bibliography

Agricultural & Processed Food Products Export Development Authority (APEDA). (2020). Export-Ready Agro-Processing Units in India.

Amul Dairy. (2021). Agro-Processing and Cold Chain Management for India's Dairy Sector: A Case Study on Amul.

APEDA. (2021). Advancements in Agro-Processing and Cold Storage for Export-Oriented Products.

Banerjee, A. & Das, S. (2019). "Emerging Technologies in Agro-Processing and Their Impact on Indian Agriculture." Indian Journal of Food Science & Technology, 56(1), 109-126.

BigBasket. (2021). E-Commerce & Agro-Processing: The Role of Digital Supply Chains in India.

Bihar Agricultural University. (2020). Scope of Agro-Processing Centres in Eastern India.

Britannia Industries. (2019). Supply Chain Management for Perishable Food Products in India.

Chand, R. (2019). Agri-Business and Supply Chain in India. ICAR Publications.

CII. (2020). Trends in Agro-Processing Industry & Supply Chain Innovations.

CII. (2021). Enhancing Agro-Processing Sector Growth through Innovations.

CSIR-CFTRI. (2020). Food Processing & Preservation: Innovations for Indian Agro-Industry.

CSIR-CFTRI. (2021). Food Processing & Quality Control: Indian Perspectives.

Department of Commerce, Government of India. (2021). Export Potential for Indian Agro-Processed Products.

FICCI. (2021). Processing & Value Addition: A Strategy for Doubling Farmers' Income.

FICCI. (2021). The Future of Agro-Processing Centres in India: Trends & Opportunities.

Food Processing Journal India. (2020). Advancements in Value-Added Products from Indian Agriculture.

Food Safety and Standards Authority of India (FSSAI). (2019). Guidelines for Hygienic Practices in Agro-Processing Units.

Food Safety and Standards Authority of India (FSSAI). (2019). Regulatory Framework for Agro-Processing Centres in India.

Godrej Agrovet. (2021). Sustainable Supply Chains for Agro-Processing in India.

Gujarat Agro Industries Corporation (GAIC). (2020). Agro-Processing and Value Addition in Gujarat: Investment & Growth Opportunities.

Haldiram's. (2020). Frozen Foods and Agro-Processing Management in India.

ICAR-CIPHET. (2020). Advances in Agro-Processing Technologies in India.

ICAR-CIPHET. (2022). Advancements in Agro-Processing Technology in India. Ludhiana: ICAR-CIPHET Publications.

ICAR-National Research Centre on Agro-Processing. (2020). Post-Harvest Engineering & Value Addition in Indian Agriculture.

ICRISAT. (2021). Postharvest Technologies for Pulses and Cereals in India.

IIFT. (2021). Export Potential of Indian Agro-Processed Products. New Delhi: Indian Institute of Foreign Trade.

Indian Agricultural Research Institute (IARI). (2021). Innovative Agro-Processing Technologies for Small Farmers.

Indian Council of Agricultural Research (ICAR). (2018). Agro-Processing Industries and Cold Storage Development in India.

Indian Institute of Horticultural Research (IIHR). (2021). Postharvest Management of Fruits and Vegetables in India: Challenges and Opportunities.

Indian Institute of Packaging. (2019). Role of Packaging in Enhancing Shelf Life of Agro-Processed Products.

Indian Institute of Packaging. (2022). Sustainable Packaging Solutions for Agro-Processed Goods.

ITC Limited. (2021). Agro-Processing & Value Addition: A Business Perspective.

ITC Limited. (2022). Agri-Business Innovations: Building Future-Ready Agro-Processing Centres.

Jain, K. & Bhatt, S. (2021). "Logistics and Cold Chain Infrastructure for Multi-Commodity Agro-Processing." Journal of Logistics & Transportation Studies, 10(1), 54-69.

Jha, S. N., Vishwakarma, R. K., Ahmad, T., Rai, A., & Dixit, A. K. (2020). Smart Technologies for Food Processing: Indian Innovations and Applications. Springer.

Joshi, B., & Sharma, K. (2021). "Sustainable Agro-Processing Strategies for Small Farmers in India." International Journal of Rural Development, 18(2), 89-103.

Joshi, M. & Sinha, A. (2021). "Technological Interventions in Agro-Processing Centres for Multi-Commodity Handling." Journal of AgriTech Research, 9(3), 67-81.

Karnataka State Agricultural Produce Processing Board. (2019). Processing and Value Addition in Karnataka's Agricultural Sector.

Kumar, A. (2021). Cold Storage & Supply Chain Infrastructure in India: A Comprehensive Study. McGraw Hill.

Kumar, V. & Sharma, A. (2018). "Postharvest Losses in Agro-Processing: A Study of Indian Markets." Indian Journal of Postharvest Technology, 5(1), 89-102.

Madhya Pradesh State Agro Industries Corporation Ltd. (2021). Agro-Processing & Value Addition for Farmers in Madhya Pradesh.

Maharashtra State Agricultural Marketing Board (MSAMB). (2021). Development of Multi-Commodity Agro-Processing in Maharashtra.

Malhotra, T. & Singh, P. (2020). "Impact of Cold Chain Logistics on India's Agro-Processing Sector." Indian Journal of Agricultural Economics, 74(3), 312-329.

McKinsey India. (2021). Future of Agro-Processing in India: Emerging Trends & Opportunities.

McKinsey India. (2022). Transforming Agro-Processing through Smart Technologies.

Mehta, P., & Sharma, A. (2022). Post-Harvest Processing & Agro-Industry Development in India. New Delhi: Oxford University Press.

Mehta, R. & Iyer, A. (2022). "Enhancing Value Addition in Fruits and Vegetables: The Role of Agro-Processing Centres." Journal of Agribusiness & Food Technology, 7(3), 56-71.

Ministry of Agriculture & Farmers Welfare. (2021). Enhancing Value Addition & Processing for Indian Farmers: A Roadmap to Growth.

Ministry of Agriculture & Farmers Welfare. (2021). Farm-Gate Processing: Enhancing Farmers' Income through Value Addition.

Ministry of Food Processing Industries (MoFPI). (2020). Status of Agro-Processing Centres in India and Future Prospects.

MoFPI. (2020). Food Processing Infrastructure Development: A Policy Framework for India. New Delhi: Government of India.

MoFPI. (2020). Mega Food Parks Scheme: Guidelines and Implementation Strategies. Government of India.

Mother Dairy. (2019). Milk Processing & Dairy Agro-Processing in India: Innovations and Growth.

NABARD. (2019). Agro-Processing and Value Addition in India: Financial Support & Development Policies.

NABARD. (2019). Financing Agro-Processing Centres: Policies and Opportunities in India.

NABARD. (2021). Innovative Financing for Agro-Processing Units in India. Mumbai: NABARD Reports.

NASSCOM. (2021). Digital Technologies for Agro-Processing & Cold Chain in India.

National Centre for Cold Chain Development (NCCD). (2020). Challenges in Multi-Commodity Agro-Processing and Possible Solutions.

National Institute of Food Technology Entrepreneurship and Management (NIFTEM). (2019). Technology-Based Startups in Agro-Processing: Case Studies from India.

National Institute of Food Technology Entrepreneurship and Management (NIFTEM). (2021). Emerging Trends in Agro-Processing Technologies for Multi-Commodity Handling.

Rajasthan Agricultural Marketing Board. (2021). Boosting Agro-Processing Units in Rajasthan: Opportunities and Challenges.

Reddy, K. & Rao, S. (2021). "Post-Harvest Technologies for Enhancing Shelf-Life of Perishables." Journal of AgriTech, 15(4), 204-221.

Singh, D. & Malhotra, R. (2020). "Value Addition in Indian Agro-Processing Industry: Trends and Challenges." International Journal of Food Processing, 6(2), 102-118.

Uttar Pradesh Food Processing Policy. (2021). Mega Food Parks & Processing Units in Uttar Pradesh.

Verma, P. & Aggarwal, R. (2019). Small & Medium Agro-Processing Enterprises in India: Market, Challenges, and Growth Strategies. New Delhi: Sage Publications.

Warehousing Development and Regulatory Authority (WDRA). (2018). Cold Storage & Agro-Processing for Perishable Goods in India.

Warehousing Development and Regulatory Authority (WDRA). (2021). Cold Chain Development and Storage Infrastructure in India.

West Bengal Department of Food Processing. (2020). Cold Chain and Agro-Processing Potential in West Bengal.

World Bank Group. (2021). Agro-Industrial Parks in India: Best Practices and Implementation Strategies.

Index